William Butler

Mexico in Transition From the Power of Political Romanism

To Civil & Religious Liberty. Fourth Edition

William Butler

Mexico in Transition From the Power of Political Romanism
To Civil & Religious Liberty. Fourth Edition

ISBN/EAN: 9783337041687

Printed in Europe, USA, Canada, Australia, Japan

Cover: Foto ©Suzi / pixelio.de

More available books at **www.hansebooks.com**

BENITO JUAREZ,
The " Washington " of Mexico.

MEXICO IN TRANSITION

FROM

THE POWER OF POLITICAL ROMANISM

TO

CIVIL AND RELIGIOUS LIBERTY

BY WILLIAM BUTLER, D.D.

ILLUSTRATED

SEAL OF MEXICO

"THERE IS A WAKING ON THE MIGHTY HILLS,
A KINDLING WITH THE SPIRIT OF THE MORN."

FOURTH EDITION—REVISED

NEW YORK: HUNT & EATON
CINCINNATI: CRANSTON & CURTS

THIS WORK
IS DEDICATED
TO
Rev. C. C. McCabe, D.D.,
AND THOSE KIND FRIENDS "WHO STAND BEHIND HIM,"
IN MEMORY OF THEIR GENEROSITY
IN FURNISHING THE MEANS ENABLING THE WRITER
TO VISIT MEXICO AND THERE COLLECT
THE NECESSARY MATERIAL FOR THE PUBLICATION OF THIS VOLUME,
BY THEIR GRATEFUL SERVANT IN CHRIST,
THE AUTHOR.

PREFACE.

In view of the false representations which were so industriously disseminated during the struggle described in this work by those who had an interest in the wrongs which Mexico so long endured, it is hoped that our readers may kindly excuse the constant quotations and documentary aspect of much of the text. Only by going back to original evidence and furnishing the authority for our statements could these falsehoods be exposed and the whole truth be placed before our readers. This for the author was a long, slow, and laborious process. But we believe it has been amply justified, and that the reading public has now at last Mexico's side of the question placed before it, with its evidences, so that it can form a more intelligent opinion upon the merits of the mighty struggle which was so providentially guided to an issue that, while it overwhelmed the enemies of the rights of the Mexican people, at the same time and in due order vindicated and established those rights upon foundations which it is expected will stand while sun and moon endure.

The errors corrected the reader will find to have been very many; some of them as willful and baseless as that which so daringly asserted that " Colonel López was a traitor, who sold his sovereign and the password to the Republicans for thirty thousand dollars," and thus loaded down that officer for twenty years with an opprobrium that was heavy enough to have sunk him into a dishonored grave, while at the time his lips were closed in his own defense until the hour came, three years ago, when the commanding general broke the seal of silence and released the colonel from the peculiar and undeserved misery which he had so long endured under a sense of loyalty to the express wishes of Maximilian, adding another illustration to the maxim that " Truth is often stranger than fiction."

While these pages were being prepared for the press, to illustrate the merciful intervention of Almighty God on behalf of those who are wronged and denied the rights of popular government, a remarkable utterance, and from a high quarter, for a contrary doctrine made its appearance. The United States senator from Kansas—regarded by his admirers as being " brainy, brilliant, and audacious "—saw fit to choose his opportunity lightly to pour his contempt upon convictions to which multitudes of thoughtful people give their earnest sympathy. Standing upon the battle-field of Gettysburg—upon ground hallowed by the blood of thousands of American heroes—this man is reported as having given utterance to the following peculiar and amazing language :

The purification of politics is an iridescent dream.   Government is force.   Politics is a battle for supremacy.   Parties are the armies.   The decalogue and the golden rule have no place in a political campaign. The object is success.   To defeat the antagonist and expel the party in power is the purpose.   In war it is lawful to deceive the adversary, to hire Hessians, to purchase mercenaries, to mutilate, to kill, to destroy. The commander who lost a battle through the activity of his moral nature would be the derision and jest of history.   This modern cant about the corruption of politics is fatiguing in the extreme.   It proceeds from the tea-custard and syllabub dillctanteism, the frivolous and desultory sentimentalism of epicenes.

No doubt but this would be welcome news to the enemies of the reign of law and personal and social purity everywhere, people who hate to be rebuked or controlled by either God or man, by law or by conscience. The decalogue and the sermon on the mount stand very much in the way of such persons, and it would have been greatly to their comfort and liberty of action had the senator been able to add the *proof* that they were really abrogated, as he said, and that such persons had nothing to fear from them either now or hereafter.

But this book will show that it was not with such a creed as this that the wronged and suffering Liberals of Mexico struggled up through their forty years of agony and effort to the joy of a purified political system which at last gave their country rest and peace. And surely the Christian and patriotic dead beneath that senator's feet in that cemetery, who gave up home, family, and life itself to rectify that "corruption of politics" which flung over our fair land treason, rebellion, and death, could they have risen from their graves, would have indignantly confronted him as he thus characterized convictions like theirs as "modern cant," etc.

The conscience of the nation was shocked by this ill-omened utterance, and Kansas herself resented it as every way unworthy of her own convictions. For a few weeks after, when the time for the re-election of her senator came round, she retired this man to private life and elected another in his place. Nor will the lesson be lost. It does not pay public men, and especially those in prominent positions, in the long run, to get into conflict with the Author of the ten commandments or the golden rule, or to turn an indifferent ear to the earnest appeals of the men or the women who look to them for sympathy and help in their struggles against sin and wrong.

It seems singular that the refuge of divine law should be unwelcome to any human being, or that men can be found who would object to have religion operate in this sphere of ours as though it were an intrusion to be tolerated only in the clouds above and the world beyond, but not to dictate here to the hearts and lives of men nor aim to control their private ways, much less their public acts and policies. Sooner or later an awakening comes to such dreamers, and they have to learn—often too late—that the ten commandments and the sermon on the mount were not given as laws of life to saints and angels in heaven, but to men and sinners down here in this wicked world, and that their mothers were right when they taught their infant lips to pray, "Thy kingdom come, thy will be done on EARTH as it is done in heaven." Any attempt to exclude public life and its responsibilities from the sphere of conscience and the divine control, and then "to teach men so," is a high crime and misdemeanor, not only against the souls of men, but also against patriotism as well as religion, against love of country and love of God, all of which go hand in hand and constitute the "righteousness which exalteth a nation," and is equally exalting to its leading men.

Rectification of wrong is the only true foundation of tranquillity; "first pure, then peaceable." "There is no peace, saith God, to the wicked," and never can be. The most perfect and permanent of all governments is that of the reigning Redeemer, of whose blessed administration the eternal Father testifies: "Unto the Son he saith, Thy throne, O God, is for ever and ever: a scepter of righteousness is the scepter of thy kingdom. Thou hast loved righteousness, and hated iniquity; therefore God, even thy God, hath anointed thee with the oil of gladness above thy fellows." He is the very model for legislators and governors. The anthem that inaugurated his administration has gone on sounding round the world ever since, "Glory to God in the highest, and on earth peace, good-will toward men." He evidently maintains that purified politics and Christian prayer-meetings can go well together, that caucuses and class meetings stand related to each other, and that a man can be president of one of earth's mightiest empires and yet be a saint like Daniel, who bends his knees to the God whose help he implores. Thank Heaven, the men who recognize God in political life bear the names that humanity now loves to remember and honor—Protestant, Catholic, and heathen alike; and the number of such pure patriots is on the increase. It is not necessary that we quote illustrative instances. One alone shall speak a brief word for the whole class in decided contradiction of the unworthy utterance against which we here protest.

The Marquis of Dalhousie was regarded by his contemporaries as the most distinguished governor-general that England ever sent to rule her Oriental empire. This honored man, during the eight years that he held this great responsibility, ruled and guided nearly one sixth of the human family. His

feeble frame bent down at last beneath the mighty load, but
God, whom he had so long honored, enabled him to finish his
duty. The day on which his successor, Lord Canning, arrived,
in 1856, he was ready to leave. They tenderly bore him from
the viceregal palace in Calcutta down to the ship that awaited
him, and laid him in the berth from which he was unable to rise
till the voyage ended. As he lay there he wrote, with feeble
hand, using pencil and tablets by his side, his last report to the
Court of Directors. In that report he found room for God,
and here is the finishing sentiment of his public life, so ger-
mane to our subject here:

These papers are an instance of the principle that we should do right
without fear of consequences. To fear God and to have no other fear is a
maxim of religion, but the truth of it and the wisdom of it are proved
every day in politics.

The golden rule abrogated! Nay, verily. "Heaven and
earth shall pass away, but His word shall not pass away!"
That word is pledged to help the oppressed of every land.
"The meek shall inherit the earth and delight themselves in
the abundance of peace." For nineteen hundred years since
the Lord Jesus Christ announced his mission in Capernaum
(Luke iv, 18) his has been the "power working for righteousness" in all lands; for this he lives and reigns. As immortal,
while he may make haste, he does not need to hurry. He can
take his time, for the future is all his own, and is sure to come
to him for the completion of his great task. Wisely and effectively is he now mightily working in "subduing all things
unto himself" and guiding the elements in motion to the grand
conclusions which will surely bring, by the attractions of his
cross, the wide world to his feet in loving and adoring homage.
Already there are millions of men and women who would willingly lay down their lives for him to evidence that love; and
the number of such is daily increasing. Long after the men
who have slighted his authority have passed away and been
forgotten better men will be filling the positions which they

were unworthy to occupy, and this glorious Deliverer will be closing up to completion the high mission of his manifestation.

"In his name shall the Gentiles trust," not merely for the salvation of the soul, but also for the rectification of every wrong and the vindication of every right to "life, liberty, and the pursuit of happiness," for all the good available in "the life that now is, as well as for that which is to come." This "King of kings and Lord of lords," whose cross redeemed the world, is yet to sway its happy populations by his golden rule until even "the isles shall wait for his law." For ages this has been the expectation and prayer of Christians and lovers of the Bible, who have been looking forward to that

"One far-off divine event
To which the whole creation moves."

CONTENTS.

CHAPTER V.

CHAPTER VI.

CHAPTER VII.

CHAPTER VIII.

CHAPTER IX.

2

TABLE OF ILLUSTRATIONS.

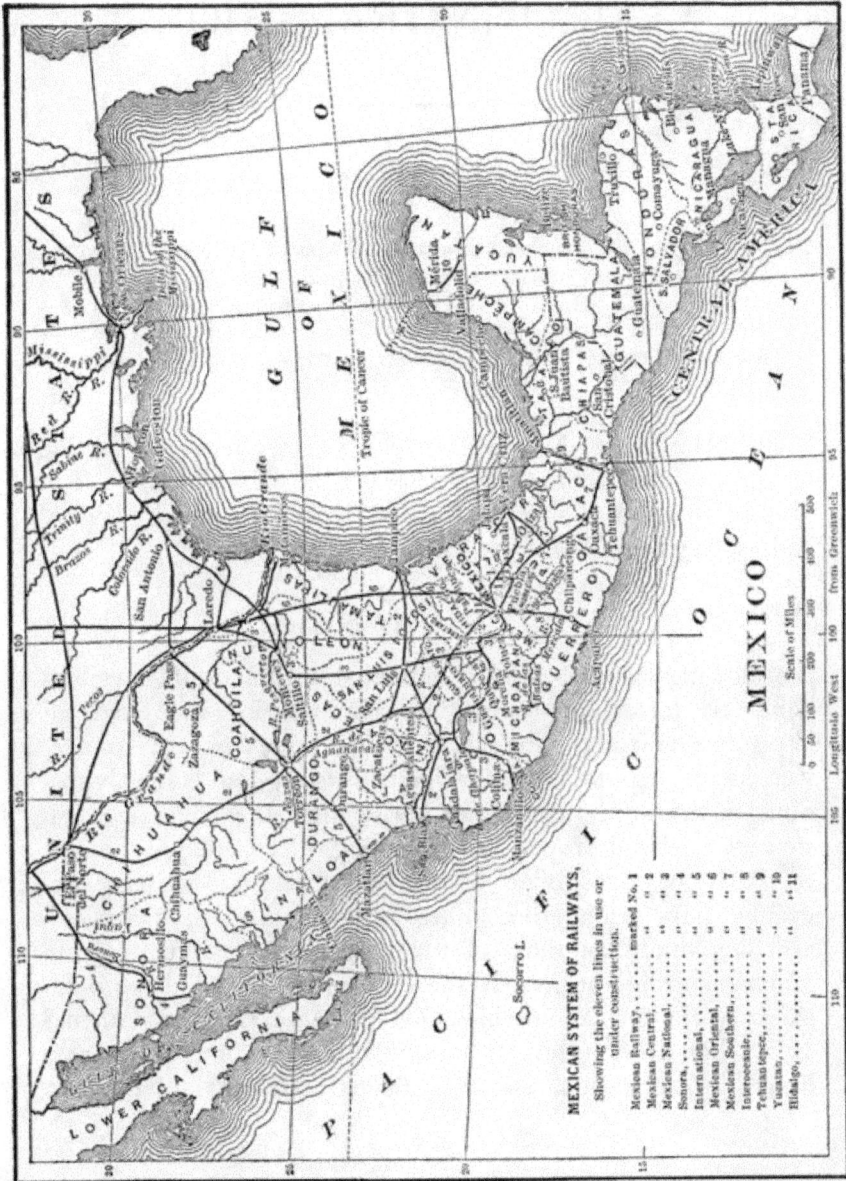

MEXICO

Scale of Miles

0   50 100 200   300   400   500   600

Longitude West   from Greenwich

MEXICAN SYSTEM OF RAILWAYS,

Showing the eleven lines in use or
under construction.

Mexican Railway, ... marked No. 1
Mexican Central, ...   "   "   2
Mexican National, ...   "   "   3
Sonora, ...   "   "   4
International, ...   "   "   5
Mexican Oriental, ...   "   "   6
Mexican Southern, ...   "   "   7
Interoceanic, ...   "   "   8
Tehuantepec, ...   "   "   9
Yucatan, ...   "   " 10
Hidalgo, ...   "   " 11

MEXICO IN TRANSITION.

CHAPTER I.

My interest in the events which this work is to describe originated in a Sabbath service toward the close of 1851. The congregation were singing Bishop Heber's missionary hymn, and as they reached the couplet

"Till, like a sea of glory,
It spreads from pole to pole,"

the glowing words seemed illuminated with a significance beyond any former apprehension. My attention was fixed, all else forgotten for the time, and questionings, new and strange, were speaking to my heart and insisting on being heard. Some of these questions ran on in this line: Does this congregation comprehend properly the meaning of the sublime thought to which they are giving utterance? Are they realizing the exalted hope which those lines express? Of what "poles" are they thinking—those of the eastern hemisphere, or those of our own continent, where the best connection of those poles exists by the formation which God has conferred upon them? Here, then, where Heber's lines, in this sense, find their most literal interpretation, is the audience really anticipating the hour when from the most northern of human homes the "sea of glory" is to illumine and bless the dwellers of the three Americas till it reaches the southern cape and crowns it with the cross of the world's Redeemer? Or, was the glowing song a mere poetic sentiment to fan for a moment the affections of these worshipers and, without further significance, sacrifice, or personal duty, to pass from their minds and be forgotten?

There was at least one heart in that assembly which was not to forget them while life shall last. The halo that invested those two lines was to draw its attention and stimulate its faith and hope, until now, after more than forty years, the great public events that have meanwhile transpired upon these continents have been seen and understood with increasing clearness in the illumination of that hour, and it has apprehended how wondrously God is moving in those lands to turn the hope of Heber's hymn into the bright reality of the perfect evangelical day, when the whole American hemisphere shall be radiant with the glory of the Lord. This book is the result of these increasing and glad convictions, and the author's hope is that, when his readers have examined the facts traced and united here, they too will share his confidence and be ready to address themselves, "as workers together with God," to the sacrifices and duties which the hour and the divine call demand for their realization from the Church of Christ.

The interest thus aroused developed into an anxiety to ascertain what was the actual political, social, and religious condition of the nations existing between our own border and the southern pole. Those seventeen States had then an aggregate population exceeding that of the United States and Canada combined. The results of this inquiry, faithfully prosecuted for a considerable length of time, through an extensive examination and correspondence, were sad indeed. In this advanced day people can hardly appreciate the fearful darkness and destitution which then prevailed over Central and South America, or realize that there was not then among the nearly forty-eight millions of human beings between our Texan border and Cape Horn one

missionary of evangelical Christianity addressing those millions
in their own tongue! All was darkness and spiritual death!
Nearly every one of those States were bound hand and foot in
concordat relations with the papal power, these concordats
requiring the executive of each nation to make ecclesiastical
matters paramount in his administration; to repress all dissent,
even to the extent of the forfeiture of freedom or property—
sometimes even of life itself; to maintain, unquestioned and unchallenged, the stern rule of the papacy over these benighted
millions. This had been going on for centuries past, and it was
fully purposed to perpetuate the same dark dominion for ages
yet to come! No Bible, no missionary, no light from any
source was to be permitted to enter or disturb this reign of ignorance and sin. It seemed in some respects a worse condition
than that of any heathenism on earth, because more cruel, repressive, and unreformable. Sufficient evidence of this will be
forthcoming, most of it furnished by the very people whom
Rome had overburdened for centuries, till at last, unable to endure longer, they have risen in their wrath, one State after
another, and taken vengeance upon their clerical oppressors.
They have snatched from their hands the civil and religious
freedom which had been so long withheld, and secularized the
vast church property which their clergy had unlawfully acquired and so long employed for their own selfish purposes.
This hour of divine relief had not dawned in 1851. Years
of agony had yet to be endured ere it appeared, and the suffering friends and martyrs of freedom and a purer faith had to
wait and still cry to the Almighty, under their bitter pressure,
"How long, O Lord, how long?"

Santa Anna was then in power, in the third term of his dictatorship, and this record will evidence that a more unscrupulous tool of the papacy never held a scepter. Since the first
blow was struck for freedom in Mexico, and the life of its
noblest martyr was sacrificed, in 1811, occasional rumors
reached the outside world revealing something of the struggles
which the lovers of liberty were maintaining against fearful

odds, and how the strong hand of the Church and the Spanish
party were cruelly repressing their aspirations, endeavoring to
extinguish them.

It seems strange now, as we look back, how unconscious our
people generally were of the condition of things in Mexico,
how little they realized the depth of the degradation in which
her millions were perishing, or how long she had agonized to be
lifted up to the condition of our land. We dreamed not of
the debt we owed to her, and the nations beyond, but left them
to their fate. Meanwhile we were loud enough in our jubilation over our own happy condition, unconscious that we were
side by side with a race of people, then more numerous than
ourselves, who were under the dread control of the darkest
Romanism on earth!

Forty years ago, in a circle of friends, some of whom expressed fears of national difficulties to grow out of the unsettled north-eastern and north-western boundaries, Daniel Webster
said:

No, gentlemen, our great national difficulty lies not in that direction.
Our greatest danger is that we have a sister republic on our southern
border, almost in mortal agony, and no one amongst us seems willing to
lend it a helping hand.

Truly to comprehend the Mexican question we need to recall the professed Warrant for the Conquest. The origin of the
title by which Spain and the Church of Rome claimed Mexico,
and indeed the entire western hemisphere, as their exclusive
domain, was an audacious act of the Roman pontiff at the close
of the fifteenth century. The craze of the Crusades led men
to imagine that the kingdom of Christ could be extended by
the sword, and the maritime nations of the age waxed jealous
of each other's share in the work and the gain it involved.
Add to this motive the love of adventure and military glory,
and the passion of avarice, and you have the elements which
moved men, and often the vilest of men, to volunteer for such
enterprises. As a warrant for all they undertook they looked
to the pope to bestow the sanction of Heaven upon their vent-

ures. The pope, nothing loath, readily authorized such expeditions, and that on the most extensive scale. Alexander VI., in 1494, settled the conflicting claims of the kings of Spain and Portugal by dividing the world between them. The account runs thus:

He divided the undiscovered regions of the earth by an imaginary line of longitude, running through the Atlantic Ocean, from pole to pole, three hundred and seventy miles west of the Azores. He gave the Portuguese unlimited sway over all the countries that they might discover to the east of that line, and pledged himself to confirm to Ferdinand and Isabella of Spain the right to every isle, continent, and sea where they should plant their flag on the western hemisphere. Hence in every picture of the landing of Columbus the first act in the scene is the planting of the flag of the Spanish crown.*

This authority was to be unlimited and to cover all things temporal and spiritual; the bodies and souls, the property and services of the conquered nations were to be their peculiar inheritance, and that of their successors forever. Such was the title-deed of Ferdinand and Isabella to North, Central, and South America. This wonderful grant of Alexander VI. was confirmed by his successor, Pope Julius II., to the Spanish monarchy. Thus the whole continent, "from pole to pole," all the kingdoms of this New World, were assumed to be handed over to a dynasty by a pontiff who did not own and had no right to a foot of the territory or a single human being upon it.

But where are the two empires so pompously divided to Portugal and Spain? Where the "Conquest" made under the authority of Alexander VI., and consolidated with such crushing force on poor humanity, especially in Mexico? What of the proud claims which Spaniards made when they engraved across their maps of the western world the words "New Spain," which were made to stretch from the Gulf of Mexico to the Pacific coast, and from the St. Lawrence to the southern cape, territorially the greatest empire that the world had ever seen? The pontifical gift has been wrested out of their blood-stained hands

* *Mexico and the United States,* by Gorham D. Abbot, p. 21. Putnam.

by a mightier Power than their own ; her sons who did all this wrong have been shaken out of this New World ; the boundaries which she obliterated have been restored ; the races which she so cruelly oppressed have risen again in this wonderful day to power, and her proud title has been erased from the maps of this hemisphere.

The assumptions of Alexander VI. would have had far less significance to the world had not the papacy supposed they had found in them a clew to universal dominion over mankind. This idea was followed out, and Pope Paul III. convoked a council in the city of Trent, in 1545, which was to legislate, under the professed authority of the Holy Spirit, a body of canons that were to subject all mankind for all ages to the will of one man in the papal chair. This council was composed of 247 bishops, of whom 187 were Italians, 32 Spaniards, 26 French, and 2 Germans, and a majority vote (124) of these men undertook to make the laws by which the millions of the human race in all lands and ages were to be bound, under fearful penalties, to accept and obey as the edicts of Almighty God !

Though Mexico to-day retains only a part of the immense area which she once called her own, yet her present size is stated as " ten times larger than Great Britain, and nearly equal in extent to France, Spain, Austria, Lombardy, and the British Isles combined." The physical facts of this great country are presented by Mr. Winston as follows :

It extends from about the fourteenth to the thirty-second parallel of north latitude, and from the eighty-sixth to the one hundred and seventh degree of west longitude, being in length from north to south about two thousand miles, and in breadth from one hundred and forty miles at Tehuantepec, on the south, to over a thousand miles where it joins our own southern borders. It has a sea-coast on the Gulf of Mexico of about one thousand miles, and on the Pacific Ocean and the Gulf of California of over four thousand miles. Situated to a large extent within the tropics, its coasts and the land near them possess a tropical climate, while the plains of the interior rise to an altitude of seventy-five hundred feet above the level of the sea, securing a temperate climate, although within the tropics. Thus almost every product of fruit and grain is found within its borders. On no island in the southern seas is there a greater luxuriance and beauty of tree and plant and flower, from the majestic palm to the creeping vines which cover the ground and trees and overrun their dwellings, than in the south and east of Mexico, while in the north all the products of our own land can be successfully cultivated. Its silver mines have been and are the richest in the world. It has gold also, with iron and other useful metals and minerals. Its majestic snow-clad mountains, its beautiful valleys and hills, its luxuriant verdure and abundant plants present rare pictures to all true lovers of nature.

The natives speak of their country as divided into three zones, the lowlands along the coast as the *tierras calientes* (hot lands), the range above as *tierras templadas* (temperate lands), and the still higher table-lands as the *tierras frias* (cold lands). In these last are seen those great volcanoes which are such a striking feature in the scenery of Mexico. The height of the five leading ones, as given by Humboldt, is:

Orizava	17,879	feet.
Popocatepetl	17,726	"
Ixtaccihuatl	15,705	"
Toluca	15,168	"
Colima	12,005	"

The summits of these are covered with perpetual snow. Popocatepetl and Ixtaccihuatl rise in their sublimity on the eastern side of the valley of Mexico, hoary guardians of the Aztec capital, the first towering ten thousand feet above the city. A railroad, wonderful for its engineering, that has overcome such immense difficulties of construction, winds its way up from the sea-shore at Vera Cruz to the city of Mexico, a distance of two hundred and sixty-two miles, and an elevation of seventy-five hundred feet. Some of the scenery on this road, and on other lines lately constructed down to the coast, is unsurpassed in grandeur in the world. Passing through all these zones garden products are brought to the markets of Mexico, and dwellers in that city enjoy fresh fruits and vegetables and flowers every day in the year. The sweep of the mild currents of air from the tropical ocean below, united with the rarefied air of the elevated table-lands, afford one of the most balmy and equable climates in

the world, free from extremes, so that in the valley of Mexico
the mercury seldom rises over eighty-five degrees, or falls much
below forty-five degrees, and nature seems in its growth to be
a perpetual spring. This wonderful land, so gifted by nature's
God, if her people were only blest with evangelical religion,
and the freedom, peace, and intelligence it brings in its train,
might become like "the garden of the Lord," where "thanksgiving and the voice of praise" might be perpetually resounding.

In 1888 Mexico had an estimated population of 11,632,924.
Of these 12 per cent. are supposed to be of European extrac-
tion, 28 per cent. mixed, and 60 per cent. aborigines. Such is
the fertility of the land that it is estimated it could sustain more
than one hundred millions of population. God has bestowed with
bountiful hand, so that it has been truly said, she has "every
herb bearing seed, and every tree that is pleasant to the sight
and good for food," while her mines are rich with the precious
metals. The single fact of Mexico's mineral wealth should have
saved her from her wretchedness. Ages before our Nevadas
were heard of Mexico was the wealthiest of all lands, and
specialists have calculated that fully one half of the silver of
commerce was extracted from her mines since the Conquest.
An enumeration of the wealth from Mexican mines which passed
through the custom-houses of Spain from the Conquest to 1825
gives the enormous amount of £2,040,000,000, being an annual
revenue to the Spanish monarch of £6,800,000 for the three
hundred years then closing.* Nor is this all, for Robertson
gives his authorities for the conclusion that the sum above
named is less than the amount fraudulently introduced into
Spain without paying the fifth part which was the king's duty
on the importation.† No wonder this profusion of treasure
astonished mankind, who had hitherto gleaned a limited supply
of these precious metals from the scanty stores in the mines of
the eastern hemisphere.

Pampered with unsanctified wealth, gained by fraud and

---

* See King's Proclamation, printed at Havana, Sept. 6, 1831.
† Robertson's *History of America*, p. 366, and note on p. 519.

HERNANDO CORTÉZ,
Marquis of the Valley of Oaxaca, Conqueror of this New World, and its
first Captain-General, 1521.

oppression, Spain became proud and overbearing, rejected the Bible and the great Reformation, and in the intoxication of her bigotry madly essayed to dominate the world by terrorizing weak nations, while at home she energized her abominable Inquisition in the interests of her intolerant Church. She then rashly attempted to extinguish in cruelty and blood the Reformation in its chosen home, by invading the country of Elizabeth. The preparations for this purpose were characteristic of the monarchy which had reduced the free Aztecs to peonage and degradation, and which was exulting in the anticipation of imposing a similar yoke on the necks of Englishmen. With the money of Mexico the Armada was built and outfitted, and then ostentatiously baptized the *Invincible,* as it sailed away to accomplish its purpose. But in one short week the wreckage of that vast fleet was strewing the Atlantic Ocean, or dashed up on the shores of the land which sent it forth. The terrible overthrow inspired the Protestant nations to build fleets to compete with this relentless tyrant of the seas. The Dutch and English began to prey on the commerce of their common enemy, and many a Spanish galleon had to lower her flag and resign her treasure to build up the greatness of these powers. From that time the decadence of Spain commenced, until her argosies ceased to cross the ocean and rotted within her silent ports. "The Lord had them in derision."

The wealth of Mexico has continued to flow, but no longer to enrich her spoilers. It is now building up the commerce of free and evangelical nations. Twice a month the transatlantic steamer leaves Vera Cruz, bearing it away to London, where it is turned into exchange for the East, and is soon reminted in Calcutta, and circulates in India, China, and Japan.

The conquest of Mexico by Hernando Cortéz, in the early part of the sixteenth century, is one of the most interesting subjects in all history. To overthrow an empire like that of Montezuma with the mere handful of men whom Cortéz led seems incredible. The original account of this conquest is contained in the four dispatches of Cortéz to his emperor.

Charles V. The representation is one-sided; the conquered race have never until now had the opportunity of appealing to the considerate judgment of mankind by recounting the story of their wrongs, and the cruelties which they endured from the fanatical invaders of their country. The destruction of their civilization, their monuments, their literature and records, has swept away till the judgment-day the proof which they should have possessed. Zumarraga, the first Archbishop of Mexico, was prominent among the iconoclasts who so recklessly destroyed their valuable manuscripts and monuments. Brantz Mayer describes the immense bonfire that he made of all the Aztec manuscripts he could collect "in and round the city of Mexico and Tlatelolco."* Of course the "pious" soldiers in this "holy war" zealously followed the example of their chief prelate, and so treasures which might have thrown light on the history of Mexico and of the continent, invaluable to the historian and antiquarian, were ruthlessly consumed by these ignorant vandals. The vast number of ruins of *teocallis* (temples or sacred places) that still remain evidence the immense population which Mexico contained at the time of the Conquest, and seem to justify the conclusion reached by Humboldt, that at that period the empire of Montezuma may have "had a population of not less than thirty millions," and "the city of Mexico a population of three hundred thousand."

The Christianization of such a mass of humanity by a mere handful of military adventurers and their few clerical helpers, by the off-hand methods which they employed, frequently at the sword's point, is an awful part of the record that has come down to us. The world never before witnessed any such process as they adopted in "Christianizing" those whom their cruelty spared. Robertson gives the authority (Romish, of course) for his statement :

While this rage of conversion continued a single clergyman baptized in one day about five thousand Mexicans, and did not desist until he was so exhausted by fatigue that he was unable to lift his hands. In the course

* Brantz Mayer, vol. i, p. 93.

of a few years after the reduction of the Mexican Empire the sacrament of baptism was administered to more than four millions. Proselytes adopted with such inconsiderate haste, and who were neither instructed in the nature of the tenets to which it was supposed they had given assent, nor taught the absurdity of those which they were required to relinquish, retained their veneration for their ancient superstitions in full force, or mingled an attachment to their doctrines and rites with that slender knowledge of Christianity which they had acquired. These sentiments the new converts transmitted to their posterity, into whose minds they have sunk so deep that the Spanish ecclesiastics, with all their industry, have not been able to eradicate them.*

"Conversion" and "baptism" are interchangeable in the language of such people, and cases are quoted where their doctrine of "baptismal regeneration" enabled two of their missionaries to boast that "their ordinary day's work was from ten to twenty thousand souls!" The "fruits" of such a Christianity are manifest to-day in Mexico, as they have been for three hundred years past, and Humboldt is fully justified in his statement when he says:

The introduction of the Romish religion had no other effect upon the Mexicans than to substitute new ceremonies and symbols for the rites of a sanguinary worship. Dogma has not succeeded dogma, but only ceremony to ceremony. I have seen them, marked and adorned with tinkling bells, perform savage dances around the altar while a monk of St. Francis elevated the Host.

And equally true is Dr. Abbot's sad conclusion, that

Christianity, instead of fulfilling its mission of enlightening, converting, and sanctifying the natives, was itself *converted*. Paganism was *baptized*, Christianity *paganized*.

Cortéz was not above the temptation to represent his opponents in the worst possible light and to magnify greatly his own victories as well as the number and character of those opposed to him, in order to dazzle his government and his countrymen with the splendor of his services and the proportionate rewards that were due to him, and those who served with him in his crusade against a peaceable nation in the ends of the earth, who

* Robertson's *America*, p. 364.

3

had offered him neither wrong nor insult, and of whose hospitality he took the meanest advantages and then punished their heroic defense with robbery, slavery, and death! But who then dared to doubt the correctness of the narrations by Cortéz? Every document for the public eye had first to be submitted to the examination of the official censor, and without his license no work could be published. Cortéz was too useful as a son of the Church and too valuable as a subject of the crown to have any of his statements qualified or denied. Bernal Diaz (one of his associates and a historian of the Conquest) ventures in a very meek way to withhold his approval of some such statements, in these words:

It may be that the person whom Gomara mentions as having appeared on a mottled gray horse was the glorious apostle San Jago or San Pedro, and that I as being a sinner, was not worthy to see him. This I know, that I saw Juan Francisco de Morla on such a horse, but, as an unworthy transgressor, did not deserve to see any of the holy apostles. It may have been the will of God; that it was so as Gomara relates, but until I read his chronicle I never heard among any of the conquerors that such a thing had happened. (Chap. xxxiv.)

The statements of Cortéz went forth accepted as facts by the "Holy Office," and were commended to the belief of the uneducated millions of Spain. The emblazoned cross upon his standard covered even the claims of miraculous assistance, the presence of the saints (St. James and St. Peter especially) with his army, and "the inspiration of the Holy Ghost," to guide in his policy. All of which is indorsed by no less an authority than Lorenzana, Archbishop of Mexico, in his *Notes on the Letters of Cortéz*, published in 1770. To eulogize such a man as a "saintly" character was an insult to the moral sense of even worldly men. The glamour of his course has now departed, and candid criticism has weighed him in her balance and found him wanting. Abundant evidence—much of it under his own hand—has shown him to have been impure, untruthful, avaricious, and cruel, and to-day his character is most discounted where he was best known. The races which he so deeply wronged execrate his memory, and one of their first acts as freemen was to raise the question whether the soil of their land should shelter his remains, so that hastily and secretly his ashes were removed, to avoid the indignities to which the excited people might have subjected them! If any desire evidence to satisfy them that this is not too strong condemnation of his character, let them turn to the authorities given below (all from Roman Catholic writers), which are but samples of the many such testimonies which could be added.*

The exaggerations of Cortéz and his followers were on a scale with their barbarities, and constitute a perpetual difficulty for all who attempt to describe his conquest. Time and closer examination only intensify this difficulty and throw a deeper shade over their credibility. Nearly all visitors to Mexico who have studied the subject, even partially, find themselves led to doubt the amazing statements of the Dispatches and become convinced that Prescott should have discriminated in regard to many of these wild assertions of Cortéz. We have not room to spare for the many illustrative instances at hand, but in passing we will note that the victory of Otumba, after the night of dreadful loss, called the *Noche Triste* (or Sad Night), where four or five hundred exhausted men are said to have conquered "more than one hundred thousand" Aztecs, may be regarded as on a par with his story of the "one hundred and thirty-six thousand skulls of the victims of the teocalli," which he says he saw there, or the equally incredible number of human sacrifices offered yearly on their reeking altars.† Even Clavigero, the Jesuit historian of Mexico, is forced to pause and decline to set down such monstrous figures in his history.‡ But, on the contrary, he states that "the victors [Spaniards], in one year of merciless massacre, sacrificed more human victims to avarice and ambition than the Indians, during the

* *Dispatches of Cortéz*, pp. 362, 398, 405. Robertson's *History of the Discovery and Settlement of America*, pp. 252, 257, 485, 488, 494.

† Helps's *Life of Cortéz*, vol. ii, p. 305.

‡ *History of Mexico*, by Abbé F. S. Clavigero, vol. i, p. 281.

existence of their empire, devoted in chaste worship to their native gods." *

Cortéz's own lips have furnished the real secret to his character, and proves that "the cursed lust for gold" was the leading motive that impelled him. Without hesitation he relates the following incident. At an entertainment which he gave to the officers of Montezuma on his first journey from the coast to the city of Mexico he inquired of them if their emperor had any gold, and, being answered in the affirmative, Cortéz said : "Let him send it to me, for I and my companions have a complaint, a disease of the heart, which is cured by gold." † Montezuma soon sent all that he could spare, hoping to get rid of the unwelcome visitor, but he had not enough to "cure" the disease. It was a spasm of the same complaint, when he had captured the valiant Cuatemoctzin, the nephew and successor of Montezuma, who led the defense of the city when the emperor was a prisoner, that induced Cortéz to commit the fearful crime that will forever stain the records of his great conquest. The booty which fell into his hands was so small, "only one hundred and twenty thousand pesos gold," that he believed Cuatemoctzin had secreted the treasure, and therefore ordered the princely man to be tortured, with his chief noble, by roasting their feet before a strong fire. The noble died under the torture, which was then suspended in the case of Cuatemoctzin, only to be renewed later, before he was hung by the conqueror, for refusing to reveal the secret. ‡ So far from being ashamed of this diabolical act, the anniversary of the capture of Cuatemoctzin and the fall of the city which he so valiantly defended was regularly celebrated during the three hundred years of Spanish rule, till the independence, in 1821, brought the native race to the front and terminated the insulting celebration. With such ample facts before us, what are we to think of the indorsement given to Cortéz by Archbishop Lorenzana (already mentioned), who

* *History of Mexico,* by Abbé F. S. Clavigero, vol. ii, p. 194.
† Helps's *Life of Cortéz,* vol. i, p. 56.
‡ Robertson's *History,* pp. 252, 257.

annotated the Dispatches of Cortéz to Charles V.? In his closing note he says:

The Conquest took place in 1521, and in three years after Cortéz, in this dispatch, speaks as if fifty years of wise government had elapsed. I shall ever reverence Cortéz, and respect his name as that of a civil, military, and *religious* hero, unexampled in his career ; a subject who bore the freaks of fortune with fortitude and constancy, and a man destined by God to add to the possessions of the Catholic king a new and larger world. (P. 431.)

We pause to note how completely the judgment of the archbishop was reversed by the divine providence. All that Cortéz established has been swept away, to the last remnant of the despotic civilization imposed upon the long-suffering race, whose enlightened sons are once more in possession of their country. On the 21st of August, 1889, the Mexicans dedicated on the Paseo de la Reforma—the magnificent drive leading from the city to the palace of Chapultepec—a colossal bronze statue of Cuatemoctzin, in honor of their valiant prince and last emperor. One of the largest assemblies of the aborigines ever seen in Mexico city was present to witness the solemnities, each bearing his garland to grace the monument which memorializes their deliverance from ages of bitter humiliation. The triumphant oration was pronounced in the Aztec language by Colonel Don Prospero Cahuantzin, Governor of the State of Tlaxcala. The national anthem was enthusiastically sung and the royal salute of twenty-one guns thundered out, during which President Diaz advanced and laid a wreath of roses and laurel at the foot of the statue. Need we wonder that Cuatemoctzin's race is now claiming a reversal of many of those popular opinions on the Conquest which Spanish historians and those who were misdirected by them, have imposed on the world as the facts of history?

In settling down to enjoy the results of their unjust invasion the *Conquistadores* (as Cortéz and his associates then were called) adopted a social system of a very oppressive character. Large portions of the land were parceled out into immense estates, and titles were conferred upon their Spanish owners,

while the millions of the Aztec race were reduced to a condition
of peonage. In the center of each estate *haciendas* (fortified farm-houses) were erected ; and here the natives had to live
under the eye of the owner, or of his administrator, when the
owner was non-resident, as was frequently the case. The
owner, called a *hacendado,* fixed the rate of wages and required the peons to draw their supplies from his store, giving
him a double profit on their toil. A church was also erected, a
Spanish priest appointed to the charge, pledged to add spiritual
authority to sustain the claims of the hacendado. The Dominican monks were introduced, and under their administration
branches of the Spanish Inquisition were established in the
cities of Mexico and Puebla, for the repression of all dissent
and the punishment of any heresy. Under the weight of this
Spanish civilization the conquered race began their new life.
Without education, on the most scanty subsistence, without
owning the miserable hut of a single room that sheltered them,
they dragged on for three centuries, ranking among the most
ignorant and hopeless of the human race. Laws were passed
by the viceroys, who were appointed by the King of Spain, to
suit the situation, one of which was that the peons of one hacienda were not at liberty to transfer themselves to another without the written permit of the hacendado or his agent, if they
were in debt to the amount of twenty dollars. The estate owners took good care that their hands should be in debt to this
extent all the time, so as to secure the control of their labor.
Worse than this, many of these wretched people were formally
reduced to the condition of absolute slavery, and some were even
branded as such with the owner's initials by a red-hot iron,
women as well as men !* while the middle class, the real back-
bone of the nation, perished from the land.

It is no wonder that Las Casas, the Bishop of Chiapas, protested so earnestly against his countrymen's barbarities, which he
declared threatened to exterminate the Aztec race, nor that he
twice crossed the Atlantic to lay the sorrowful story of their

* Wilson's *Mexico*, p. 209.

wrongs before Ferdinand and Charles V. A grateful Mexican artist—Felix Parra—has immortalized the good bishop's humanity in that famous picture which occup'.s the place of honor in the Academy of Fine Arts in the city of Mexico. It is entitled "Las Casas Protecting the Indians," and represents the venerable man standing, while at his feet is the bleeding body of an Aztec, whose anguished wife clings to his robe as he raises the cross for their protection, and his face, uplifted, is illumined as he appeals to Heaven for help for the oppressed. Who that has looked upon that pleading countenance can ever forget it? The historians of the Conquest admit that the merciless Spaniards subjected not only the common people to these barbarous conditions of life, but also many of the *caziques*—nobles and governors—were degraded to the condition of peonage on the haciendas or to work in the mines.

The monks of the Franciscan order were soon imported to Catholicize the native people and thus complete the work of Cortéz. Magnificent endowments were provided for this order to carry on this work, until their head-quarters in the center of the city of Mexico became one of the most extensive and wealthy monastic-institutions in Christendom.

A hundred years after Cortéz reached Mexico, with this creed and civilization, the Pilgrim Fathers landed on Plymouth Rock, and, notwithstanding all the natural disadvantages, from which Mexico is so happily free, they planted a faith and a freedom which have made the wilderness, the sterile soil, and the rock-bound coast a true commonwealth, and consolidated a glorious civilization of peace, intelligence, and prosperity without a rival on earth—the very reverse of the debasement to which Spain and Rome degraded Montezuma's race and country. If the Romish Church became an utter failure in Mexico, as well as in Central and South America, that failure cannot be accounted for at a future day by any lack of material or adequate, even absolute, power for the accomplishment of the purposes to which Christianity aspires. She secured also boundless resources by means which she alone employs; she chose her methods, took all the time necessary to work out the results, and the world sees and laments her failure.

Notwithstanding her efforts to conceal the vast accumulations she had been sweeping into her treasuries for three hundred years, rendering no account to the nation, either as to their extent or use, deliberately and contemptuously refusing to contribute a single dollar toward the public burdens, while claiming all immunities, some approximation of the amount had been made manifest to the nation she had so impoverished, and successive governments have investigated in the hope that some portion of it might be made to fulfill its duty in helping bear the public burdens, especially when it became apparent that the lay estate could no longer carry all, or save the State from bankruptcy.

The most successful of these efforts was made by the Liberal government in 1850, when Señor Lerdo, then minister of public works, compiled a synopsis of the Mexican hierarchy, of the religious houses, their endowments, revenues, salaries, etc. While he could approximate very closely in regard to the monasteries, nunneries, their inmates, and the ecclesiastical staff, it was still in the power of the clericals to evade his investigations in regard to the bulk of the church property of Rome in Mexico, which they alone knew, and which for so many years they were using to fight against freedom in the land.

Señor Lerdo's exhibit was approved by the " Mexican Society of Geography and Statistics " as worthy of public confidence, and it created a sensation. Men knew that but a part of the resources of this foreign Church was laid bare, but what had been ascertained revealed vast sums lavished upon institutions and orders of indolent, ignorant monks and nuns, who were consuming in idleness wealth for want of which their poor suffering countrymen were steeped in poverty and their government without resources. It was then calculated that the Church of Rome owned " 861 estates valued at \$71,000,000, and 22,000 city lots at \$113,000,000—a total of \$184,000,000." Some writers value the property thus held at \$300,000,000, and the yearly income at $25,000,000, while the floating capital under the control of the archbishop and his chapter amounted to about $20,000,000, and was employed largely in loans and mortgages. The money power wielded by the Church was only second to her spiritual power, and she had a practical monopoly of both. Even as late as 1873, when we entered Mexico, there were only two or three banks in the republic. Yet there was plenty of money to be loaned, and at moderate rates of interest. For security they preferred bonds and mortgages, the expectation being that before the spirit left the dying frame influences could be brought to bear to lead the owner to leave a suitable part to be used for masses for his soul.

Señor Lerdo estimates the amount consumed in the maintenance of the 3,223 ecclesiastics was annually $20,000,000, besides the large amounts expended in the repairs and ornaments of an enormous number of churches. In 1793 the twelve bishops had $539,000 appropriated to their support, but now their revenues are so mixed up with the revenues of the Church that it is impossible to say how much these twelve "successors of the apostles" appropriate for their support.* Of this sum, it is understood, the Archbishop of Mexico received as his yearly salary $130,000, the Bishop of Puebla and Valladolid (Morelia) $110,000 each, and the rest in due proportion. These facts led several competent men to investigate the subject. Their substantial agreement renders it unnecessary that we should add statements to the representations which we have quoted and which are accepted in Mexico as sufficiently near to the facts of the case for all needful information.

As to the object for which these means were employed and the power that they conferred to accomplish them, Mr. Wilson remarks, in 1854:

In place of the Inquisition, which the reformed Spanish government took away from the Church of Mexico, the Church now wields the power of wealth, almost fabulous in amount, which is practically in the hands of

---

* *Mexico To-day*, by Brocklehurst. London, 1883. *Mexico*, 1861–62, by Dr. Lempriere. Wilson's *Mexico*, p. 322.

a close corporation sole. *The influence of the archbishop, as the substantial owner of nearly half the property in the city of Mexico,* gives him a power over his tenants unknown under our system of laws. Besides this a large portion of the church property is in money, and the archbishop is the great loan and trust company of Mexico. Nor is this power by any means an insignificant one. A bankrupt government is overawed by it. Men of intellect are crushed into silence, and no opposition can successfully stand against the influence of the Church Lord, who carries in his hand the treasures of heaven and in his money-bags the material that moves the world. To understand the full force of his power of money it must be borne in mind that Mexico is a country proverbial for recklessness in all conditions of life; for extravagant living and extravagant equipages; a country where a man's position in society is determined by the state he maintains; a country the basis of whose wealth is the mines of precious metal, where princely fortunes are quickly acquired and suddenly lost, and where hired labor has hardly a cash value. In such a country the power and influence of money has a meaning beyond any idea we can form. Look at a prominent man making an ostentatious display of his devotion; his example is of advantage to the Church, and the Church may be of advantage to him, for it has an abundance of money at six per cent. per annum, while the outside money-lenders charge him two per cent. per month. The Church, too, may have a mortgage upon his house overdue; and woe betide him if he should undertake a crusade against the Church. This is a string that the Church can pull upon, which is strong enough to overawe government itself. (P. 323.)

What has she to show the impoverished nation for these hundreds of millions which she has extracted from it ? A people without intelligence or morality or self-respect, steeped to the lips in ignorance, poverty, and peonage as the Mexicans were thirty years ago, and had been ever since the Conquest.

What became of all this wealth? Two or three quotations will indicate for what *purposes* it has been so prodigally employed, while the poor nation from which it was taken was perishing for the improved conditions which that wealth would surely have brought. Instead of that, this is the use of it in which they have gloried. Madame Calderon writes:

Innumerable were the churches we visited that evening. . . . The cathedral (in Mexico city) was the first we entered, and its magnificence struck us with amazement. Its gold and silver and jewels, its innumerable ornaments and holy vessels, the rich dresses of the priests, all seemed burning with almost intolerable brightness. The high altar was the most magnificent; the second, with its pure white marble pillars, the most imposing. . . . Each church had vied with the others in putting forth all its splendors of jewelry, of lights, of dresses, and of music. . . . There are between sixty and eighty others, some of them possessing little less wealth than the cathedral. (P. 108.)

We were also shown the jewels, which they keep buried in case of a revolution. The *custodia*, the gold stand in which they carry the Host, is entirely incrusted with large diamonds, pearls, emeralds, amethysts, topazes, and rubies. The chalices are equally rich. There are four sets of jewels for the bishop. One of his crosses is of emeralds and diamonds, another of topazes and diamonds, with great rings of the same belonging to each. (P. 274.)

To the right of the altar of the Cathedral of Puebla is the gem of the building. It is a figure of the Virgin Mary, near the size of life. Dressed in the richest embroidered satin, she displays strings of the largest pearls, hanging from her neck to below her knees. Around her brow is clasped a crown of gold, inlaid with emeralds of marvelous size. Her waist is bound with a zone of diamonds, from the center of which blaze numbers of enormous brilliants.

To cap this climax we need only quote one more testimony concerning the shrine

In which rest the figure of the "Virgin of Remedios," who enjoys the exclusive right, amid her other treasures, to three petticoats, one of them embroidered with pearls, another with emeralds, and a third with diamonds, the value of which is credibly stated at not less than three millions of dollars.

In addition to all this wealth hidden in her churches, Rome increased the burdens upon the nation by her monastic system, which she jealously secluded from any governmental inspection, or the influence of public opinion as to the personnel, property, or the rights and liberties of the thousands around whom she erected those massive walls. Señor Lerdo's statistics give their number. How fearful is the fact stated by Robertson: "In the city of Mexico alone there are more than fifty convents, male and female, containing three thousand three hundred individuals" (p. 515). The unfortunate city had borne this load for centuries notwithstanding all her protests. In proof of this Robertson adds:

In the year 1644 the city of Mexico presented a petition to the King of Spain, praying that no new monastery be founded, and that the revenues of those already established might be circumscribed; otherwise the religious houses would soon acquire the property of the whole country. . . . The abuse must have been enormous indeed, when even the bigoted Spanish Americans were induced to remonstrate against them.

He also states that these numerous clergy "were generally native Spaniards, devoted to the interests of the king, the Church, and the Inquisition, passing their lives in criminal indulgence or luxurious repose." The Spaniards took good care to reserve all the positions of their political system, as well as the case of the monastic establishments for men of their own race, and systematically excluded all Aztecs from the priesthood.

Clavigero took exception to this statement of Dr. Robertson, but on referring the question to Madrid the representations were amply vindicated (p. 518). It was a foreign priesthood from first to last that wrought out the sad condition that we deplore in Mexico.

Let us contemplate a single item of this heavy burden which dragged so long upon the resources of the land. Of the fifty convents, in the capital alone, the most important and wealthy was that of San Francisco. We speak of this one from our personal knowledge. It was in the center of the city, and covered an area equivalent to four large blocks of ground. It contained an immense church and four suffragan chapels. In the center was a magnificent patio, or cloister, where the monks promenaded, which, with its pillars and carved arches, must have cost a very large amount of money to erect. There were also residences of the superior, refectories, gardens, and orchards, with suitable equipments, the whole inclosed with massive walls. Its resources were so ample that it was regarded as the most wealthy monastic establishment in the New World, with few, if any, in the Old World to surpass it.

In this establishment, as in all the rest of its kind throughout the land, millions of the money of Mexico, extracted from its people by many questionable expedients, were locked up in costly buildings, while other millions were invested so as to yield large revenues for the luxurious use of the Spanish ecclesiastics who occupied them. They scorned the idea of owing any responsibility for their vast revenues or paying taxation toward the support of the government of the country, while they were ever ready to furnish funds to aid every effort to crush the party of freedom in order to perpetuate their own exclusive privileges. When the Liberals at last struggled up to power, and had to face the question, and under Benito Juarez became strong enough to enforce the decree of sequestration, in spite of the stubborn defense of the church party, which refused all compromise and threatened the government and the Congress with all the maledictions and ghostly penalties in their power, they began with this monastery of San Francisco, by a demand for admission and the keys. From within the monks refused. The general commanding sent for the engineer corps of his brigade, and led them to the center of the outer wall, where it was about twelve or fourteen feet high. Ladders were raised, and with pickax and crowbar the great stones were soon loosened. They broke down the wall to the ground, and while part remained to clear away the *débris* the rest went across the garden and began their work on the opposite wall, and when this was open a street, now known as Calle de Independencia, was completed right through the establishment. The monks were then informed that the government was in possession, and that they must leave. A small pension was assigned them for their old age. The fraudulent aspect of the whole affair was laid bare when it was discovered that this massive establishment and its revenues were monopolized by the *fourteen* old monks who stood there before the Liberal general!

The place was mapped out and divided into lots to suit purchasers, as were more than one hundred and fifty similar communities, and was turned to all sorts of uses—dwellings, schools, stores, florist's garden, places of amusement, and of manufacture. Being so many, they were sold at prices ridiculously low, considering their original cost. It became the duty of the writer to purchase a portion of this property of this San Francisco establishment, for our mission purposes, the part of it already mentioned as the "cloisters," for which we paid $16,300. The extent of the monastery may be imagined from the statement that this portión, though one hundred and eighty feet in depth, was not more than one fiftieth part of the property which had sheltered so many generations of lazy monks who added nothing to the resources of the country, but lived and died like

> " Idle drones,
> Born to consume the produce of the soil."

No wonder the freemen of Mexico wished to end this folly and deliver Mexico from the incubus of their presence. The archbishop protested, and threatened excommunication, but when all was done tried to force the purchasers into the concession of paying a second price to him as a condition of release from his interdicts, and giving the sanction of the Church to their title. A very few timid souls may have yielded to the illegal demand. The writer was artfully approached with the same purpose, but promptly declined to discredit the government of the republic by any such concession.

The great wealth she so long enjoyed corrupted the Church. In her self-sufficiency she arranged to elevate herself above all responsibility to any other power, and claimed inviolability and immunity from secular jurisdiction. The clericals should be amenable only to clerical courts, not merely for their own persons, but their property as well—a repetition of the prerogatives insisted on by the clergy of the mediæval ages, as lately shown by II. C. Lea, in his *History of the Inquisition.* These privileges were denominated *fueros*, under which

They established courts, in which every question relating to their own character, their functions, their property, was tried and pleaded, and obtained almost total exemption from the authority of civil law and civil judges.*

* Robertson's *Charles V.,* p. 34.

THE PLAZA, OR GREAT SQUARE, OF MEXICO.

This position, under which she could not be called to any responsibility by the State, immensely increased her power for doing mischief. With her abundance of money and the co-operation of the aristocracy, and the service of her partisans of every class, bound to her by all motives in heaven and earth, this ecclesiastical despotism dominated Mexico. It knew the price of the corrupt generals, and could furnish the funds for a "pronunciamento," under which the liberal administration of the hour would be overthrown, and the executive that replaced it would be required to furnish assurance that ecclesiastical matters should be held paramount in his administration. We have in our possession a body of photographs, fifty-two in number, portraits of the persons who have governed Mexico, under various titles, during the fifty-eight years from 1821 to 1879. Let three of these be deducted of those who ruled longest, Juarez, Maximilian, and Diaz, nearly seventeen years between them; there remain then fifty governors for forty-one years, or an average reign to each of about nine months and twenty-one days. The terrible fact is that each of these frequent changes was the result of a "pronunciamento," a conflict, bloodshed, and waste of money. It may be asked here whether there is a parallel to this atrocious case in all the history of Christendom.

Most of these sudden and expensive changes transpired in the great plaza, or square, shown in the opposite picture. This is the most historic spot in all Mexico. To the left is the great cathedral, built on the site of the Teocalli, or Temple, of Montezuma, so often referred to in the histories, and where so much of the wealth of the Church is stored. Back from the garden and where the flag waves is the National Palace, frequently called the "Halls of Montezuma." To the right, and under the tall flag, is the Municipal Palace, where the city government and courts are situated. The whole area is very extensive and is a great center of business and wealth.

Leaving the past out of view for the time, we present, from unquestioned evidence, some samples of their peculiar Catholicism and its practices, which will explain the degradation into

4

which Mexico has sunk. In doing this very little Protestant
testimony will be quoted—as some of our readers might hardly
resist the fear that such representations would be prejudiced—
nor will any Roman Catholic evidence be presented except that
of the highest character.

The two witnesses whose testimony will abundantly prove on
this ground the necessity of introducing the reformed faith
into Mexico are both of the highest class, prominent Romanists,
one from Spain and the other from France. The witness
from Spain is a lady, the accomplished wife of the first Spanish
embassador to Mexico, Madame Calderon De La Barca. The
reader is aware that as a result of the wars of the first Napoleon
and the state of things inaugurated in Spain by him something
approaching constitutional rule was established there—the Inquisition was abolished both in Spain and her dependencies. Mexico
felt the thrill of the better day and welcomed it heartily, and
before the despotism of the Spanish monarch, Ferdinand VII.,
could be restored, Mexico proclaimed her independence, which
was finally achieved in 1822. A feeble attempt was made to
regain the lost province, but that failed, and Mexico was henceforth to govern herself as well as she could, amid the struggle
with the Church and the aristocracy against the people. For
fifteen years Spain remained aggrieved, when, finding she was
only doing herself disadvantage by refusing to open diplomatic
relations with her revolted dependency, she concluded, in
1839, to forget her wounded pride, and, acknowledging the
independence of Mexico, appointed a minister to represent her.
The choice fell upon Señor Calderon De La Barca, who was well
suited for the purpose. His wife was eminently fitted to adorn
her high position by a splendid education, her many accomplish-
ments, and other qualities which enabled her to fill most acceptably the delicate duties of her position. Coming by the
United States, they left their daughters at school in New York,
and reached Mexico in December of 1839, where they were
received in the most cordial manner by the government and
the people. Madame Calderon became a special favorite, and

was indeed a privileged person. She was truly devout as well as accomplished. The clergy were delighted with her, and she had the *entrée* to every thing that a lady might see and study during the nearly three years that their term of office lasted. She was regarded as lending the luster of the Spanish court and aristocracy to the society of Mexico by her presence and courtesies.

Meanwhile, to interest her daughters, she wrote a regular series of letters, giving them full particulars of all she was privileged to see and enjoy, without any expectation that they would ever go into print. But W. H. Prescott, the historian, had meanwhile made the acquaintance of the family, and was allowed to hear these interesting letters. He recommended so earnestly that such rich stores of instruction and amusement should not be reserved for the eyes of a few friends only, but that they should be given to the world, that after Madame Calderon's return from Mexico she consented to do so, having made such alterations and omissions as were necessary in a private correspondence. They were accordingly published in a volume under the title *Life in Mexico.* How little she imagined the tumult of feeling the publication would cause among the clericals of Mexico! And yet there is not a bitter word or a false accusation in the whole book; nor could she imagine that the simple truth would hurt either their feelings or their interests. Yet it did, though so gently spoken, because they did not wish the light let in upon their doings.

The other person whose testimony is so important in regard to the state of things in Mexico was the Abbé Emanuel Domenech, chaplain of the French Expeditionary Force, the trusted representative of Napoleon III., of whose admissions we shall have more to say later on, when we reach the "Intervention" period, but whom we here introduce for his testimony in regard to what he found in Mexico after the failure of the French, and the death of Maximilian, when, his first office having ended, he was required before leaving Mexico to go through the land on a tour of observation, and report on the truth of the rumors which had reached the outside world as to the low

moral and religious condition of the clergy and Church of Rome
in Mexico. This duty he fulfilled thoroughly, and on his return
published his report in Paris, in 1867, entitled *Mexico As It Is,
the Truth Respecting its Climate, its Inhabitants, and its Government.* His account is a fearful record. Nothing worse, probably, was ever published of a Church and people than what his
pages contain. And yet the abbé was a prominent clergyman
of the Romish Church of France, describing the clergy and
people of the same Church in Mexico. The book was published
in French, and was evidently not intended for the Protestant
eye. As to the character of the religious sentiments which
the Mexican clergy have so long fostered and still sustain, the
abbé, writing in 1867, says :

Mexican faith is a dead faith. The abuse of external ceremonies, the
facility of reconciling the devil with God, the absence of internal exercises
of piety, *have killed the faith* in Mexico. It is in vain to seek good fruit
from the worthless tree, which makes Mexican religion a singular as-
semblage of heartless devotion, shameful ignorance, insane superstition,
and hideous vice. . . . The idolatrous character of Mexican Catholicism
is a fact well known to all travelers. The worship of saints and madon-
nas so absorbs the devotion of the people that little time is left to think
about God. Religious ceremonies are performed with a most lamentable
indifference and want of decorum. The Indians go to hear mass with
their poultry and vegetables which they are carrying to market. I have
had to abandon the Cathedral of Mexico, where I used to go every morning, because I could not collect my thoughts there. The gobble of
the turkeys, the crowing of cocks, the barking of dogs, the mewing
of cats, the chirping of birds in their nests in the ceiling, and the flea-
bites rendered meditation impossible to me, unaccustomed to live in such
a menagerie. . . . One day I was present at an Indian dance, celebrated
in honor of the patron saint of the village. Twenty-four boys and girls
were dancing in the church, in the presence of the priest. An Indian,
with his face concealed under a mask of an imaginary divinity resembling
the devil, with horns and claws, was directing the figures of the dance,
which reminded me of that of the Redskins! I remarked to the priest,
who, for all that, was an excellent priest, that it was very incongruous to
permit such a frolic in a church.

"The old customs," he replied, "are respectable; it is well to preserve
them, only taking care that they do not degenerate into orgies." . . .

During holy week I have seen processions of three thousand persons stripped and covered only with sackcloth, so coarse as to show that the individual had not even a shirt. The different phases of the passion of Christ were represented by groups of painted statues large as life, and by men and women placed upon stages, borne on the shoulders of hundreds of Indians. The bearers, bending under the weight of their burden, would go, from time to time, to refresh themselves at the liquor shops, leaving in the middle of the streets the groups representing the passion. Jews and Romans, decked with helmets of tin plate, breastplates of pasteboard, and breeches embroidered with silver, made a part of the procession.

The mysteries of the Middle Ages are utterly outdone by the burlesque ceremonies of the Mexicans. The accouchement of the Virgin on Christmas night appears to me indecent. In France the police would forbid the ceremony as a shock to public morals. But public morality being a thing unknown in Mexico the custom of representing the accouchement of the Virgin in many of the churches offends no one.

But we forbear any further quotations from this paragraph. The abbé finds himself forced to the sad conclusion, after their three hundred years of opportunity, which he expresses in the two sentences following :

It would require volumes to relate the Indian superstitions of an idolatrous character which exist to this day. For want of serious instruction you find in the Catholicism of the Indians numerous remains of the old Aztec paganism.

The observations I have made of the religious sentiments of the Mexicans are not confined to the ignorant classes. They apply equally to those who are well-to-do.*

As further samples of their religious practices we take from Madame Calderon's work the following extracts :

All Mexicans at present, men and women, are engaged in what are called the *desagracios*, a public penance performed at this season in the churches during thirty-five days. The women attend church in the morning, no man being permitted to enter, and men in the evening, when women are not permitted. Both rules are occasionally broken.

The other night I was present at a much stranger scene, at the discipline performed by the men, admission having been procured for us by certain means, *private but powerful*. Accordingly, when it was dark, enveloped from head to foot in large cloaks, and without the slightest idea of what

---

* See *Mexico and the United States*, by Gorman D. Abbot, p. 203, etc.

it was, we went on foot through the streets to the Church of San Augus-
tin. . . . The scene was curious. About one hundred and fifty men, enveloped in cloaks and serapes, their faces entirely concealed, were assembled in the body of the church. A monk had just mounted the pulpit,
and the church was dimly lighted, except where he stood in bold relief,
with his gray robes and cowl thrown back, giving a full view of his high
bald forehead and expressive face.

His discourse was a rude but very forcible and eloquent description of
the torments prepared in hell for impenitent sinners. The effect of the
whole was very solemn. It appeared like a preparation or the execution of a multitude of condemned criminals. When the discourse was finished they all joined in prayer with much fervor and enthusiasm, beating
their breasts and falling upon their faces. Then the monk stood up and
in a very distinct voice read several passages of Scripture descriptive of
the sufferings of Christ. The organ then struck up the *Miserere*, and all
of a sudden the church was plunged in profound darkness, all but a
sculptured representation of the crucifixion, which seemed to hang in the
air illuminated. I felt rather frightened, and would have been very glad
to leave the church, but it would have been impossible in the darkness.
Suddenly a terrible voice in the dark cried, "My brothers, when Christ
was fastened to the pillar by the Jews he was *scourged!*" At these words
the bright figure disappeared and the darkness became total. Suddenly
we heard the sound of hundreds of scourges descending upon the bare
flesh. I cannot conceive any thing more horrible. Before ten minutes
had passed the sound became *splashing*, from the blood that was flowing.

Incredible as it may seem, this awful penance continued, without in-
termission, for half an hour! If they scourged *each other* their energy
might be less astonishing.

We could not leave the church, but it was perfectly sickening; and
had I not been able to take hold of the Señora ——'s hand, and feel
something human beside me, I could have fancied myself transported into
a congregation of evil spirits. Now and then, but very seldom, a suppressed groan was heard, and occasionally the voice of the monk encouraging them by ejaculations or by short passages of Scripture. Sometimes
the organ struck up, and the poor wretches, in a faint voice, tried to join
in the *Miserere*. The sound of the scourging is indescribable. At the end
of half an hour a little bell was rung, and the voice of the monk was
heard calling upon them to desist; but such was their enthusiasm that the
horrible lashing continued louder and fiercer than ever.

In vain he entreated them not to kill themselves, and assured them
that Heaven would be satisfied and that human nature could not endure
beyond a certain point. No answer but the loud sound of the scourges,

which are, many of them, of iron, with sharp points that enter the flesh. At length, as if they were perfectly exhausted, the sound grew fainter, and little by little ceased altogether. We then got up, and with great difficulty groped our way in the pitch darkness through the galleries and down the stairs till we reached the door and had the pleasure of feeling the fresh air again. They say that the church floor is frequently covered with blood after one of those penances, and that a man died the other day in consequence of his wounds." *

In the Santa Teresa convent, in the refectory . . . they showed us a crown of thorns, which on certain days is worn by one of their number by way of penance. It is made of iron, so that the nails, entering inward, run into the head and make it bleed. . . .

We visited the different cells, and were horror-struck at the self-inflicted tortures. Each bed consists of a wooden plank raised in the middle, and on days of penance crossed by wooden bars. The pillow is wooden, with a cross lying on it, which they hold in their hands when they lie down. The nun lies on this penitential couch, embracing the cross, and her feet hanging out, as the bed is made too short for her upon principle. Round her waist she occasionally wears a band with iron points turning inward; on her breast a cross with nails, of which the points enter the flesh, of the truth of which I had melancholy ocular demonstration. Thus, after having scourged herself with a whip covered with iron nails, she lies down for a few hours on the wooden bars, and rises at four o'clock. All these instruments of discipline, which each nun keeps in a little box beside her bed, look as if their fitting place would be in the dungeons of the Inquisition. They made me try their *bed and board*, which I told them would give me a very decided taste for early rising.†

These are some of the ceremonies of modern Romanism in Mexico. My readers can imagine what St. Paul would have said had he stood with Madame Calderon on these occasions and had been asked if this were Christianity. Or the prophet Elijah, to whom it might have recalled the dreadful scene on Mount Carmel, when confronted by the one hundred and fifty priests of Baal, who "cried aloud and cut themselves with knives and lancets until the blood gushed out upon them." Was the above scene any higher, as worship or atonement, than what we missionaries witness of the self-

* *Life in Mexico*, by Madame Calderon, p. 213. Chapman & Hall, London, 1843.
† Ibid., pp. 223, 224.

torturing fakirs in India? Nay, verily, they are alike heathen abominations in the sight of God, and of no value to the soul. We brought from Mexico a full set of these instruments of torture, purchased from those who had used them. They are bloodstained and rusty from use, and are here presented photographed on a reduced scale. The set includes five articles. Number 1 is the scourge referred to by Madame Calderon, and is used in the more public penance, which she was allowed, as a special favor, to witness. It is about eighteen inches long, and the steel points project a full half inch on all sides. The lash is swept over both shoulders and strikes down to the waist. Numbers 3, 4, and 5 are for more private infliction, and are worn under the clothing. Number 2 is a circlet, called "the crown," for the head, the points being about an eighth of an inch long, and is to be tightened around the head. Number 3 and the rest have points nearly a quarter of an inch long, and are designed for the arms and limbs. Number 5 is for the waist, and has a strong buckle at the end, by which it may be tightened as much as the poor sufferer can endure. The tighter they are worn the more meritorious is the penance. So unmercifully are they used that they often make the blood trickle down into the stockings and shoes!

Now let us hear the abbé further as to the character of the *religion* which is professed in connection with these ceremonies. He says :

The Mexican is not a Catholic ; he is simply a Christian, because he has been baptized. I speak of the masses, and not of the numerous exceptions to be met with in all classes of society.

I say that Mexico is not a Catholic country :

1. Because a majority of the native population are semi-idolaters.

2. Because the majority of the Mexicans carry ignorance of religion to such a point that they have no other worship than that of form. It is materialism without a doubt. They do not know what it is to worship God in spirit and in truth, according to the Gospel. . . . If the pope should abolish all simoniacal livings, and excommunicate all the priests having concubines, the Mexican clergy would be reduced to a very small affair. Nevertheless, there are some worthy men among them, whose

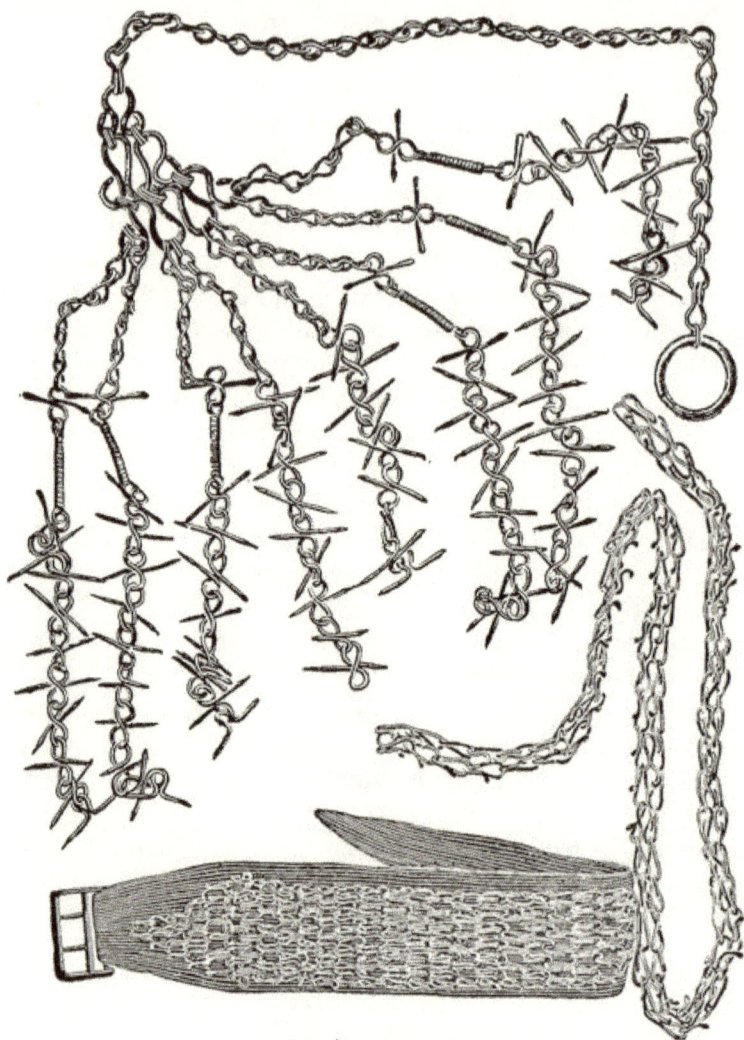

THE "DISCIPLINAS,"
Used on the body for self-torture.

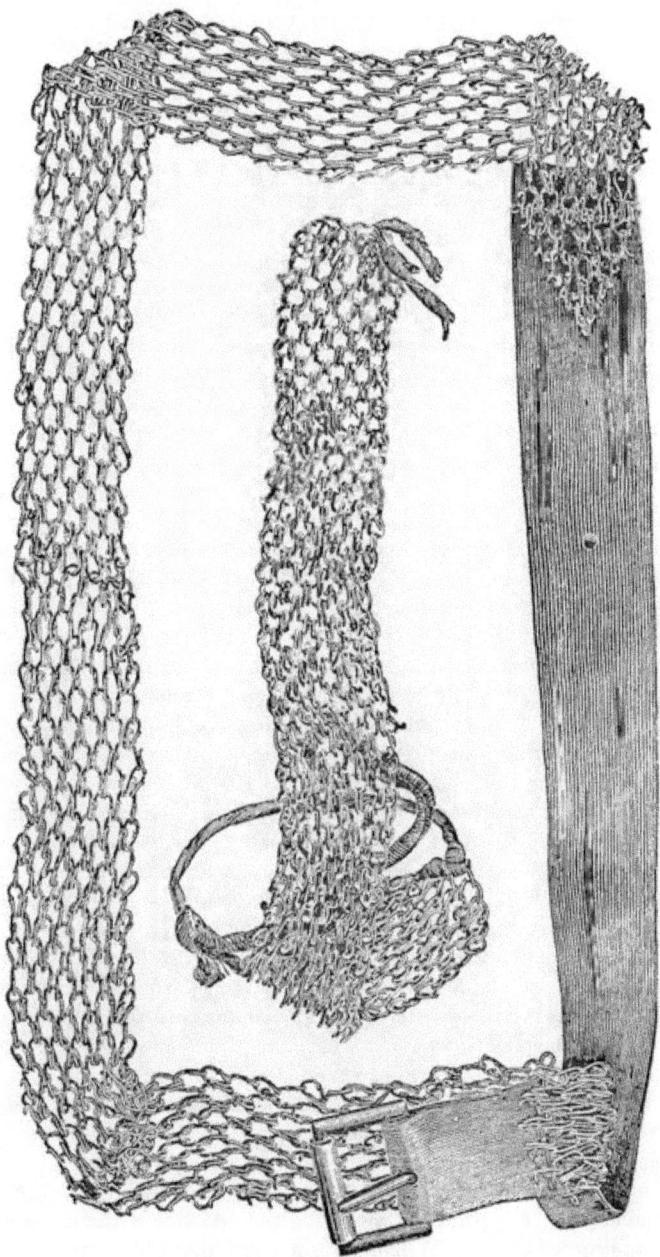

THE "DISCIPLINAS,"
Used on the body for self-torture.

conduct as priests is irreproachable. . . . In all Spanish America there are found, among the priests, the veriest wretches—knaves deserving the gallows—men who make an infamous traffic of religion. Mexico has her share of these wretches. Whose fault is it? In the past it has been Spanish manners—climate. In the present it is the episcopate. If the bishops had good seminaries, where pupils could receive a sound and serious education; if the bishops had more energy; if they were more cautious in the choice of candidates for the priesthood; if they required others to observe, and observed themselves, more scrupulously, the canonical laws of the Church, they would not see the disorder of which they are now the first to complain. . . . I have known, in the south and in the north of the Mexican Empire, pastors who gave balls at their houses and never thought the least in the world that it would be better to distribute bread to the poor than to give champagne and refreshments to the danseuses.

The clergy carry their love of the family to that of paternity. In my travels in the interior of Mexico many pastors have refused me hospitality in order to prevent my seeing their *nieces* and *cousins*, and their *children*. It is difficult to determine the character of these connections. Priests who are recognized as fathers of families are by no means rare. The people consider it natural enough, and do not rail at the conduct of their pastors, excepting when they are not contented with *one* wife. . . . I remember that one of these prelates, passing through a village near the episcopal city, the priest said to him, " Sire, have the goodness to bless my children and their mother." The good bishop blessed them. There was a chamberful. Another did better still. He baptized the child of one of his priests. Can a clergy of such character make saints ? I doubt. Nevertheless, they must not be taken for heretics. . . .

They make merchandise of the sacraments, and make money by every religious ceremony, without thinking that they are guilty of simony, and expose themselves to the censures of the Church. If Roman justice had its course in Mexico one half of the Mexican clergy would be excommunicated. . . . The well-instructed priests, disinterested and animated by a truly apostolical spirit, holy souls whose religious sentiments are of good character, constitute an insignificant minority. . . .

But is it not a lie to God and men to make a vow of poverty and then live in the midst of abundance and comfort, as the ecclesiastics of all Spanish America do?

One of the greatest evils in Mexico is the exorbitant fee for the marriage ceremony. The priests compel the poor to live without marriage, by demanding for the nuptial benediction a sum that a Mexican mechanic, with his slender wages, can scarcely accumulate in fifty years of the strictest economy. This is no exaggeration. The consequences of the excessive demands for perquisites in general are as lamentable to public morality as to religion. One of the first duties of the Mexican episcopate should be, in my opinion, to reduce the fee for baptisms, marriages, dispensations, and every thing else indispensable to the performance of religious duties.*

Another 'brief testimony from Madame Calderon which is especially pointed. The evil existing in monastic institutions was concealed as far as possible from her; yet, doubtless with a sad heart, she made this entry:

Some of these convents are not entirely free from scandal. Among the monks there are many who are openly a disgrace to their calling, though I firmly believe that by far the greater number lead a life of privation and virtue.

Once more, as it intrudes itself on her view even in the public streets, she is reminded of the attempts of the Viceroy Revillagigedo, as long ago as his time, to restrain the profligacy of these monks by stern expulsion. She adds:

Alas! could his excellency have lived in these degenerate days and beheld certain monks of a certain order drinking *pulque* and otherwise disporting themselves, nay, seen one, as we but just now did from the window, strolling along the street by lamp-light, with an *Yndita* (Indian girl) tucked under his arm! (Pp. 153, 238.)

In one of the quotations from the abbé we read, " The Mexican is not a Catholic; he is simply a Christian because he has been baptized." This distinction is amusing to a Protestant. How a " semi-idolater," " ignorant of spiritual worship," can be a Christian in any sense acceptable to God is something evangelicals cannot realize, and it shows how sacred terms are perverted by the false theology of Romanism. He would explain his remark by the doctrine of baptismal regeneration. The poor Indian having been baptized by one in the " apostolic succession " was therein regenerated, notwithstanding all his " insane superstition " and " hideous vice." Poor Mexico! Romanism has not saved her; she needs the true Gospel

* *Mexico and the United States*, pp. 195, etc.

of the Lord Jesus, offering her the mercy that she requires, freely.

The perversion has been so great and the abolition of biblical ideas of truth and purity so complete in the ruin wrought by this fallen Church upon the nation that the evangelization of Mexico has thus been made the most difficult work to which the Church of Christ can now address herself. If it were not for the promised power of the Holy Spirit, to whose blessed agency all things are possible, the condition would seem almost hopeless. But with this co-operation it is our privilege to believe and expect that the mercy and consolation reserved for this deeply injured people will all the more transcend the weight of sorrow through which they have passed, so that "where sin abounded grace shall much more abound."

Rome began her rule in Mexico by sweeping away by red-handed violence the intellectual stamina of the nation as well as its records and literature. On this point Baron Humboldt's testimony is conclusive. His great learning and thorough inquiry in examinations conducted on the ground itself enable him to speak with full authority. Of the original wrong and destruction of the middle class, which wrecked the nation, he writes :

The Christian fanaticism broke out in a particular manner against the Aztec priests and the teopiqui, or ministers of the divinity, and all those who inhabited the teocallis, or houses of God, who might be considered as the depositaries of the historical, mythological, and astronomical knowledge of the country, were exterminated; for the priests observed the meridian shade in the gnomons and regulated the calendar. The monks burned the hieroglyphical paintings by which every kind of knowledge had been transmitted from generation to generation. The people, deprived of these means of instruction, were plunged in an ignorance so much the deeper, as the missionaries were unskilled in the Mexican languages and could substitute few new ideas in place of the old. The better sort of Indians, among whom a certain degree of culture and intellect might be supposed, perished in great part at the commencement of the Spanish conquest, the victims of European ferocity. The natives who remained consisted only of the most indigent race—poor cultivators, artisans, weavers—porters who were used as beasts of burden. How shall we judge, then, from these miserable remains of a powerful people, of the degree of cultivation to which it had risen from the twelfth to the sixteenth century, and of the intellectual development of which it is susceptible ? If all that remained of the French or German nation were a few poor agriculturists, could we read in their features that they belonged to nations which had produced a Descartes and a Clairaut, a Kepler and a Leibnitz ? *

In General Lew Wallace's valuable work entitled *Quetzel, or The Fair God*, the author has united together the incidental evidence which history and legend still hold of Montezuma's empire and people as they were before the Spaniards invaded their country and savagely destroyed their prosperity. It was a worthy service to render to Mexico, and may well rank in this sense next to that which he embodied in *Ben Hur*, when presenting to the world the civilization which characterized the period of the Incarnation and the nature of the foreign rule which had displaced the native dynasty of the Jewish people. Even Nero's despotic government left uninjured the conquered race in the very particulars in which the Roman Church and Spanish government crushed life and freedom and hope out of the Aztec people. This conviction was ingrained into the minds of many of the intelligent native gentlemen of Mexico. One such said to the writer in 1875 :

My countrymen are to-day in a far worse condition than they were when Cortéz burned his ships behind him in the harbor of Vera Cruz and marched to the conquest of Montezuma's empire—worse fed, worse clad, worse housed, and more ignorant than they were that day.

Few that know Mexico would call this terrible accusation in question ; while the quotations which we have made from the work of the Abbé Domenech (whose veracity no Romanist will call in question) show that it is the Church and not the State that must be held responsible for the guilt involved in the above charge. Take the single fact of the burning shame so long festering in the social life of Mexico, which is one of the charges that the abbé brings against his Church, the absence of

* *Essai Politique,* vol. i, p. 117.

marriage and the consequent general prevalence of illegitimacy over the land.

Nor was it from the poor uninstructed millions of the Otomí or Aztec race alone that she took away the "key of knowledge," as we learned when fitting up a church in the city of Mexico. The Ten Commandments were placed on either side of the pulpit. Intelligent Mexican gentlemen were constantly coming in to see the changes going forward in the building, and they would stand in front of the second commandment and read every word of it, read it again, as those who had never seen it before, and sometimes would turn to us and ask if that "was really in the Bible?"

Then, mark the universal practice of image worship, the doctrine of purgatory, with its corresponding tenet of indulgences; without the Bible or the school, terrorized by the Inquisition, and threatened with the "major excommunication," or the perpetual pains of hell, if they desired a change or claimed freedom to worship God. It seems incredible that a Church could thus crowd a nation into destitution and ignorance, but the testimony cannot be questioned. Beyond the impoverishment caused by her extravagant church demands, there was another means more potent still to draw from the people their resources, by masses and indulgences for the souls of the dead. General Waddy Thompson, United States embassador in Mexico, expresses his amazement at what he saw in 1845. He writes:

The immense wealth which is collected in the churches is not by any means all, or even the larger portion, of the wealth of the Mexican Church and clergy. They own very many of the finest houses in Mexico and other cities (the rents of which must be enormous), besides valuable real estates all over the republic. Almost every person leaves a bequest in his will for masses for his soul, which constitute an encumbrance upon the estate, and thus nearly all the estates of the small proprietors are mortgaged to the Church.

As a means of raising money I would not give the single institution of the Catholic religion of masses and indulgences for the benefit of the souls of the dead for the power of taxation possessed by any government. Of all the artifices of cunning and venality to extort money from credulous

weakness there is none so potential as a mass for the benefit of the souls
in purgatory. Our own more rational faith teaches that when a man dies
his account is closed and his destiny for good or evil is fixed forever, and
that he is to be judged by "the deeds done in the body;" but another
creed inculcates that that destiny may be modified or changed by prayers
at once posthumous, vicarious, and venal. It would seem to be in direct
contradiction to the Saviour in the comparison of the camel passing
through the eye of a needle. Nothing is easier than for a rich man to
enter the kingdom of heaven; he purchases that entrance with money.
I do not know how the fee for these masses is exacted, but I do know that
it is regularly paid, and that, without the fee, the mass would be regarded
of no value or efficacy. I remember that my washerwoman once asked me
to lend her two dollars. I asked her what she wanted with it. She told
me that there was a particular mass to be said on that day which relieved
the souls in purgatory from ten thousand years of torment, and that she
wished to secure the benefit of it for her mother. I asked her if she was
fool enough to believe it. She answered, "Why, yes, sir; is it not true?"
and with a countenance of as much surprise as if I had denied that the
sun was shining. I have seen stuck up on the door of the Church of San
Francisco, one of the largest and most magnificent in Mexico, an adver-
tisement, of which the following was the substance :

"His holiness the pope (and certain bishops which were named) have
granted thirty-two thousand three hundred years, ten days, and six hours
of indulgence for this mass."

The manifest object of this particularity is to secure the more effectual belief in the imposture. By thus giving to it the air of a business
transaction, a sort of contract between the devotee and the Almighty,
by his authorized agent and vicegerent on earth, the pope, is established. I tremble at the apparent blasphemy of even describing these
things.*

Such indulgences are constantly seen, as advertisements on
the church doors in Mexico, without any attempt at conceal-
ment. These facts justify Father Gavazzi's assertion that " the
dogma of purgatory became the true California of the priests,
the best gold-mine of the papal system."

The pictures of purgatory, provided to make the requisite
impressions on those who have lost friends, are frightful. One
of them, purchased in Mexico, lies before us. It represents a
lady shut up in this miniature hell, surrounded by thick walls

* *Recollections of Mexico*, p. 43.

and the window barred with heavy irons. On her wrists is fastened a yard of heavy chain, while the lurid flames rise round her to the height of her shoulders. In agony she lifts up her manacled hands as in imploring supplication to her living friends to furnish the aid that shall end her misery and deliver her from the place of torment. No wonder that such pictures, among ignorant people, do the work they were intended to accomplish. Well did that vile peddler of such indulgences, sent out with full powers by Pope Leo X., in 1507, to dispose of them, know how to raise the requisite terror in the imagination of the crowds that stood around him in Germany, then so ignorant and superstitious. But Roman greed outdid itself when God's agent, Martin Luther, entered the crowd and heard the audacious Tetzel finish his harangue with the words, "The very moment the money clicks on the bottom of this chest the soul escapes from purgatory and flies to heaven! Bring your money, bring money, bring money!" Luther was horrified with the profanation, and within a few days nailed up the ninety-five immortal theses on the doors of the Cathedral of Wittenberg, and the great Reformation was born. Our characteristic designation sprang from the protest of this honest monk. We are, and will remain, Pro-test-ants in the name of Almighty God, against all doctrines that cannot be deduced from his Holy Bible.

But, alas for the Mexican people! Denied the word of God, they have no way of ascertaining that the doctrine is of man's invention, a perversion of the Gospel, and a dishonor to the Redeemer's office. He is represented as interceding for the *salvation* of all who "come unto God by him." But if multitudes of them are in purgatory, as Romanism teaches, they are practically beyond his help. He can do nothing for them, as the pope alone holds the key. There they may remain for ages, unless they have left money for masses, or their friends supply the lack. "The power of the keys"—a phrase which they boastingly use—is only exerted where money furnishes the motive, so that it has been bitterly said of these conditions,

5

"Where there is high money there is high mass, low money, low mass, and no money, no mass."

One trembles on reflecting what will be the ultimate vengeance of God upon a system that so daringly misrepresents his mercy and the sole efficacy of the sacrifice of his Son. Now being the "accepted time, and this the day of salvation," by "the precious blood of Christ, which cleanseth from all sin," this leaves nothing for purgatory or priest to cleanse after death, and its special honor is that it is offered to all, "without money and without price." A glorious Gospel for even the poorest sinner on earth.

Many of the educated men of Mexico, disgusted with the manifestations of this money-getting system of Romanism, are infidels or free-thinkers, like the same class of men in France and Italy, while many of them who are not infidels cannot reconcile this doctrine of their Church with common sense or with the justice of God. Madame Calderon refers to a conversation with one such after attending a "high mass" for the release of a mutual friend :

C——n received an invitation some time ago to attend the *honras* of the daughter of the Marquis of S——a. M. was observing to-day that if this Catholic doctrine was firmly believed, and that the prayers of the Church are indeed availing to shorten the sufferings of those who have gone before us, to relieve those whom we love from thousands of years of torture, it is astonishing how the rich do not become poor and the poor beggars in furtherance of this object; and that if the idea be purely human it showed a wonderful knowledge of human nature on the part of the inventor, as what source of profit could be more sure? (P. 81.)

Madame Calderon evidently sympathized with the idea presented. How can men really believe as the priests of Rome profess to do and act so heartlessly? Here is the pope, who upholds so strongly the belief in purgatory and in his own power of release from it, and yet only *money* can move him to open those dreadful doors and let out the sufferers. If this man truly believed in his doctrine and his power to meet the dreadful emergency of multitudes—of millions—shut up, as they declare, in fires " only a little less hot than hell itself," how could he rest day or night ?   Should we not expect that his zeal would consume him in his efforts to issue indulgences and offer these releasing masses from early morning to late at night, not waiting for any other motive but the promptings of compassion alone, to free them daily by the thousands from their tortures? And would not the Mexican clergy, if they sincerely maintained this doctrine, instead of waiting for the low motive of money to arouse them, rush to the rescue and be on their altars from dawn to dark to relieve such sufferers, and especially the poor who have nothing with which to pay for their release ?

CHAPTER II.

WE should not do our subject justice if we failed to present
to our readers one of their religious peculiarities, and perhaps
the most awful of them all—for the extent to which it has de-
based the nation. It is equally unscriptural and irrational with
those already named, and amazes strangers who visit the land.
Even Romanists, who come not merely from Protestant countries, where religious competition has saved them from descending to the sad depths in which they find their Church in Mexico, but natives of Spain and Italy as well, are pained to behold what they witness here. Madame Calderon will be again
our impartial guide. Here, too, we shall be conscious of that
occasional quiet humor which she could not quite repress as the
amazing stories were told her by bishops and others. Though
a devoted Romanist, there was a revulsion in her intelligent
mind as she witnessed these absurd and wicked idolatries of her
Church in Mexico. Their splendor and costly decorations could
not blind her as to their true character. We are referring to the
practices of the *Mariolatry*, which has no parallel in any other
land, and which has raised up two Virgins for the adoration of
the Mexican people!

Madame Calderon tells the story of the first of these Virgins
as follows :

We went lately to pay a visit to the celebrated " Virgin de los Remedios," the Spanish patroness and rival of "Our Lady of Guadalupe."

This Virgin was brought over from Spain by the army of Cortéz, and on the night of the *Noche Triste* the image disappeared, and nothing further was known of it, until, on the top of a barren mountain in the heart of a large maguey, it was found. Her restoration was joyfully hailed by the Spaniards. A church was erected on the spot. A priest was appointed to take charge of the miraculous image. Her fame spread abroad. Gifts of immense value were brought to her shrine. A treasurer was appointed to take care of her jewels, a camarista (a keeper of robes) to superintend her rich wardrobe. No wealthy dowager died in peace until she had bequeathed to Our Lady of Remedies her largest diamond or her richest pearl. In seasons of drought she is brought in from her dwelling in the mountain and carried in procession through the streets. The viceroy himself on foot used to lead the holy train. One of the highest rank drives the chariot in which she is seated. In succession she visits the principal convents, and as she is carried through the cloistered precincts the nuns are ranged on their knees in humble adoration. Plentiful rains immediately follow her arrival or pestilences are terminated. . . . It is true that there came a time when the famous curate Hidalgo the prime mover in the revolution, having taken as his standard an image of the Virgin of Guadalupe, an increased rivalry arose between her and the Spanish Virgin; and Hidalgo being defeated and forced to fly, the image of the Virgin de los Remedios was conducted to Mexico dressed as a general and invoked as the patroness of Spain. . . .

The church where she is enshrined is handsome, and above the altar is a copy of the original Virgin. After we had remained there a little while we were admitted into the sanctum, where the identical Virgin of Cortéz, with a large silver maguey, occupies her splendid shrine. The priest retired and put on his robes, and then returning, and all kneeling before the altar, he recited the *Credo*. This over, he mounted the steps, and, opening the shrine where the Virgin was incased, knelt down and removed her in his arms. He then presented her to each one of us in succession, every one kissing the hem of her satin robe. She was afterward replaced with the same ceremony.

The image is a wooden doll about a foot high, holding in its arms an infant Jesus, both faces evidently carved with a rude penknife, two holes for the eyes and another for the mouth. The doll was dressed in blue satin and pearls, with a crown upon her head, and a quantity of hair fastened onto the crown. No Indian idol could be much uglier. As she has been a good deal scratched and destroyed in the lapse of ages, C——n observed that he was astonished that they had not tried to restore her a little. To this the padre replied that the attempt had been made by several artists, each one of whom had sickened and died. He also mentioned as one of her miracles that living on a solitary mountain she had never been robbed; but I fear the good padre is somewhat oblivious, as this sacrilege has happened more than once. On one occasion, a crowd of léperos (beggars) being collected, and the image carried round to be kissed, one of them, affecting intense devotion, bit off the large pearl that adorned her dress in front, and before the theft was discovered he had mingled with the crowd and escaped. When reminded of the circumstance the padre said it was true, but that the thief was a Frenchman! (P. 120.)

This ill-conditioned image has been for more than three centuries the special idol of the Spanish aristocracy in Mexico. She was served with great splendor, and was the owner of the famous petticoats valued at $3,000,000. Waddy Thompson describes one of her processions which he witnessed, "numbering some forty to fifty thousand persons, including all the high dignitaries of the government, the Church, and the army," all professing to believe the priestly story that every attempt to repair the broken nose or to supply the lost eye "ended in the death of the daring sinner who would attempt to improve an image made in heaven." The Empress Carlota, on her arrival in Mexico in 1864, accepted this Virgin as her protectress, and resolved to serve her with an earnestness that would popularize her with the nation. Those who were present and saw her do it described to the writer how zealously she headed the procession of Mexican ladies, she, as each of them, carrying an immense burning wax taper as they walked through the dusty streets of the capital in honor of this image. The poor lady evidently knew not all the facts involved in her action, or how much too late it was to restore the popularity that had been waning ever since the republican movements, which began in 1810, bringing to the front another idol—another Virgin Mary—instead of this one, formerly the popular image of Mexico.

We should say that the picture of this Virgin which we here present and which is the accepted type, brought from Mexico, rather *flatters* the original! The artist evidently did not follow copy in this case and give the world a faithful representation of the image which is so truly described as "rude and ugly." Of course one is expected to make allowance for a lady who not

THE VIRGIN OF REMEDIOS,
The Patroness of the Spaniards in Mexico.

only went through the vicissitudes and hard experiences of "the Conquest," but who in addition has added three hundred and fifty to her years of earthly life and shows now the effect of both! In January, 1874, I paid a visit to this shrine to see and hear for myself what there was remaining of this once famous image. The church and its surroundings was a picture of desolation. The only power that could have restored its prestige and glory had been overthrown when the cause of Maximilian and Carlota had been crushed. She shared their fate. The church, once so resplendent, was shut up, but three or four poor people, who were hanging round in expectation of an occasional visitor, on seeing us approach started off to call the priest of the church. He soon appeared, the doors were opened, and after robing himself he took down the image from her shrine with the usual large amount of formality and many genuflections, and presented her to our view, and then lowered her near enough for us to kiss the hem of her garment, if so disposed, and seemed rather disappointed when we declined the honor. Our lack of service and reverence, however, was made up by the three or four beggars who had come in when we entered. They adoringly kissed the "sacred" margin of her petticoat and crossed themselves.

As we stood at that altar and contemplated this image our hearts went out in deep compassion to the misguided millions of Mexico who have been taught to trust in and worship *such* a rival of Almighty God as this is, and at the same time became conscious of a deeper feeling than we have ever felt before of the guilt of a clergy who could thus mislead their fellow-beings. This idolatry explained the poverty, ignorance, and degradation of the people. I asked the priest why the Virgin no longer went in grand processions to Mexico, as of old, and he sadly replied, "Ah, Señor, the Virgin of Remedios goes no more in processions until the 'Laws of Reform' are repealed!" All right. Then she will probably stay where she is, more and more deserted, for the liberty-loving Mexicans are not likely to go back on their grand record of freedom. While the Mexicans are greatly to be pitied, we have no reason to suppose that we should have been in a better state had we for three hundred years been bearing the burdens they have carried. Give the United States to the absolute control of the same Church and the same kind of clergy, let them inculcate the same doctrines and practices, place the same restrictions on freedom of thought and the Bible, grant them an established Church and the parochial school system, with political corruption in national affairs, and what reason have we to suppose that in half the time they have thus wielded power in the land of the Aztecs, say one hundred and fifty years, we would not show an equal ruin and degradation?

Still, we have not completed our showing of the unique situation in Mexico. The second image of the Virgin, which has figured as a bitter rival of this one, shall have her story presented to us by Madame Calderon, who had the narration from the lips of the resident bishop, on the occasion of her visit to the grand shrine of the Virgin of Guadalupe, with all the surroundings of the gorgeous cathedral to impress her favorably.

The "divine painting" of the Virgin of Guadalupe represents her in a blue cloak covered with stars, a garment of crimson and gold, her hands clasped, and her foot on a crescent, supported by a cherub. The original painting is coarse, and only remarkable for the tradition attached to it. Madame Calderon's narrative is as follows:

We went to call on the bishop, the Ylustrisimo Señor Campos, whom we found in his canonicals, and who seems a good little old man, but no conjurer. . . . Folding his hands and looking down, he proceeded to recount the history of the miraculous apparition, pretty much as follows:

"In 1531, ten years and four months after the conquest of Mexico, a fortunate Indian, whose name was Juan Diego, passing by the mountain of Tepeyac, a short distance south of Mexico city, the holy Virgin suddenly appeared before him and ordered him to go in her name to the bishop, the Ylustrisimo D. Fr. Juan de Zumarraga, and to make known to him that she desired to have a place of worship erected in her honor on that spot. The next day the Indian passed by the same place, when again the holy Virgin appeared before him and demanded the result of his commission. Juan Diego replied that in spite of his endeavor he had not been able to obtain an audience of the bishop. 'Return,' said the Virgin, 'and say that it is I, the Virgin Mary, mother of God, who sends thee.' Juan Diego obeyed the divine orders, yet still the bishop would not give him credence, merely desiring him to bring some sign or token of the Virgin's will. He returned with this message on the 12th of December, when, for the third time, he beheld the apparition of the Virgin. She now commanded him to climb to the top of the barren rock of Tepeyac, to gather the roses which he should find there, and to bring them to her. The humble messenger obeyed, though well knowing that on that spot were neither flowers nor any trace of vegetation. Nevertheless, he found the roses, which he gathered and brought to the Virgin Mary, who, throwing them into his *tilma* [blanket], said, 'Return, show these to the bishop, and tell him that these are the credentials of thy mission.' Juan Diego set out for the episcopal residence, and when he found himself in the presence of the prelate he unfolded his *tilma* to show him the roses, when there appeared imprinted on it the miraculous image which has existed for more than three centuries.

"When the bishop beheld it he was seized with astonishment and awe, and conveyed it in a solemn procession to his own oratory, and shortly after this splendid church was erected in honor of the patroness of New Spain. From all parts of the country," continued the old bishop, "people flocked in crowds to see our Lady of Guadalupe, and esteem it an honor to obtain sight of her. What must be *my* happiness, who can see her most gracious majesty every hour and every minute of the day? I would not quit Guadalupe for any other part of the world, nor for any temptation that could be held out to me;" and the pious man remained for a few moments as if rapt in ecstasy.*

The old bishop's account is borrowed, but in very much abridged form, from a printed sermon of Cardinal de Lorenzana, Archbishop of Mexico in 1760; and that sermon and description, be it observed, is the general source from whence all writers take in presenting this legend, though its value as to veracity is brought much into question by the fact that the cardinal did not give the story to the world until two hundred and twenty-seven years after the events were said to have occurred! Those who desire the fuller account of the legend will find it in

* *Life in Mexico*, p. 60.

Brantz Mayer's valuable work.* His account is taken from that printed by Ignatio Barillo y Perez.

All persons visiting this now famous cathedral corroborate the account of the wealth and splendor which have been lavished on this shrine until the facts seem bewildering, and the extravagant ceremonial of her anniversary every December may well be reckoned among the amazing facts of this world, especially considering the ponderous edifice that the clericals have ventured to build upon such a slender foundation as this story of the poor Indian peon and his blanket. Robertson describes the splendor of the scene which he witnessed on the anniversary. He says:

The interior decorations of the church are sumptuous in the extreme. The altar at the north end, and the canopy and the pillars around it, are of the finest marbles. Above it, in a frame of solid gold, covered with a crystal plate, is the figure of the Virgin, painted on the Indian's *tilma*, presented in the picture on the opposite page here. On each side of the image, within the frame, and extending its whole length, are strips of gold literally crusted with emeralds, diamonds, and pearls. At the feet of the figure there are again large clusters of the same costly gems. From each side of the frame issues a circle of golden rays, while above it, as if floating in the air, hangs the figure of a dove of solid silver as large as a goose in size.†

We here present this second Virgin of Mexico to our readers. This picture, gorgeously illuminated, of her whom they delight to call "The Patron Saint and Protectress of Mexico" is found in nearly all the homes in the land, in every variety, from cheap engravings to costly paintings. With her devotees the greatest day in the whole year is the 12th of December, the anniversary of her miraculous appearance, when the crowds come from all parts to witness the rites instituted in her honor. Until recently the whole pompous ceremonial was countenanced by the presence and apparent devotion of all the high officers of the government, including the president himself. In evi-

* *Mexico: Aztec, Spanish, and Republican*, in two volumes, Drake & Co., Hartford, vol. i, p. 256, etc.

† *A Visit to Mexico*, by W. P. Robertson, vol. ii. London, 1853.

NON FECIT TALITER OMNI NATIONI.

THE VIRGIN OF GUADALUPE,
The Patroness of the native Mexicans.

dence of this amazing folly notice the testimony of General Thompson. After describing the scene and its prodigality of wealth in honor of this idol of Mexico, he says:

If the reader should ask, "Does any body believe this?" I answer, that on the anniversary of this miracle I went to the Church of Guadalupe, where more than fifty thousand people were assembled, among them President Bravo and all his cabinet, the archbishop, and, in short, every body in high station in Mexico. An oration in commemoration of the event was delivered by a distinguished member of the Mexican Congress. He described all the circumstances of the affair as I have given them, but with all the extravagance of Mexican rhetoric, just as one of our Fourth of July orators would narrate the events of the Revolution. The president and others exchanged all the while smiles and glances of pride and exultation.*

Eleven years later R. A. Wilson, of Rochester, visited Mexico and made a thorough examination of their ceremonies in this Gaudalupe cathedral. Two of his Sabbaths were given to the matter. He says:

The State and the Church were duly represented upon the platform by the president [then Santa Anna], the nuncio, and the archbishop. Beneath the platform, and within the silver railing, were the official representatives of foreign nations, who were easily distinguished by a strip of gold or silver lace upon the collars and lapels of their coats. To this uniformity of dress there was a single exception in the person of the new American embassador, Mr. Gadsden, whose plain black dress and clerical appearance would have conveyed the impression that he was a Methodist preacher, had he not been engaged, with all the awkwardness of a novice, upon his knees in crossing himself. . . . On the next Sabbath I attended the Indian celebration of the appearance of "the most blessed Virgin." During the Christmas holidays in the country of the Pintos I had seen Indians dressed up in whimsical attire, enacting plays, and singing and dancing; but this was the first time that I had ever seen, in a house dedicated to the worship of God, or, rather, in a temple consecrated to the adoration of the Virgin, fantastic dances performed by Indians under the supervision of priests and bishops. When I found out what the entertainment was I was heartily vexed that I should be at such a place on the Sabbath day. The dancing and singing were bad enough, but the climax was reached when the priest came down from the altar, with an array of attendants

* *Recollections of Mexico*, p. 112.

having immense candles, to the side-door, where the procession stopped to witness the discharge at midday of a large amount of fire-works in honor of the Virgin Mary.

I hurried home from this profanation of the Lord's day, and sat down and comtemplated the old Aztec god, who had been deified for his wisdom, and could not but regret the change that had been imposed upon these Indians. The next Sabbath after this was the national anniversary of the miraculous apparition; but having seen enough of this sort of thing I concluded that my Sabbath would be better spent in staying at home and reading a Spanish Testament, which had been brought into the country in violation of the law. When I was first at the city of Mexico, Governor Letcher related to me the stratagem by which he contrived to smuggle an American Bible agent out of the country when the police were after him, on an accusation of selling prohibited books; for in such a country as this the word of God is a prohibited book.[*]

One is surprised that so competent an observer as Madame Calderon is so deficient in her account of the services at Guadalupe. It could not be for lack of opportunity, for she remained in Mexico for more than two years, and must have seen it all, especially at the time of the great festivals. Her silence, to us, can be accounted for in two ways—either the fact of her Spanish interests leading her to sympathize rather with the Virgin of Remedies, or else she had witnessed the scenes at Guadalupe and had been so grieved that she was unwilling to describe them.

A recent witness, Mrs. F. C. Gooch, describes the occurrences in 1887. A change for the better has certainly come at Guadalupe, especially in the entire withdrawal of government patronage; yet these observations evidence that enough remains of these manifestations of folly and profanity in the name of religion to grieve the heart of every intelligent Romanist who visits Mexico. She writes:

A party of Americans, of which I was one, with a few Mexicans, went to Guadalupe the night before the grand *fiesta* was to take place. To adequately describe the scene would require the pen of a Dickens. The poor, the lame, the halt, and the blind had been there congregated as well as the hale and the hearty. The babel of voices, the songs of the Indians,

---

[*] *Mexico and its Religion*, p. 230, by R. A. Wilson. Harper & Co., 1856.

the fire-crackers and sky-rockets, suggested to us, instead of a religious congregation, rather a demoniacal pandemonium. Gambling was in full force. . . . The air was filled with an indiscriminate jangle of unearthly sounds, from a variety of very earthly instruments, which, with the dust, the odor of the meat cooking, and the fumes from the crowd, made us hurry along to the chapel on the hill, where a treat was in store for us. The Indians from the fastnesses of the Sierras, in the far north, were to dance in their peculiar costumes.

Animated by insatiable curiosity, and anxious to witness the entire ceremonials, I pressed through the crowd of poor people to the inner circle. What a scene! The wildest, most fantastically decked beings that mortal eye ever beheld were in the inner space. . . . Then the dance! They formed circles, the men on the outer circle and the women on the first inner circle, and again other circles of the younger Indians of both sexes, forming one within the other. The everlasting jangle and trumtrum of the ghastly *jarana* covered with the skin of an armadillo, looking like an exhumed skeleton, with the finery of flaunting ribbons floating around it, its harsh notes mingling with the drowning wail of the wild musician who played as though in a frenzy, were in keeping with the whole scene. . . . It was the wildest, most mournful dance that mortal could invent; and it seemed as if the souls of the devotees were in the movement. It was a sort of paroxysm of physical devotion, and seemed to exhaust its votaries.

Having concluded the dance to the honor and glory of Guadalupe, they filed into the church chanting a low, monotonous hymn. I was the first to enter after them, followed closely by my friends. When they reached the altar, where a large picture of the Virgin was suspended, all dropped on their knees in regular lines of fours, and began crossing themselves and murmuring their *paternosters*.

The man who played on the *jarana* recited prayers, the others responding. After this they sang a litany, accompanied by low, moaning sounds, as if in anguish of spirit, while every eye was fixed steadily upon the patron saint in mute appeal, and tears streamed down their bronzed and hardened faces.

After half an hour thus spent upon their knees they arose, and still accompanied by the strange music from the ghastly instrument, that seemed to have taken on a more unearthly character, moved backward, making a low courtesy at each step, and as they filed out sang in chorus in their strange tongue:

" From heaven she descended,
Triumphant and glorious,
To favor us—
La Guadalupana.

6

"Farewell, Guadalupe !
Queen of the Indians !
Our life is thine,
This kingdom is thine."

When they withdrew from the church, our party following closely, the dancing was renewed with added fervor. But before we had gone down ten of the almost countless steps, one of the most picturesquely attired of all the Indians was walking by my side, making a bargain with me for the sale of his crown and feathers!

While the scene I had just witnessed had at times an effect to excite merriment the contrary feeling of sadness and almost reverence prevailed. I could not but feel awe in the presence of those dark children of the wild mountains as they performed their mystical devotions and sang the rude barbaric songs that had in their tones the strangeness of another world.*

All this heathenism in the house of God! More Aztec by far than Christian; for, save the person supposed to be represented on the " blanket " within the golden frame, there is not one Christian idea about the whole service.   Yet these occasions are regarded as the most meritorious of the year in Mexico. The scene, taken altogether, is matchless on the earth.   A vast multitude of people, all bent on these wild, idolatrous practices ; the sales of the sacred medals, ribbons, scapulars, and other devices ; the crowd around the sacred well struggling for a share of the " holy " water, to carry to their distant homes, while the women and boys push vigorously the sale of the tickets for the lottery.   One asks, " Is it possible that this scene is authorized by the Roman Catholic Church ? "   It is, all authorized.   Look into the center of that crowd at the church door and see. A busy man stands behind a table selling bright medals, which are oblong in shape, and about an inch and a half long.   On one side is the image of the Virgin of Guadalupe, with the inscription, " N. S. D. Guadalupe de Mexico;" on the obverse, " Non fecit taliter omni nationi."   Each is delivered to the purchaser wrapped in a little piece of printed paper, on which you read :

Our most holy father, the sovereign Pope Pius VI., by his brief of the 13th of April, 1785, has conceded plenary indulgence in the hour of death

* *Face to Face with the Mexicans*, by F. C. Gooch, p. 257.

to all those who shall then have upon them one of the *medals of Our Lady of Guadalupe*, which, ready blest, are sold in her sanctuary.*

So the highest authority in the Church of Rome has indorsed all this perversion of Christianity, and even professes to carry its supposed benefits through death into eternity! The poor, misguided people accept the assurance of their pontiff and venture their soul's welfare upon the possession of the medal!

They also furnish a document to show that this "miraculous appearance of the mother of God upon earth," the year and at the place aforesaid, was proved before the Congregation of Rites at Rome. And Benedict XIV. was so fully persuaded of the truth of the tradition that he made

cordial devotion to our Lady of Guadalupe, conceded the proper mass and ritual of devotion. He also made mention of it in the lesson of the second nocturnal, . . . declaring from the high throne of the Vatican that Mary, most holy, *non fecit taliter omni nationi.*

All this resting upon the slender foundation of the story of an Indian peon, "though, like many of his race, he was probably an habitual liar, yet when he bears testimony to a miracle he is presumed to speak the truth.† " Those who have examined the "miraculous" picture closely are very doubtful of the "blanket" part of it. Mr. W. E. Curtis, in 1888, while on a mission from our government, carefully examined the matter, and gives his conclusion:

According to the story, the portrait is stamped upon the serape or blanket of the shepherd, and this Catholics in Mexico devoutly believe. But a close examination reveals the fact that it is done in ordinary *oil colors* upon a piece of ordinary *canvas*, and that the pigments peel off like those of any poorly executed piece of work.‡

This testimony is confirmed by Colonel Evans in *Our Sister Republic*, p. 349.

General Thompson was one day looking at this picture in company with a Mexican friend, and directing his attention to

---

* See *A Visit to Mexico*, Robertson, vol. ii, p. 154.

† Wilson's *Mexico*, pp. 231, 232.   ‡ *The Capitals of Spanish America*, p. 21.

the Latin sentence, *Non fecit taliter omni nationi*, which is no doubt quoted from the Vulgate of Psalm cxlvii, 20, where the psalmist is exulting in the distinguishing favors which the Lord Jehovah had conferred upon Israel, saying, "He hath not dealt so with any nation." Unaware that he was putting a question to his friend which intelligent Mexicans are reluctant to answer to a foreigner, he asked the meaning of the words, whereupon his friend promptly replied that it meant, " She had never made such cursed fools of any other people ! "

The gentleman's exposition may pass unchallenged, though its utterance a few years earlier might have sent him to the Inquisition ; for there is no worse degradation than is here exhibited, which this dreadful departure from primitive Christianity has entailed upon this people for generations.

So far as we can trace back the origin of this legend we remember that the *conquistadores* found it impossible to complete the catholicizing of Mexico by force and cruelty. They found it equally difficult to attract the conquered natives to the worship of the *Spanish* Virgin Mary, whose image and pictures they sought to induce the Aztecs to accept and set up in their homes for worship. The conquered people could not forget that the figure of this Spanish Virgin was borne on the standards of their victorious oppressors, and aided, as they supposed, in their enslavement. This foreign goddess they therefore rejected, unless when compelled to worship her. Their own temples and idols had all been destroyed, and they longed for something to trust in and adore. So, a new policy to meet the case had to be thought out, and erelong the idea was conceived of a *native* Virgin Mary—not Spanish but Mexican—manifesting herself as such to the Aztec race as their own Virgin and patroness. It was not hard to find a suitable tool with which to try the experiment, and Juan Diego, being well backed up, worked out the problem successfully. It did not seem to give the conspirators who invented this new Virgin Mary much consideration that the two ladies must necessarily be rivals and the whole affair become ridiculous in its results. It was enough for them that the Spaniards could worship one Virgin Mary and the Aztecs worship the other, each with the services and rites which they preferred, and all would go conveniently.

Wealth remained with the Spanish Virgin for a long time, but the one of Guadalupe had the crowds, and their devotion led them to emulate the liberality of the other party and in time to exceed it, though in doing so they made their own impoverishment perpetual, so that every stranger visiting the land is amazed at the incongruity of the poverty of the worshipers and the wealth and splendor of the services.

When the great struggle for deliverance from the Spanish yoke culminated in the effort for independence led by Hidalgo, in 1810, the patriot priest saw that he could rally the oppressed native races best by putting the image of the Virgin of Guadalupe on his flag of freedom. The Spaniards met this by painting the image of the Virgin of Remedios on their flag. Under this leading the conflict was fought out most bitterly for twelve years, when the native blood and determination proved the stronger, and "Nuestra Señora de los Remedios," used by the Spaniards as their war-cry, was silenced, and herself and shrine sunk into disregard, deserted by all save the few Spanish families that remain and still adhere to her. Iturbide, when, in 1822, he joined the party of freedom as the leader of the creole class, was wise enough to discern that with the "Guadalupana" —as the Spanish aristocracy designate the "Indian Virgin"— was the best prospect of victory, and he thus united a considerable section of the wealth and intelligence of the cities with the cause represented by the Virgin of Guadalupe. The failure of the French intervention and overthrow of Maximilian's empire, as already intimated, extinguished the last hope of the partisans of the Virgin of Remedios for her recovery of her former glory and influence.

During the years of the dreadful conflict waged by the devotees of their two Virgins it is almost amusing to contemplate how much and how earnestly these two ridiculous dolls were regarded and treated as real personages, whose active influence

was looked for to crown the cause of their respective devotees
with the victory which they implored. On one occasion, when
the republican cause seemed to be getting the worst of it, the
fact was attributed to the presence and favor of the Virgin of
Remedios, and her expulsion from Mexico was therefore resolved upon. The general-in-chief made out her passport in
due form, and is said to have gone with some of his staff to her
shrine, where he tore the general's scarf, which she wore, from
her waist, and, delivering her passport to the attendant priests,
ordered her immediate expulsion from Mexico! This order
her devotees, however, found means to avoid, and she remained.
After peace was won and the republic established it was
deemed necessary to end the disgraceful squabbles and liability
of conflict between the partisans of the two Virgins by forbidding either party to take their favorite in public processions
through the streets. The "Laws of Reform" made this excellent rule perpetual.

The utter absurdity of this condition of things in religion,
running on through the centuries, was endured by the distracted nation without either party seeming to realize how
unworthy of reason and common sense was the pretension to
divine authority in either case. We are here reminded of Madame Calderon's excuse for some scenes not very unlike these
which she describes, probably the only one she, as a Roman
Catholic, could offer: "However childish and superstitious all
this may seem, I doubt whether it may not be as well thus to
impress certain religious truths on the minds of a people too
ignorant to understand them by any other process" (p. 108).
This is a poor explanation to offer for a wealthy Church which
had these millions in her power for three centuries, and whose
first duty it was to cure them of their "ignorance" and "superstition" and to elevate them in sacred knowledge and morality.
Alas, what a *failure* is Romanism in Mexico! Over this wide
world Protestant mission work needs no excuses, nor has it anywhere any such failures to answer for. Its converts are a
credit to it, no matter how brief the period it has had them

under training. Where it has had them for even a fourth part of the time above mentioned they have become a self-supporting, intelligent, and missionary Christianity, an honor and a blessing to the lands whose highest positions some of them are to-day filling.

Before leaving the subject it is our painful duty to ask the reader's attention to one more aspect of the utterly unwarranted idolatrous extravagance of doctrine which this Church built up on the ruins of Aztec heathenism. Those who only know Romanism as they see it in the United States or in England—for there it is astute and careful—can have little idea of the practices which that Church has encouraged in Mexico. Not only has she failed to give them the Gospel of Christ, but she presented them with "another gospel," in the sense which St. Paul so plainly condemns.

We are conscious of the seriousness of the words which we now use, but the painful evidence is too abundant to be overlooked. We will present only a very few out of the many samples, each from their own acknowledged authorities, to justify the charge which Protestantism brings against the terrible departure from the teachings of revealed religion. These errors center around the person of the mother of our Lord, who has by them been exalted out of the sphere which she occupies in the evangelical narrative, clothed with divine attributes and made the supreme object of human trust in the matter of salvation. All this without any warrant from the word of God, and in defiance of its spirit and teaching.

Let us take a few of the titles which Mexicans have been taught to employ in common with their co-religionists elsewhere before introducing what is special in the teaching of the hierarchy of Mexico. One of these is that the Virgin Mary is "the mother of God;" and because evangelical Christians object to such a title being applied to any creature, and being in strict language impossible in itself, the Romish clergy there bitterly misrepresent us and our teaching and try to raise the hatred of their fanatical followers against us as " revilers of the Virgin Mary."

A human creature "the mother of God" is an utter impossibility. The stream cannot rise higher than its source. She became, as the Scriptures call her, " the mother of Jesus," who derived his manhood from her, but not his godhead. That godhead existed in all its perfection a whole eternity before the Virgin Mary was born, and therefore could not be born of her in time. She gave him all she had to give, her humanity, and that was all that her mission called for. " The man Christ Jesus " was her child, and to this humanity the divine and eternal Son of God united himself and became " Emmanuel " by the unity, and was thus qualified to become the atoning Saviour of the human race.

Another of those titles invented to lend color to the claim which they have set up to invest her with superhuman attributes and give her a title to divine honors is that of "the divinized mother of God."* Concerning this pure and honored woman no one knows any thing beyond what is written in the four gospels and Acts of the Apostles, because her name is not once mentioned in any of the epistles, while the five apostolic fathers of the first century after Christ say nothing about her save what is given as above. " Mary, of whom was born Jesus, who is called Christ " (Matt. i, 16), is the opening of the simple and beautiful record. Now let us put by the side of this the amazing and awful designations invented by Romanism to prove her to be " divinized," and as such the object of human trust and adoration.

The announcement of the new doctrine of " the Immaculate Conception " of the Virgin Mary, in December, 1854, by Pope Pius IX., revised the shocking profanity of the rosary of " the Blessed St. Anne, Mother of the Blessed Virgin, and GRANDMOTHER OF GOD ALMIGHTY ! " † All this blasphemous language is recklessly employed to commend " the divinized mother of God" to the adoration of her worshipers, while

* *Christian World*, vol. xiv, p. 254.   † *Ibid.*, vol. vi, p. 163.

true Christians grieve and infidels mock at such impossible assumptions.

Still another of these unauthorized titles adopted for this humble woman is that of "Queen of Heaven." As such she is represented in their picture on page 44, crowned with the infant Saviour in her arms. There is nothing to justify this picture; it is manifestly false to the facts. Mary was the wife of a poor carpenter in a humble home, and the bauble of a crown never rested upon her brow. If answered that the picture represents her as she appears in heaven, that view of it is equally false, for it is impossible for her to appear as this represents in the eternal world, where Christ sits—not in her lap or in her arms, but "on the right hand of the Majesty on high."

There seems something very unworthy in this constant attempt to keep Jesus in his babyhood before the minds of Roman Catholic people. It minifies him, and eclipses the true glory of his immortal manhood and priestly functions by thus exalting his mother's patronage and power over him, notwithstanding that eighteen hundred years have passed since she had the opportunity of such responsibility.

Pius IX. took special delight in thus exalting the Virgin Mary. He says in his encyclical letter to the bishops of the Catholic world, December, 1864, that the Virgin Mary, "who, sitting as a queen upon the right hand of her Son, our Lord Jesus Christ, in a golden vestment, shining with various adornments, knows nothing which she cannot obtain from the sovereign Master." *

The old gentleman does not condescend to inform the world by what authority he states this as to her position, the dress she wears, and the ornaments with which she is decorated. His word is to be accepted without question. He knows, however, no more about these things than the humblest person who reads his pompous encyclical. Her spirit, no doubt, is before the throne, waiting, like all the true saints, for the glorious resurrection of the dead. And yet in this false and unwarranted

* _Christian World_, vol. xvi, p. 200.

teaching she is represented as embodied clothed in cloth of gold, wearing a crown and exercising her mediation for sinners here on earth as the great "Queen of Heaven." But heaven has no queen. The term is drawn from the Sabian idolatry, and as such is denounced and condemned by Almighty God in Jeremiah vii, 18, and xliv, 17.

The two most popular books of devotion which they use are *The Litany of the Dolorous Virgin Mary*, prepared by Pope Pius VII., and *The Glories of Mary*, by Ligouri. These books contain ascriptions to the Virgin of nearly every attribute of Almighty God; but the climax is reached where she is represented as having by the act of the divine Father superseded the adorable Saviour as being more tender-hearted toward the sinner than he can be! It is expressly taught in these books of their devotions that "the Lord Christ has assumed the administration of justice and punishment" toward men " and resigned to her the functions of grace and mercy!" So the poor, misguided souls are taught to transfer their appeals and hopes to her in such prayers as these : " O Mary, we poor sinners know *no refuge but thee. Thou art our only hope.* To thee we *intrust* our salvation" (p. 130). This shocking inversion of the Gospel is then wound up in a grand doxology, putting her on a par with the adorable Trinity, at which I tremble as I copy it :

I salute thee, O Great Mediatrix of peace between men and God; O Mother of Jesus our Lord, the love of all men and of God : *to thee be honor and blessing with the Father and with the Holy Spirit. Amen.**

With assumptions and ascriptions like these Pius IX. carried his point and gave forth to the world, on the 8th of December, 1854, as an article of faith henceforth "necessary to salvation," his dogma of the Immaculate Conception of the Virgin Mary. In his missive he tells Christendom that he did this

with a particular filial devotion and with our whole heart, to adore the blessed Virgin and to promote all that tended to her praise and glory, and whereby her worship might be more and more extended.†

* *The Glories of Mary,* by Ligouri, and *Christian World,* vol. xxi, p. 10.
† *Christian World,* vol. vi, pp. 212, 213.

One might suppose that the widest departure from the Bible and apostolic Christianity had been reached when the above were written, but there was one step more that might be taken, and Catholicism in Mexico has not shrunk from taking it. We now, with a heavy heart, present this additional evidence of the peculiar Mariolatry for the invention of which the Church has incurred such a fearful accountability to the Holy Trinity, as well as to the judgment of the Christian world, whose sensibilities have been shocked as the facts became known that Romanists in Mexico have dared to adopt such language on such a subject. To be cautious to the fullest degree, I have had the inscription carefully copied from the tablet on the immense "reja," or iron screen, of the third chapel on the left as one enters the great cathedral in the city of Puebla. This is, next to the cathedral in the city of Mexico, regarded as the most imposing church on this continent. The tablet hangs in front of the Chapel of the Virgin of Guadalupe, and the inscription is in the form of a prayer to her. We give first the original Spanish and then the translation :

ORACIÓN.

Vírgen santísima de Guadalupe, admirable Hija de Dios Padre, Madre de Dios Hijo, y Esposa de Dios Espíritu Santo, Señora mía consagrada, primero santificada que creada, suplícote Patrona y Señora mía, que si en este dia, en este instante, en esta hora, ó en lo restante de mi vida, ó en la muerte, contra mí ó contra cosa mía alguna sentencia fuere dada, sea por vuestra intercesion revocada, y por mano de tu Hijo nuestro Señor Jesucristo sea perdonada. Amen, Jesús.

The translation is as follows :

PRAYER.

Most holy Virgin of Guadalupe, glorious daughter of God the Father, mother of God the Son, and wife of God the Holy Spirit, my Lady consecrated and sanctified before thou wast created: I pray thee, my patron saint and Lady, that if to-day, if this moment, if this hour, or if during the remainder of my life, or in death, any sentence should be passed against me or against any thing of mine, it may by thy intercession be revoked, and by the hand of thy Son our Lord Jesus Christ be turned aside. Amen, Jesus.

This awful language is not a thing allowed in the past times
of ignorance only; but in the recent issue of the *Novena*, or
manual for nine days' prayer to the Virgin of Guadalupe, authorized by the members of the "Chapter of Holy Mary of
Guadalupe," in 1885, and printed by J. J. Little & Co., New
York, the same expressions are found on the eleventh page,
ending with these words:

> The Holy Spirit also has made thee the dispenser of all his gifts and
> graces. All the three divine persons concurred to crown thee at thy glo-
> rious ascension to the heavens, and then there was conferred upon thee
> absolute power over all created in heaven and on earth.

How heart-sickening to think that these extracts and that
doxology are sanctioned by highest authority in the Roman
Church! No wonder that the millions of Mexicans have failed
to find their Saviour, and that their services have degenerated
into the heathenish spectacles such as we have presented.

Thoughtful students of history, as they note the difference
between nations, are impressed by the fact that wherever image-
worship is met, there ignorance, degradation, and wretchedness
abound. There is an adequate cause for this that can only be
accounted for by the recognition that there exists an all-power-
ful Being whose decalogue is the supreme law of this world.
The Almighty avows his position and purposes toward the violators of his holy law as expressed in the second commandment,
who, making any "graven image, or any likeness of any thing
in heaven above, or on the earth beneath," do "bow down to
it, or serve it." The reason is given why he punishes this fearful sin not merely with individual but with national judgments: "For I the Lord thy God am a jealous God, visiting
the iniquity of the fathers upon the children unto the third
and fourth generation of them that hate me; and showing
mercy unto thousands of them that love me, and keep my commandments."

No wonder the Romish priests fear to let their people
"search the Scriptures;" no wonder that they exclude the

second commandment from many of their catechisms and nearly all their books of devotion. But it is a wonder that they do not realize the fearful responsibility which they assume in so doing, nor the account that they may yet have to render to God and to their people for having done so.

Keeping close, as we Protestants do, to the Bible teachings, and ready at any hour to have our opinions brought to the test of the word of God, it is unjust to call us "heretics." Contrast our position with the fluctuations and theological novelties of the following list of dates of the doctrines now held by the Roman Church, not one of which is in the Bible, nor can be proved thereby, but several of which we have shown here to be contrary to its teaching, and it will be easy to decide who are the "heretics."

DATES OF ROMISH DOGMAS.

The Church of Rome claims to be apostolic, immutable, and infallible. The following table will show how far this is from being true:

Prayer for the dead began...........................A. D.	200
Worship of saints, martyrs, and angels..................	350
Worship of the Virgin Mary was developed about........	431
Worship in an unknown tongue........................	600
Papal supremacy......................................	606
Worship of images and relics imposed.................	788
Obligatory celibacy of the priests......................	1000
Infallibility of the Church............................	1076
Sale of indulgences...................................	1190
The dogma of transubstantiation officially decreed........	1215
Auricular confession officially imposed..................	1215
The cup kept back from the laity officially sanctioned....	1415
Purgatory officially recognized........................	1439
Romish tradition put on a level with the Scriptures......	1540
Worship of the Virgin of Guadalupe sanctioned by the pope.	1785
The Immaculate Conception proclaimed................	1854
The pope's temporal power proclaimed..................	1864
Papal infallibility proclaimed.........................	1870

The last pope made the belief in the three items which he proclaimed a necessary condition of grace and salvation.

CHAPTER III.

From darkness to dawn through conflict and suffering—Spanish rule—Viceroys —"Patriarch of Mexican Independence"—His "Grito" and helpers—The Bravos—Odds against freedom—Iturbide and coronation—Unfortunate return—Monroe doctrine—Texan war and its object—McNamara and "Methodist wolves"—General Fremont—War with United States—Treachery at Cherubusco—The hand of God—Hidden refuge for Bible study in the Cañadas.

From the year 1535 until the year 1821, when Mexico obtained her independence, the country was governed by sixty-one viceroys appointed by the Spanish crown. Their term of service extended over a period of two hundred and eighty-six years, giving to each viceroy an average of more than four years. Among these Spanish rulers there was occasionally found one of benevolent disposition and liberal ideas. But it must be conceded that in the main the Spanish rule in New Spain was one of iron despotism, in which priest and soldier bore an equal part, until several millions of human beings, the constitutional elements of whose character were gentleness and docility, rose against their oppressors with the determination of driving them from the land.

The Spaniards had acted so domineeringly in the exercise of their absolute rule, and in the monopoly of all places of trust and power, that they oppressed and insulted the native Mexicans until positive hatred was the result. Not only so, but they had also made the public service so close that even the " creole " class were by law excluded from any participation in it. The creoles were descendants of the Spaniards, members of their own families ; but under the rule that no country-born person should be allowed to participate in the government of the colonies in the slightest degree they were made to feel the inferiority of their birth.

The legislation prepared in Spain for the government of these "colonies of the crown" was equally exclusive and oppressive, though New Spain was a hundred times larger than Old Spain, and far more populous; yet at every point the laws were made to discriminate against the former, to the extent that the mulberry-tree or the silk-worm were not allowed to be cultivated, nor the vine grown (though both so genial to the soil). Mexico must purchase her wine and her silk of the mother-country or do without them, nor could her poor raise and sell them elsewhere and so assist themselves to this extent by their industry.

The Spaniards were, in many cases, non-resident, living in Spain on the incomes remitted from their Mexican estates, and the rest occupying their high positions in the capital and leading points of the country. The creoles numbered several hundred thousand. The Roman Church stood with the Spaniards, with all her influence and wealth, as against the popular wishes, save in those very few cases where some of the humble clergy (better than their system) ventured to sympathize with their poor people in the heavy burdens which they endured. Early in this century a movement had begun with the creole class to have the Spaniards share with them political rights, and in this desire the then viceroy, Iturrigaray, was disposed to concur, in the interest of peace, if not of justice. It was a great blow aimed at *caste* after nearly three hundred years of monopoly! But this kind concession cost the viceroy his position. He was removed, and the Archbishop of. Mexico was placed in power, until a new viceroy, of a sterner kind, was sent from Spain.

The French Revolution and the changes made by the movements of Napoleon I., including the removal of the Bourbons from the throne of Spain, reduced the prestige of the Spanish rule in Mexico and seriously lessened the power of the viceroys. This was intensified when the emperor placed his brother on the Spanish throne, thus giving a heavy shock to the doctrine of the "divine right of kings," and the immutability of established order, and raising hopes that changes in the interests of liberty and right were to be expected and welcomed, and, if need be, fought for, by those who appreciated the sentiment, "Who would be free himself must strike the blow!" The spirit of liberty became infectious, and was strengthened by the Constitution granted by the new Cortes of Spain in 1812, which abolished the Inquisition and gave to Mexico more freedom than she had known since the Conquest. The viceroy was a cruel absolutist, and had no heart to welcome the beneficent 'change, and longed for its overthrow. The fall of Napoleon was followed by the removal of his brother and the change of the liberal regimen in Spain. Ferdinand VII., who was restored to the throne by the policy of the "Allied Powers," who met in Paris to reconstruct the map of Europe, was one of the most despotic of the Bourbons. He abolished the Constitution, restored the Inquisition, and absolute government once more oppressed the inhabitants of the Spanish peninsula. Stern orders were sent to withdraw all that had been conceded to the people of Mexico. Fearing the progress of the liberal ideas in that country as well as in the South American colonies, Ferdinand was intending to dispatch a fleet and army to bring the Mexico and South American colonies into submission. Before it was ready to sail the discovery was made that many of the officers had become infected with "this new fever of liberty," and even dared to express their displeasure at the service demanded of them, and were, indeed, more likely to lead the revolt in Mexico than to suppress it. None others could take their places, and Ferdinand and his clerical sympathizers were openly criticised for their despotic plans till, alarmed for the stability of his throne, the Constitution was restored and the hostile expedition to Mexico abandoned.

Next to personal redemption, that in which man most needs the intervention of Almighty God is in his aspirations for justice and freedom. Of these it is true that "every good gift, and every perfect gift, is from above." The apostles of liberty, as those of religion, are messengers of God, the author of liberty. The martyrs of both are under his vindication, accepting their

MIGUEL HIDALGO,
The "Patriarch of Mexican Independence."

work and crowning their efforts with success. So that in this
sense also we hold that

> "The proper place for man to die
> Is where he dies for man;"

or, better still, as they sang so enthusiastically during our civil
war:

> "As He died to make men holy,
> Let us die to make them free!"

The honored men who laid the foundations of our republic,
and the devoted man who dared to abolish slavery forever within
our borders, appealed to the "considerate judgment of mankind and the gracious favor of Almighty God" for the rectitude
of their intentions and the successful prosecution of the work
before them. So also in Mexico the divine Spirit raised up devoted men who dared to face danger and death to secure the
"good gift" of freedom for the millions around them. We
have no doubt, when the facts are fairly stated, generous Americans will admit that these are as worthy as any to be held in
"everlasting remembrance."

We now present to our readers the head of this illustrious line,
Hidalgo, whom the Mexicans so delight to honor. He is called
"The Liberator of Mexico," "The first Governor of Mexico by
the National Will;" and "The Patriarch of Mexican Independence." Miguel Hidalgo y Costilla was born on the 8th of May,
1753, received a liberal education, entered the Roman Catholic priesthood, and at the time of his great effort was curate
in the town of Dolores, in the State of Guanajuato. He was
fully devoted to the welfare of his parishioners. Among other
things he taught them the culture of the vine and the silk-worm,
the making of porcelain and other small industries, by which
their temporal condition began to improve. Although the spirit
of freedom was in the air in 1810, and some relaxation of the
cruel prohibitions of Spain against Mexico might have been
taken for granted, these humble efforts of the kind-hearted curate were disapproved at head-quarters as a daring innovation

not to be tolerated. The viceroy gave orders for the destruction of the industries, and there was some talk of passing over Hidalgo to the Inquisition, where his notions might be inquired into, for he was known to entertain liberal views.

When the agents of the viceroy reached Dolores, and Hidalgo saw with indignant sorrow all that he had accomplished for his people destroyed, the vines rooted up, the mulberry trees cut down, and the other works overthrown, the tyrannous act incensed him and his people, as it also aroused the general disapprobation of the nation. He was then nearly sixty years of age, and had previously been in correspondence with other lovers of liberty. The thought of independence had grown stronger in view of the weakening of the Spanish monarchy. Hidalgo had several persons on whom he could rely, some of them, priests of good reputation, assured him of their co-operation if he would lead the way. Satisfied that the time had come to strike the blow, Hidalgo prepared his declaration of independence, made his flag, and on the 16th of September, 1810, displayed that flag and gave forth the " Grito," or cry of independence. His own people and the country around took up the cry, thousands flocked to his standard and placed themselves under his leadership.

His first move was toward Guanajuato, where he believed some creole officers would join him with the men under their command. That city of 70,000 inhabitants is the center of the silver mining of the district. Hidalgo and his army were cordially welcomed and remained there for ten days organizing his troops. Again, and more formally, he proclaimed the independence of Mexico, and was announced as " captain-general " of the forces. In the government treasury he found $1,000,000, which very opportunely supplied him with the sinews of war. The increasing crowd that he led was but half armed and entirely undisciplined, and it need not be wondered at that in the first hour of their power the arrogant conduct of their Spanish oppressors was remembered, and in that bitter resentment for the wrongs so long endured by their race vengeance was taken upon some of them before Hidalgo and the leaders could restrain their men. Soon Valladolid, Guadalajara, and other cities fell into their hands. More patriots reached their camp, foremost among whom were the priests Morelos and Matamoros. This army swept on, the country rising in favor of the cause of independence, enthusiastically recognizing Hidalgo and his chiefs as representing the national will, and justly claiming the allegiance and help of all who loved their native country.

In a few days they reached the crest of the great valley of Mexico, and a halt was there made to take council as to their movements. Right before them in the center of that valley was the capital, the possession of which would add thousands of sympathizers to their numbers and soon place the whole country in their power. But a royal garrison held it, amply provided with the best armaments of the times, including artillery, and having well-disciplined cavalry. Hidalgo hesitated to lead his followers into a conflict so unequal. Numbers and courage were under his command, ample for any effort, but discipline, weapons, artillery, and cavalry he had not, and while some were for taking all the risks involved, and desirous of prompt attack, the leader and his officers concluded that it was safer for the sacred cause they had in charge to retire toward the United States frontier, where, with the money in hand, they could purchase all that they required, and meanwhile discipline and training would be organizing their followers to return again, better fitted for a conflict which now seemed so unequal.

The order was given to turn northward. But the vigilant agent of the viceroy, General Calleja, was watching their movements and saw that he had them at a disadvantage. He concentrated his troops and followed, attacking them at Aculco and again at Calderon, inflicting terrible damages upon the undisciplined crowd. The main body still held together and reached Saltillo in January, 1811. Here Hidalgo left Rayon in command, and with an escort pushed on for the Texan frontier to purchase the military equipment so much required. Unfortunately, just before reaching it he and his party were betrayed, by a former friend named Elizondo, into the hands of the Spanards. Hidalgo and his three chiefs were at once loaded with chains and cast into prison. On the 29th of July he was led before the ecclesiastical tribunal, clad in clerical robes, for degradation from the priesthood. He was stripped of his sacerdotal garb, the chains and fetters put upon him again, and then was handed over for execution to the civil authority.

It is narrated of him by those who witnessed the trying scenes that " even the chains and shackles could not detract from the dignity and patience that characterized him." He was led out to be shot on the morning of July 30, 1811. He faced his executioners with courage, and placed his hand over his heart as a guide to the soldiers' aim; but it required the fifth volley to extinguish his noble life, the veneration in which he was held probably interfering with the accuracy of their aim. His officers, Jimenez, Aldama, and Santa Maria, had been executed three days before. The heads of all four were placed on spikes and elevated on the corners of the castle of Granaditas, in Guanajuato, and their bodies in the chapel of the Franciscans. When his cause was triumphant, twelve years later, the grateful nation decreed them a public funeral, and the remains of these heroes were tenderly brought from the scene of their sufferings and deposited beneath the "Altar of the Three Kings," under the dome of the cathedral of the capital of the country for whose liberty they died.

Certainly Hidalgo could not have dreamed of the glorious part which his tattered flag should bear in the future. On the eve of the 16th of September, the highest national holiday, at eleven o'clock P. M., in the Hall of Representatives, the president, his cabinet, and the members of Congress, public men of Mexico, with all the brilliancy of society in the capital, crowd the structure and wait for the moment when the hands of the clock reach the hour at which Hidalgo first raised the cry of independence. Then the President of Mexico raises the old flag, waves it three times, and repeats the "Grito," "*Viva la*

Libertad! Viva la República! Viva Mexico! " and the great audience rises to join in the shout, "*Viva la República!* " as if they would lift the roof off the building. The thunder of the artillery gives its response to the popular joy, and the more than three hundred thousand people in the capital, and, indeed, the whole nation, remember gratefully the man who died to make them free. Visitors who are privileged to witness the scene can never forget its deep enthusiasm or fail to realize how much constitutional liberty cost the Mexican people and how dearly they prize it.

On the death of Hidalgo the leadership devolved upon José Maria Morelos. He was also a priest, but a born warrior, and one who earned for himself in his brief career the popular title of " the hero of a hundred battles." His army continued to increase, and many victories were gained over the royalist forces; in many cases the garrisons were surprised, the officers were imprisoned, and the troops induced to join the Republican army. Morelos became immensely popular, and men began to feel that the cause of independence was already won. In 1812 he was joined by the Bravos (father and son), Guadalupe Victoria, Bustamente, and Guerrero.

Morelos was impressed with the necessity of having the movement for independence sustain a truly national character, and that its interests should be furthered by constitutional means. A Congress was gathered representing all classes of the Mexican people. It was limited in number, as it was subject to constant movement, and could be more easily protected from the pursuing army of the viceroy. The care of this Congress devolved upon Morelos; while they deliberated, his division of the patriot forces stood over them to guard them from impending danger. A constitution was finally framed and proclaimed in October, 1814. Some time after the Congress was moving to a more distant point, when Morelos, discovering that the royalist force was gaining upon them, decided to save the representatives of the people by remaining with a small guard to check the progress of the enemy, while the larger part of the force, under Nicolas Bravo, had time to conduct them to a place of safety. Having thus secured their escape, Morelos was unable to face the greatly superior force which confronted him, and was taken prisoner on the 15th of November.

General Concha was amazed at the quiet resignation of his prisoner as he remarked, "My life is nothing if the Congress be saved ; my task was finished from the moment that an independent government was established." He was taken to the capital, degraded by the bishop from the priesthood, and handed over to the secular power for execution. To increase the degradation of his death it was ordered that he should be shot in the back as a traitor. The vindictive nature of the hierarchy, who exulted in his death, is seen in the cruel and reckless language used in the document ordering his execution. He is characterized as "an unconfessed heretic, and an abettor of heretics, a profaner of the holy sacraments, and a traitor to God, the king, and the pope." All this malignity was manufactured out of the one fact that this brave man loved liberty so much that he was willing to fight to see it established in his country. But the honorable name of Morelos could not be tarnished. His countrymen have conferred his worthy name upon the capital of one of their greatest States, and in *Morelia* his name is preserved as a shrine of freedom where men go to do homage to his memory. His portrait hangs in its principal hall, and beneath a frame holds the remnant of the silk handkerchief with which he covered his eyes in the hour of his execution, and underneath are the lines :

> " This is the venerated relic,
> The mournful bandage with which the tyrant
> Hid the gaze of Morelos,
> When the martyr of the Mexican people
> Offered to his beloved country
> His precious life as a sacrifice."

How fearful the acts against the patriots is indicated in the records of the years between 1810 and 1820. The viceroys conducted the war with a vengeance which is described as " proclamations which make the hair stand on end." So says Chevalier, and adds: "A system of extermination was ordered. An order of the day of General Cruz, even still more revolting, directed that 'the insurgents should be pursued, incarcerated, and killed like wild beasts.'"

An illustration of their spirit, which contrasts so favorably with the noble conduct of the patriotic leaders, is shown in the case of the two Bravos, father and son, both holding the rank of generals in the Republican army. The father was named Leonardo and the son Nicolas. They were devoted to each other as well as to the cause of their country. Leonardo Bravo was taken prisoner at the battle of Cuautla, was tried and condemned to be shot. Venegas, then viceroy, so highly appreciated Leonardo's abilities that he offered him his life if he would induce his brothers and son, Nicolas, to join the royalists. Leonardo scorned such an offer. Before his execution, Nicolas Bravo, having in his hands as captives three hundred Spanish prisoners—some of whom were wealthy and influential men—was authorized by Morelos to offer to exchange the whole of them for his father. But the viceroy, appreciating the value of a Bravo to the popular cause, rejected the offer and ordered the execution to take place.

The grief of Nicolas for his father was extreme, and he ordered his three hundred prisoners to be shot, and had them placed " in chapel " (religious preparation for death) for execution next morning. During the night he reflected that if his order was carried out, while he would be justified in the eyes of the world and by the usages of war in executing them under the circumstances, in retaliation for his father's death, the cause of independence, so dear to him, might be dishonored by the act. So his measures were taken, and at sunrise the next morning he was on the ground when his army stood confronting the prisoners and waiting for the order. Riding out in front, he thus addressed the doomed men :

Your lives are forfeited. Your master, Spain's minion, has murdered my father, murdered him in cold blood for choosing Mexico and liberty

before Spain and her tyrannies. Some of you are fathers, and may imagine
what my father felt in being thrust from the world without one farewell
word from his son; aye, and your sons may feel a portion of that anguish
of soul which fills my heart as thoughts arise of my father's wrongs and
cruel death. And what a master is this of yours! For one life, my
poor father's, he might have saved you all and would not! So deadly is
his hate that he would sacrifice three hundred of his friends rather than
forego this one sweet morsel of vengeance! Even I, who am no viceroy,
have three hundred lives for my father's. But there is a nobler revenge
than this. Go! You are all free! Go, find your vile master, and henceforth serve him if you can!

The effect was overwhelming. In gratitude to him for
sparing their lives, the soldiers, with tears streaming from their
eyes, rushed forward and offered their services to his cause, and
remained faithful to him and to it to the end.

General Bravo afterward bore a conspicuous share in the
history of his liberated country. He lived to take part in the
American war (1847), his last military service being at the defense of Chapultepec and Molino del Rey. He died at the age
of sixty-eight, beloved and admired by all who knew him.

Meanwhile the Congress continued its labors, and had the
courage to send a completed copy of the Constitution which
they had framed to the viceroy Calleja. The royal council
to whom he referred it solemnly condemned the document.
The viceroy had a copy of it burned in the great plaza of
Mexico by the public executioner, and ordered a similar ceremony performed in all the chief cities where Spain had a garrison. He also issued an edict which threatened with the death
penalty and confiscation of property any one who was found
with a copy of the Constitution in his possession, and forbade
any person to refer to it.

The peculiar difficulties under which the patriots of Mexico
wrought out the freedom of their country will be made the
more manifest and impressive when the actual facts are clearly
understood. While the Mexicans studied with admiration, so far
as they could from time to time obtain a view of the condition
of peace and prosperity which the United States had won for

themselves, and longed to be like them, yet there were difficulties in their way which our patriot fathers never knew, and
burdens to be borne beyond all that they ever carried, while
the shut-in condition of the Mexicans separated them from the
light and intelligence which so brightly shone to guide our way
to constitutional freedom.

Let us mark the difference more definitely, that our Mexican
neighbors may have the proper credit for the freedom which
they won against such fearful odds. When our patriot fathers
here pledged "life and fortune and sacred honor" to become
independent and free, they had not been for three hundred
years crushed down in ignorance and poverty, almost without
hope or aspiration. No powerful viceroy wielding the military
forces of a foreign despot was in power to repress every utterance for liberty or "hunt them down like beasts of prey" when
they attempted to obtain it. No great landed aristocracy,
owning every acre of the soil, laid its heavy hand upon them in
vengeance. No wealthy established Church united its ghostly
power with the civil despotism to repress them, bringing to its
aid the remorseless Inquisition and their spiritual maledictions,
adding blasphemously the terrors of God and of eternity to
utterly crush their cause and their hopes as unlawful. Nor
were they cut off from the sea and its resources or left without
one friendly nation on the earth to extend sympathy or a helping hand to them in the unequal struggle, nor so destitute of
resources that they had to win battles to obtain weapons and
ammunition to continue the conflict. All these disabilities the
patriot Mexicans had to endure for years ere they were able to
stand on equal terms with the combined and relentless foes of
their freedom. All they had to begin with was their own right
hands and noble leaders, who "loved not their lives unto the
death," to make their nation a land of liberty. Generous
Americans will give worthy credit to such a people, and to the
patriots who led them at last to the liberal institutions which
they now enjoy.

To all this we may add that the land was, from end to end,

without the Bible, the school, or the most elementary literature; that even their Constitution (when they gained one) had not the doctrine of religious liberty in it, for that they had to learn at a later day, when Benito Juarez enshrined it in his glorious Constitution of 1857, and thus crowned the freedom of his country. It surely may be questioned whether a people ever won constitutional liberty under greater disadvantages than these had to endure during their struggles from 1810 to 1857.

Matters moved slowly during the four following years, but in 1820 events in Spain again revived the hopes of the Mexican Liberals, and they renewed their efforts for independence. This led the viceroy to re-organize his army for offensive operations and to call once more to his aid the creole Colonel Augustine Iturbide, who had already made himself famous in the war against Hidalgo and Morelos. The Spanish forces then in Mexico and subject to the viceroy's orders amounted to eleven regiments, while the patriot army was estimated at twenty-four regiments; but they were more widely scattered than was the royal army, less disciplined, and but half armed. Iturbide was appointed by the viceroy to the command of the Army of the South-west.

About this time it came to be supposed that Ferdinand VII., in view of the insecurity and unrest of his Spanish throne, was considering the question of abandoning that uneasy seat in Madrid for a quieter one in Mexico, where he might find more devoted subjects and an asylum from revolutions. Some of the Liberals were led to suppose that they could obtain constitutional freedom under Ferdinand, and were willing to consider the question. This led to a temporary cessation of hostilities, and to the removal of the despotic viceroy. A man of more gentle character, named O'Donoju, was sent in his place. Yielding to the patriotic influences brought to bear on him, Iturbide had just before (February 24, 1821) issued to the nation what was called the "Plan of Iguala," or the "Constitution of the three Guarantees"—religion, independence, and union. In religion the nation was to be Roman Catholic, without toleration of any other faith—independence of the entire country from Spain; union conceding the equal rights of the native races with those of the creoles and Europeans. This proposal was such an immense advance toward freedom that the "Plan" took extensively with the masses, while the enlightened leaders, on reflection, regarded it with suspicion as being too churchly to be safe for complete liberty.

The new viceroy and Iturbide met at Cordova and discussed the situation. A few modifications in the plan satisfied the viceroy, who consented to become one of the members of the "Provisional Junta" to carry on the government until a monarch could be obtained. On reflection Ferdinand declined the offered throne. The crown-princes of Spain also refused to come. Each thought he had interests at home that would be compromised, and the whole affair dropped to the ground. During these negotiations the viceroy died, and none other had been appointed before events hurried on to a conclusion. Iturbide was now standing at the head of affairs. His "Plan" went forth to the nation, the first article of which declared as follows: "*The Mexican nation is independent of the Spanish nation, and of every other, even on its own continent.*" By this act Mexico virtually became independent of Spain, and Spain was then so much disturbed and impoverished that she was unable to do more than protest; and so Mexico and South America were left, at least for the present, to organize themselves as they chose under the circumstances. But it does seem singular that after all the long years of strife Mexico should have effected her independence without shedding another drop of blood. The Spanish flag, after having floated for just three hundred years, was hauled down on the 24th of February, 1821, and thus the good seed sown by Hidalgo and his followers was in great part harvested by the hand of Iturbide eleven years afterward.

Iturbide had already secured an understanding with Guerrero, the Republican leader, for uniting the two armies in view of independence. Had he been satisfied to have remained a pop-

ular leader he would probably have been promptly elected constitutional President of Mexico. But Iturbide was not a patriot,
and thought more of his own interests than of those of his
country.   Chance threw in his way the opportunity of doing a
great service to the nation without suffering or risk to himself,
and he did it, and thus earned the designation of "The Liberator of Mexico."

Those who knew him well and remembered his antecedents
believed him to be heartless and animated by personal ambition.
Republicans could not forget that Good Friday in 1814 (of
which Chevalier gives the account in his second volume), when,
to celebrate his victory at Salvatierra, two or three days previously, over the feeble patriotic forces, in the mere wantonness
of his power he resolved to "celebrate the day becomingly" by
shooting the three hundred Republican prisoners whom he had
taken, on the pretext that "they were excommunicated persons,
and that the Spanish authorities employed spiritual weapons as
well as swords, muskets, and cannon in subjugating the Inde-
pendents!"   So, to please the hierarchy and consummate their
work, Iturbide doomed those men to die like dogs—not on the
battle-field, but on the parade-ground—because the Church had
excommunicated them for taking up arms to win the liberty of
their native land! Now, however, he had done Mexico a good
turn, and men hoped he might prove worthy. A new Congress
in which the clergy were well represented was in session, and
great solicitude was felt as to the form of government. This
body stood in the way of Iturbide's ambition to reign, of which
the patriots learned with alarm. Having gained the attachment of many of the officers and promised large concessions to
the Church, his first move was to have a number of his partisans
parade the streets shouting, "Long live Augustine I.!"   The
next day the Congress debated the question, while the galleries
were crowded with adherents of Iturbide, who was also present.
Some voted to appeal to the various States, but a vote was
forced (May 19, 1822) which awarded the imperial crown to
Iturbide. The church party gave their influence, as well they

might, considering what was wrapped up in the plan of Iguala, from which the Republicans were beginning to fall away. Every thing was done to make the coronation a gorgeous ceremony. An archbishop and many bishops added their dignity to the occasion. The great cathedral was made to display all its resources of magnificence. On the 21st of June, with music, processions, illuminations, incense, joy-bells, and salvos of artillery, he was anointed and crowned at the high altar as Augustine the First. A heavy civil list was voted, an imperial court was arranged, his children were entitled as princes, and an aristocracy was instituted. The Spanish government contemptuously repudiated the movement, but was unable then to reverse it. Unfortunately for Iturbide's welfare, he soon began to presume too much upon the power of his position. The Spaniards were unduly favored in the gifts of offices and honors, the representatives of the nation were treated to some manifestations of arbitrary conduct that were unpleasant, and a demand for more centralized power in the Imperial hands was advanced. These and other kindred developments opened the eyes of the people to the consciousness that they had not gained much by this change of masters. Just here a name looms up that was to fill a large space in the future history of Mexico, and which became, by force of circumstances, better known to Americans than any other south of our own border for the following forty years. Santa Anna was at this time in military command at Vera Cruz. Hearing how matters were going on at the capital, and perceiving therein an opportunity to push himself into prominence by resistance to a man whom many were already beginning to regard as a tyrant, he raised the standard of revolt and " pronounced " against Iturbide. Yet to Iturbide he owed his own position, as he had been raised by the emperor within a few months past from the rank of captain to that of general. The Republican leaders, Victoria, Guerrero, and Nicolas Bravo, supposing Santa Anna sincere in his professions of freedom, hastened to join him with their followers.

Iturbide soon realized that he had forfeited the confidence of

his subjects, that civil war was upon him, and he was powerless
to meet it with any hope of victory. So on the 20th of March,
1823—just nine months after his elaborate coronation—he
tendered his resignation. The Congress, however, refused to .
accept it, on the ground that it had not voluntarily elected him
emperor, and proceeded to form a provisional government
composed of four revolutionary chiefs—Bravo, Victoria,
Negrete, and Guerrero. Sentence of exile was pronounced
against Iturbide, but in view of his services in securing independence the Congress voted him a pension of $24,000 per
annum, on condition of his leaving the country and residing in
Italy, without the right to return to Mexico. Accepting these
terms, Iturbide left, with his family, for Italy. Happy had it
been for him and them had he kept his word with the Mexican
nation, but on the 14th of July, 1824—only fourteen months
after his departure—he returned, with his family, to Mexico,
landing at Sota la Marina, in the State of Tamaulipas, when he
was arrested by the governor and executed. The Congress
granted a pension of $8,000 to the family, which went forthwith
to reside in the United States, where the son, Don Angel Iturbide, became a student at the Jesuit college at Georgetown,
D. C., and there married an American lady of the Romish communion, daughter of Mr. Nathaniel Green, of that city. A son
of this marriage, "Prince Augustine," as he is regarded by the
church party in Mexico, represents the dead emperor, and is the
connecting link between the past and the present. After his
father's death he remained in Mexico, with his mother, and was
there during the French intervention. Toward the close of the
empire of Maximilian, who was childless, this boy attracted the
attention of the Empress Carlota, and was adopted with the
intention of making him heir to the throne, but on the collapse
of the empire he was surrendered again to his mother. Afterward he entered the same college that his father had attended,
and on completing his course returned to Mexico, while he took
a subordinate position in the army. Here, after a couple of
years, he was charged with some acts of insubordination toward

his superior officer, and after trial was sent to prison for fifteen months. Meanwhile his mother had died, and on his release lately he left for the United States. This, no doubt, ends the probability of the Iturbide family being any further a disturbing element in Mexican history.

The fall of Iturbide closed the empire, and a republic, on the model of the United States (save the one item of full religious freedom), was established under a constitution, in October, 1824, General Victoria becoming first constitutional President of Mexico, remaining in power until April, 1829.

By this time Spain had recovered a measure of her strength and took the resolution to reconquer Mexico and South America. A small army was landed at Tampico under the command of General Barradas, but it was soon after defeated by the Republican army under Santa Anna and General Teran, and forced to quit Mexico. These events intensified the hatred of the Spaniards, already strong enough. In a moment of irritation the Congress voted the exile of all Spaniards from the country, but it was not fully carried out. From that hour, however, Spanish influence has declined, and the Mexicans have come to the front in public affairs. What remain of the Spaniards in Mexico have generally continued faithful to their preference for monarchical government, and did what they could for its re-establishment in Mexico during the following thirty years.

The events which we have now rapidly enumerated, commencing with the declaration of independence by Iturbide in 1822—an event which led the United States to acknowledge that independence in the same year—were the facts which, in the interests of the peace and political welfare of this continent, led President James Monroe to issue in 1823 that doctrine of reciprocity of non-intervention which has ever since been associated with his name, and which has done so much to preserve our own nation from entanglement with European quarrels. It had equally preserved us and the neighboring nations from disturbance from foreign powers from that time up to the

8

year 1862, when it was so maliciously violated by Napoleon III.
and led to the fearful events which the further part of this narrative is to lay before our readers. The first effect of that
doctrine was seen in the fact above intimated, that Spain never
attempted a repetition of the barbarous purpose she undertook
in 1829, to force her cruel rule on an unwilling people, while the
failure of the last attempt has, no doubt, settled that question
for this continent for all time to come.

The accepted summary of this grand doctrine, under the
protection of which the nations of North, Central, and South
America are resting, may be here presented.   It runs thus :

The American continents, by the free and independent condition they
had assumed and maintained, are no longer to be considered subjects for
colonization by European powers. Any attempt on the part of European
powers to extend their political systems to the western hemisphere would
be considered dangerous to the peace and safety of the United States. Any
interposition by such powers to oppress or control the governments that
had declared their independence and maintained it, and whose independence had been acknowledged by the United States, would be viewed as
unfriendly to the United States. The political systems of Europe could
not be extended to any portion of the American continent without endan-
gering the peace and happiness of the United States, and such extension
would not be regarded with indifference.

From 1822 to 1855 the name of Santa Anna was the most conspicuous in Mexican politics, chiefly as the most active disturber
of the peace of the nation.   His clerical patrons knew well
how to utilize his remarkable qualities, though it must be confessed that his eye to the main chance was always as keenly open
for his own advantage as for the promotion of their purposes.
His vanity and love of display are apparent in the picture
opposite, where his breast is covered with decorations that were
never won nor conferred, though they were assumed, and were
his because he had paid for them ! His despotic acts no doubt
postponed by twenty years the rest of constitutional freedom
that would have been won but for his reckless interferences.

His full name was Antonio López de Santa Anna.   His
home was at Manga de Clavo, near Jalapa, where he had an

GENERAL SANTA ANNA,
The turbulent Dictator of Mexico.

estate, the extent of which Madame Calderon tells us was twelve leagues, between that city and Vera Cruz. Mrs. F. C. Gooch truly says of him that

When only twenty years old he entered the arena of politics by disrupting the empire established by Iturbide, and the career thus begun was consistently carried out. At an early age he had so mastered the arcana of scheming and revolution as to reflect credit on a veteran in the cause, demolishing and creating sovereignties, often grasping victory from defeat, and gathering strength when all seemed lost. He was five times president, and was the means of deposing, probably, twenty rulers. As a commander of men his resources and ability were remarkable. After the most disastrous defeat he generally managed to retire from the scene still holding the confidence of his ragged, half-starved army, increasing it materially while on the move. His fertile brain was ever ready to plan a revolution or arrange a *coup d'état.*

In the change which he fomented of establishing a central system, abolishing the federal power, every State was deprived of its share of control and all authority lodged in the hands of the executive in Mexico city. No wonder that Yucatan and Texas rebelled and resolved to establish each a separate government. This was the origin of the war with Texas, and that developed into the war with the United States.

Santa Anna is best remembered by Americans for his attempt to whip back the Texans into the traces, when they made their effort for independence of Mexican control, and also for his infamous perfidy in executing the little Texan force under Colonel Fannin, after they had surrendered under written stipulation that their lives should be spared. Nor will he be soon forgotten in our history in connection with his capture by General Houston and his little army of Americans and Texans on the 21st of April, 1836, or the inordinate vanity that he displayed when led into the presence of Houston. Santa Anna laid the flattering unction to his soul that he was himself a hero of the highest class. He had already given himself the amazing title of " The Napoleon of the South! " and expected of his followers that he should be so regarded. The record tells us that even in his fallen condition as defeated and a prisoner, when he was led into the Texan camp and to Houston's presence, he pompously announced himself as "Antonio López de Santa Anna, the President of Mexico, who surrenders as your prisoner ; " and then added, as he looked at General Houston, "You are born to no common destiny, who are the conqueror of the Napoleon of the South!"

The treaty signed recognized the independence of Texas and prompt evacuation of Texas by the Mexican army, and solemnly pledged Santa Anna and his four generals (who all signed with him) to obtain its confirmation by the government of Mexico. How much value there was in the promises and the signature of this hypocritical character was evident enough when, about six months afterward, on reaching Mexico, he publicly repudiated the convention into which he had entered and had signed, on the contemptible ground that "obligations contracted by an individual under *duress* were absolutely void!" He thus proved himself to be as false and hypocritical to his own parole as he was in respecting the conditions which he violated in the case of the brave Texans who unfortunately trusted his promises at Goliad and San Antonio.

During his parole in the United States ere he returned to Mexico he visited Washington and had an interview with President Jackson, upon which he afterward liked to dilate, as the writer had opportunity to hear him do toward the end of his career. Disgraced in the eyes of his countrymen by his failure in the Texan campaign, Santa Anna retired to his estate and remained there until the following year, when a hostile visit of the French navy to Vera Cruz made his services again desirable. He was placed in command of the army at that port, and in repulsing the French troops on the 5th of December, 1838, he lost one of his legs. This mended his reputation somewhat, but laid him aside until the events of 1841 once more called him out, and he became president again, but soon took advantage of his position and proclaimed himself dictator.

It may interest the reader and throw some additional light upon the great transition through which Mexico had to pass on her way from such follies to respectability and character in her public life, if we take another glance at the whimsicalities of the man whom we leave here for the present as the arbitrary dictator of his suffering country. Some of them seem incredible, but we have the authority for them all.

"The fantastic tricks before high Heaven" which Santa Anna was so fond of playing may refer us again to that left leg, which he lost by a shot from the Prince de Joinville's artillery. He had it carefully boxed up, and sent it from Vera Cruz to his admirers in the capital, accompanied by an eloquent letter breathing great patriotism. The stratagem succeeded, and the leg was appropriately cared for until a magnificent monument, surmounted by the national insignia, was prepared to receive it. Santa Anna returned to the capital before the monument was quite finished, and it is said went in the procession to the burial of his own leg! It was deposited with all the honors. He defended the affair very laconically by remarking that, "It was a Christian leg, and deserved to have a Christian burial!" The newspapers of the day announced the event as follows:

MEXICO, *September* 28, 1842.—Yesterday was buried with pomp and solemnity, in the cemetery of St. Paul, the leg which his excellency, President Santa Anna, lost in the action of December 5, 1838. It was deposited in a monument erected for that purpose, Don Ignacio Sierra y Rosa having pronounced a funeral discourse appropriate to the subject.

Gilliam, while referring to these facts, was reminded of an event which has a good parallel in it. He says:

It is true that while Benedict Arnold, the traitor, was in London he inquired of an American what the people of the United States would do with him if he should return to his home. The American replied that the leg in which he had received an honorable wound, in his career for liberty and independence, would be separated from his body and buried with all military honors; but that his body would be hung between heaven and earth as a traitor to his country.*

As Santa Anna stood before the crowd around that monument where this singular funeral was so pompously conducted,

* *Travels over the Table-Lands and Cordilleras of Mexico during* 1843–44, by A. M. Gilliam, p. 119, and Calderon's *Life in Mexico*, p. 368.

how little he imagined what would there occur within only two
years after! During this brief term of time he could not be
satisfied with being president; he must assume dictatorial powers
and try to bend the Congress to his will. Even the archbishop,
at the head of the church party, pronounced against his tyran-
nical policy of levying a forced loan of $4,000,000—the most
odious of all imposts, because so opposed to the principal object
for which governments are founded, the security of the property of the people. His effort excited universal indignation
throughout the republic and caused his overthrow. Even his
army refused to fight for him, and deserted, so that he was now

> "The leader of a broken host,
> His standard fallen and his honor lost."

He had to surrender himself into the hands of his bitter foes,
who sent him a prisoner to the gloomy fortress of Perote, within
whose walls many of the victims of his vindictive policy had
pined in days gone by. During the tumult in December, 1844,
the monument was desecrated, and the leg it contained was
dragged from its resting-place and kicked through the streets
by the rabble! This was all the more humiliating to him because
he had during this very dictatorship indulged so freely in that
extravagance of display and vulgar love of pageantry for which
he was so noted.

After ten years of independence Texas applied for admission
to the United States. The resolutions providing for her annex-
ation awakened hot debate in Congress and violent discussions
all over the country. Into the debates entered the great question of African slavery in the Union. To annex Texas was sure
to involve the United States in a war with Mexico. To advocate
war for the sake of extending slavery and increasing the slave
power of the Union was enough to excite the most bitter opposition from the Whig and the Free Soil parties.

Texas contained two hundred thousand square miles of un-
disputed territory, out of which, Senator Benton, of Missouri,
said in Congress, "nine slave States could be made, each equal to

the State of Kentucky." This would give, he argued, a predominant slave representation in the government. *Here, then, we find the great underlying cause of the war* which so soon followed. Mr. Calhoun, also in the Senate, at the close of this Texan war, maintained the right of slave-holders to carry and hold their slaves in all the free territory acquired by conquest from Mexico.*

It is honorable to Mexico just here to call attention to the fact that, as soon as this purpose was avowed, her republican sons protested against such a desecration of the territory which they had made free by abolishing slavery forever from every part of it. But all in vain, as we shall see. Our Southern slave-holders, infatuated, forgot Him who is "higher than the highest," who was able to defeat their purposes.

At this period an event occurred which was to prove of the highest moment to the future of the United States and Mexico. The war-ships of the British and American navies were hovering off the coast of California, each anxious to arrive before the other, so as to land and run up the flag and take possession in the name of their government. Colonel Fremont, with a small force, having the same object in view, was operating in the interior. But there was another party also, representing a different government from either, who was anxiously pushing a project of his own to secure that California for *his* master and a very different future.

We have heard of that wonderful map which hangs in the library of the Propaganda at Rome, said to be the largest map of the United States in existence, on which are definitely marked all the points of interest and prospective importance and power in our great West and away to the Californian coast. It was an immense work then to ascertain and locate these points so well and so quietly, " while men slept," unconscious that the papacy was preparing to preempt in advance the strategic points of these broad lands for its own purposes. These facts were presented by Rev. Dr. Ellinwood in an able paper read

* See *History of the War with Mexico*, by H. O. Ladd.

before the General Assembly of the Presbyterian Church in 1881. We copy so much as refers to our subject. He said :

But while a Mexican dictator had grasped despotic power, and our statesmen had planned for territory which would render slavery secure, there were other schemes afloat.

Testimony now to be found in the archives of the State department at Washington shows that in the years 1845 and 1846, just as our conflict with Mexico was commencing, an Irish Catholic missionary in California, of the name of McNamara, conceived a plan for planting on a very large scale a colony of Irish Catholics in the rich valley of the San Joaquin River. In an intercepted letter to the Mexican president Father McNamara says: "I have a triple object in my proposal. I wish, first, to advance the cause of Catholicism; second, to promote the happiness and thrift of my countrymen; and, thirdly, to put an obstacle in the way of the further usurpations of that irreligious and anti-Catholic nation—the United States. And if the plan which I propose be not speedily adopted your excellency may be assured that before another year the Californias will form a part of the American nation. The Catholic institutions will become the prey of Methodist wolves, and the whole country will be inundated with cruel invaders." The grant of the land was made; and, according to the testimony given before a committee of Congress, General Castro had armed and organized the Mexican Californians, and had engaged the Indian tribes to help to exterminate the American settlers, when the whole scheme was reported at Washington.

Captain Gillespie was at once dispatched as a secret messenger to General Fremont, then on the Oregon border.

After many hair-breadth escapes from the Indians the message was delivered. Fremont turned back, rallied the American settlers, levied on horses, guns, and stores, and with the suddenness of a thunder-bolt routed the Mexican force, broke up a junta which had been appointed to negotiate with the British Admiral Seymour, then off the coast, to establish a British protectorate, and on the 5th of July, 1846, having learned of the declaration of war between Mexico and the United States, he ran up the Stars and Stripes, and California was saved for the "Methodists."

These events are wonderfully like those which had transpired in Oregon a short time before; and it is fortunate for Christian civilization that the result was the same in both cases.*

Further light is thrown upon this subject by a paper furnished to the *Century Magazine* by Mrs. Jessie Benton Fremont,

---

* *Mexico, Her Past and Present Resources*, in *The New York Evangelist*, June 30, 1887.

widow of General Fremont. From this it appears that McNamara was a British subject, but working in the interest of a project originated at Rome to checkmate the growing Protestantism of the United States. He had succeeded in interesting both the civil and religious authorities at Mexico, who had considered and indorsed this colonization plan, in which he had engaged to locate ten thousand families, to each of whom he was to apportion a square league of land. Mexican authority in that great West was then a mere shadow, without force and unable to sustain itself against the American element scattered through the country, if they would only come together and set up a government of some kind. Hence the efforts made by McNamara to hasten the British Admiral Seymour to land in California, raise his flag, and take possession. He had almost secured his prize of 13,500,000 acres, from San Francisco to the San Gabriel Mission, near Los Angeles, the San Joaquin River and the Sierra Nevada being the boundaries. The Mexican governor, Pio Pico, issued this immense tract of land to Father McNamara " on the express condition that the grant was to keep out the Americans." But Fremont and his band succeeded in raising the United States flag that very day at Monterey before Admiral Seymour could arrive and act in McNamara's interest. California was thus added to the United States, and his plan was utterly defeated. The following year the treaty of Guadalupe-Hidalgo closed the war with Mexico and confirmed by purchase as well as conquest the possession of California to our Union.*

A brief reference to our war with Mexico is necessary here. Santa Anna (who was recalled from exile to aid in the struggle) took the field at the head of twenty thousand men. He met General Zachary Taylor at Buena Vista, and suffered a heavy defeat. At Cerro Gordo he was vanquished, after which he retreated to defend the capital, but Molino del Rey, Chapultepec, and Mexico city surrendered to General Scott.

* Compiled from Mrs. Fremont's manuscript, in the *Century Magazine*, April, 1891.

The Stars and Stripes floated over the national palace in Mexico from September 14, 1847, till June 12, 1848. The concessions demanded by the United States government were embodied in the treaty signed at Guadalupe by the plenipotentiaries of both nations on the 2d of February, 1848. By this treaty Mexico surrendered territory about equal to one half of her former extent, making the enormous total of our southern and south-western border of 851,590 square miles; seventeen times the size of the great State of New York, including ten degrees of latitude on the Pacific coast, and extending a thousand miles to the east.

It is true that $15,000,000 of compensation and a release from $3,250,000 of claims of United States citizens on Mexico were tendered and accepted by the vanquished nation. But the Mexican government well knew that the acceptance of the sum offered was obligatory, though it was not, even then, more than a fraction of its value, not to mention the hundreds of millions which the mines of California were to yield in all the future to the United States! To this was added the bitter reflection to the Mexican administration that after they had, in their honest and painful efforts to establish a true republican government in their country, abolished slavery forever, and now when they entreated, in the framing of this treaty with their conquerors, that a clause should be inserted committing the United States not to permit slavery to be established in any part of the ceded territory, they were met with a disdainful refusal, and their honorable demands were rejected by the great republic, the power that of all on earth should have been to them a friend in their struggle to maintain the liberty they had established. Instead of this, our nation was led to wage this unnecessary and unjustifiable war in the interest of the Southern slave-holders and for the wider extension of their wicked institution. For abundant evidence of this fact we refer the reader to the book of Mr. Jay,* where, from page 150

* A *Review of the Causes and Consequences of the Mexican War.* Boston. Mussey & Co., 1849.

to 195, will be seen, from the action and language of our government and the debates in Congress, that the extension of the area of slavery was the paramount object of the war with Mexico.

It is enough to make any lover of freedom tremble to imagine what the result would have been to the future of the world and of Christian civilization had the purpose of the Southern oligarchy been carried out as they intended. The gain of this immense territory made them so bold that they next planned the abolition of all restriction throughout the country, so that they might have power of control over their slaves from the Canada line to the Gulf of Mexico. The Fugitive Slave Law was passed in their interest, and the hunted slave was no longer safe wherever the Stars and Stripes floated. The surprise and excitement of the nation, and especially of our liberty-loving millions, became intense, while the haters of constitutional freedom indulged their bitter sarcasm at our expense. We were on the high road to the building up, over this wide land, from the Atlantic to the Pacific, of the most colossal empire of negro slavery that the world had ever seen. It only needed time for development, and to be left unhindered by God and man to become even far worse and more awful than that " open sore of the world " of which Livingtone spoke in Africa. Worse, because the Arabs there have set that sore running under the sanction of their Koran, while our sacred Book, in its spirit and precepts, forbids such injustice.

So men who were ruled by their consciences and who feared God declared that they would not be forced to aid or to perpetuate an institution so unchristian. Slave-holders professed to laugh at our reverence for the " higher law," and our convictions, and were determined to force obedience to the Fugitive Slave Law, even declaring that they would erelong " call the roll of their slaves under the shadow of Bunker Hill." Slowly the great North arose to the duty which she owed to God and humanity to free herself from what Mr. Wesley designated as "the sum of all villainies." Judge Harrington, of Vermont, well voiced the conscience of the North in that case where the slave-hunter had overtaken his victim and brought him into court to demand his rendition, offering the proof of ownership in the bill of sale to the person whom he represented. The worthy judge closed the case when he ruled that, "This title is invalid here. I demand a bill of sale from the Almighty!" So the slave went forth to freedom.

The word of God is the instrument to unify the world, and these mighty movements were in his providence to open its way to its great mission among men. In our war with Mexico the Bible entered to begin its beneficent work in the hands of the Aztecs. There were a few there who had heard of it, though they had not seen it; but they welcomed it, for they were longing for a clearer knowledge of the way to salvation. A small number of these were priests, like Orestes, Gomez, and others. Among the laity more were anxious for its introduction, for they had learned that the Bible stood well with liberty, that Bible readers every-where were free men, that the most enlightened nations were those where the Holy Scriptures had the fullest circulation, and they desired the help of such a book in their struggle for popular freedom. When the war with Mexico was proclaimed in 1847 the American Bible Society grasped the opportunity and appointed Rev. M. Norris as agent, an edition of the Spanish Scriptures being then just published. Mr. Norris went with the army and distributed many copies, and was aided by some of the men and officers. An account of what was done in this respect was written by Major-General Casey in 1850. We will quote one fact of special interest on the subject, to show how some of the educated people looked at the wonderful book, now for the first time within their reach. He writes:

The occupying of the city of Mexico by our army, considering the obstacles which were to be overcome, naturally excited a new train of thought among the intelligent and thinking Mexicans. They would ask these questions of one another: "How is it that these people, whom we had been taught by our priests to consider as God-forsaken heretics, over-come all obstacles which have been opposed to them from Vera Cruz to this city, and then with a comparative handful of men have broken through the three lines of fortifications with which our city was surrounded and taken possession of the capital of our republic ? Our city had a popula-tion of 200,000, and besides it was under the special protection of Mary of Guadalupe, who in many priestly processions about our streets was inter-ceded by us. These people possess and are zealously distributing a book from which they profess to derive their religion, and from which we also pretend to derive ours. May it not possibly be that the priests from interested motives have corrupted the teachings of the truth ?" A little leaven has been planted in Mexico which by God's blessing will leaven the whole.

At this time General Casey held the rank of captain, and in this capacity led the storming party at Cherubusco, where the American army suffered its greatest loss, chiefly by the treachery of some of its own soldiers. His account of this affair is as follows:

On the 20th of August the battles of Contreras and Cherubusco were fought. At the latter place the principal point of attack was a fortified convent, and the American army lost 1,000 men in killed and wounded by the obstinate resistance. This was caused by the presence of more than two hundred deserters from the American army, composed mostly of Catholic Irish, who had been persuaded to desert by the instigation of the Mexican Catholic priests. Fifty of these men were afterward captured and hung, the drop at the gallows falling just as the American flag went up on the castle of Chapultepec. When the final assault on the city was made by the causeway, at the extremity of which the castle of Chapul-tepec was situated, we had but little more than 6,000 men.*

The sectarian treachery of the Irish deserters might have proved to be overwhelming. Yet Mr. Jay considers the pun-ishment as excessive.† But it is only fair to remember that this had to be judged in the light of the emergency which their desertion, and the turning of their weapons against their gov-ernment in the presence of the enemy, had created. It might have involved the destruction of the whole American force, which was so small comparatively. As it was it cost them

---

* *Christian World*, vol. xxiv, p. 47.   † *Review of the Mexican War*, p. 208.

nearly *one seventh* of their whole number. Nor should it be forgotten that this was not the first time. A few months before a similar act of treachery had occurred in General Taylor's command at Monterey, by the same class of men deserting and crossing the river to join their co-religionists on the other side and help them fight the Americans. While Christians may well seek the intervention of the Omniscient One to guard against dangers of this class, the patriot is equally bound to use his vigilance to counteract them. On some occasions yet to come the celebrated order may need to be repeated as a precaution, "Put none but Americans on guard to-night!" The spirit of that order might have saved a large part of that disheartening loss at Cherubusco.

The valley of Anahuac, in which the city of Mexico is situated, is surrounded by high mountains on every side. Between the peaks are deep gorges known as "cañadas." To one of these we went, in 1874, to see the place where a few Mexicans used to meet on the Sabbath day to listen to the reading of the word of God. A copy of the Scriptures had come into their possession, and they arranged to assemble to hear it read. The place selected was high up on the side of a mountain where a little cave was found. They dug a bank for seats on the sides, where twenty or thirty might sit, and in the center they built up with sods a little rest where the Bible could be laid, and a seat behind it for the reader to occupy. Every thing had to be done with the greatest secrecy. They could not dare to approach or leave the place together, for their Jesuit enemies would soon have suspected and discovered their retreat. So, from various directions and one by one, they came to enjoy their opportunity. Every Sabbath this little company of Mexicans met together, and the Bible was then brought from its hiding-place and read and talked over, and then they would kneel down and pray, imploring God to give them grace faithfully to follow what they had learned, and entreating him to have mercy upon their country and hasten the hour when this holy book should be free and available to all in their benighted land. While here in this favored country we were in the regular enjoyment of our luxury of the means of grace with "none to make us afraid," how little we could realize at what risk and under what difficulties these honest souls, without any man to guide them, were seeking light and help from the divine oracles! It was no ordinary privilege to visit such a place and try to realize how it looked with its worshipers only a few years before. Undoubtedly this was a sample of several such scenes over the country after the distribution of the Bible had taken place, and before the triumph of the republic had made it safe to let it be known that people were in possession of it or that they met to read or hear it read. After the departure of the American army in 1848 a raid was made by the clergy upon these holy books, and many of them were given up and destroyed by burning them publicly with indignities, especially in the cities; but yet many of them were never surrendered, and to-day some of those old and well-worn Bibles are seen and examined with a peculiar reverence. Thank Heaven, it is not the Bible-burners that have the upper hand in Mexico to-day! Their malignant power to hinder it is gone. It has at last "free course and is glorified" in all the land.

Santa Anna's failure to free the country from the presence of the United States army greatly disappointed the nation and led to the formation of factions against him, so that he felt himself forced to resign his positions of president and commander-in-chief on the 1st of February, 1848, and on the 5th of April he sailed with his family for the island of Jamaica, where for nearly five years he found a quiet asylum. But we shall see him once more as a turbulent dictator ere his final exile is pronounced. The Mexican Congress declared General Herrera constitutional president, and the nation tried to recover from its terrible experience of war and its many miseries.

9

CHAPTER IV.

This brings us to a period where we have to consider certain events transpiring in Europe which will be found to have a very intimate relation with those which have preceded and are yet to follow in Mexico—facts that proved more hostile to her aspirations for freedom than were the events now passed under review, sad as they were, but which nevertheless, in the mercy of God, contrary to their designed intent, were to help her forward.

He who would properly comprehend the crisis in Mexico which we now approach must bear in mind that her sorrows were shared by others, and that they arose from identical causes. Her great transition did not stand alone, nor was it at all isolated, while on her struggle for constitutional freedom was probably suspended the future peace and welfare of this whole continent. This was specially true of Latin America, but also, and in a very serious sense, it was true of Anglo-Saxon America. All that both in the best estate longed for in their respective futures was involved in the Mexican struggle, and, under God, depended upon her success. If she were crushed they must have been involved sooner or later in the great catastrophe; while, if she rose triumphant, the security of all the rest would be established.

The States of Central and South America had, with one exception, enthusiastically proclaimed themselves converts to the theory of constitutional freedom for all their people, which the Anglo-Saxon portion so grandly illustrates before them in its peace and prosperity, and were coming into possession of similar blessings for themselves. To gain this for their respective countries their bravest and best had given their treasure and their blood, and thousands of them had become martyrs in the glorious cause. But all this is hateful to the claims of political Romanism. That one little State of Ecuador is more to the pope's mind as to what the condition of a State should be than all the order, prosperity, and intelligence of the rest put together. Once, and only about seventy years ago, all of Central and South America were about as Ecuador is to-day, and the papacy was happy over their condition, so much so that no voice, with her sanction, was ever raised to call them to a better life of freedom or intelligence. On the contrary, Romanism did her best to rivet those chains and to proscribe and punish with disabilities and even cruel deaths, as we have already seen, those who raised the flag of freedom, even when the ever-to-be-honored men who did this were some of her own clergy.

In this regard (whatever she may say to the contrary occasionally) Rome holds that the greatest of all offenders on this hemisphere against her will and preferences is the United States. If it were not for this land of ours her rule would have been undisturbed and unchallenged over all the rest, perhaps for generations to come. We chose to be free, and at once began to talk about it quite loudly as a very good thing and desirable for every body else, and our neighbors heard and proceeded to examine our condition in order to judge for themselves, and were won by the teaching of our example. The pope and his curia are not at all in love with us and our measures, and their occasional compliments to our blessings must be taken with many grains of allowance, as their official utterances frequently evidence. It was bad enough for us to have a "free Church in a free State" for ourselves, but to "let our light so shine" that sixteen States should follow our example and cast their concordats away and declare for similar freedom—this was outrageous. In fact, we are a great concern to the pope. Worse yet, we are using our prosperity not merely as an example of freedom and safe statehood, but we are also employing our resources to evangelize the natives of the earth with such vigor that our contributions for the spread of the Gospel are double what the pope collects from his whole denomination to extend his papal missions! Hence his tears and lamentations and encyclicals bearing on the subject, and his fixed resolves to checkmate us by any means within his power.

There were other elements also that entered into the struggle in regard to Mexico. The toryism of the English nation and her high churchism found our example distasteful, illustrating as it did the capability of enlightened men for self-government and the power of the Christian Church to sustain herself and her institutions without the crutches of State support. To people who held to the "divine right of kings," and the theory of a national church establishment and such laws as those of primogeniture and entail, the United States was an unwelcome fact before the Mexican question was raised. No one can fully understand the story of the French intervention in Mexico and our relation to it if he does not comprehend how far these jealousies entered into the question as well as their sympathy for the Southern rebellion.

There are facts that seem to intimate that a purpose has been long entertained by the monarchists of Europe to neutralize the influence and example of the United States, and, if possible, to overthrow our institutions. There are those who remember the language used by the Duke of Richmond, when Governor-General of Canada in 1819, to Mr. H. G. Gates, of Montreal, and by him faithfully reported afterward. Speaking of the government of the United States, the duke is reported to have said:

It was weak, inconsistent, and bad, and could not long exist. It will be destroyed; it ought not, and will not, be permitted to exist; for many and great are the evils that have originated from the existence of that government. The curse of the French Revolution and subsequent wars and commotions in Europe are to be attributed to its example, and so long as it exists no prince will be safe upon his throne, and the sovereigns of Europe are aware of it, and they have been determined upon its destruction, and have come to an understanding upon this subject and have decided on the means to accomplish it; and they will *even finally succeed by subversion rather than conquest.*

The Church of Rome has a design upon that country, and it will, in time, be the established religion and will aid in the destruction of that republic. I have conversed with many of the sovereigns and princes of Europe, particularly with George the Third and Louis the Eighteenth, and they have unanimously expressed these opinions relative to the government of the United States and their determination to subvert it.*

Mr. Gates tells us that the duke then proceeded to show how this *plan* would be carried out. We were to be swamped by immigration; these immigrants would in time become citizens, next they would get strong enough to hold the balance of power between the parties into which the nation was divided, and finally would gain the majority, when our institutions would be overthrown and the republic abolished. This is very like the testimony and warning of the illustrious Lafayette, who well knew the hostility of Romanism to republican governments, and declared it as his conviction to Prof. Morse and others that "if ever the liberties of the United States are destroyed it will be by Romish priests." † It is somewhat startling to pause and realize how the duke's anticipations seem in process of accomplishment, and especially remembering that immigration at that date was only about 11,000 per annum and the Romish population in this country very small indeed. Now the former has risen into hundreds of thousands annually and the latter has climbed up to nearly 8,000,000. How amazed would this aristocrat become were he here to-day to see it, and how assured of the near approach to fulfillment of his anticipations! Such men, however, leave out of their calculations the divine control in human affairs and that power which is working for righteousness in this world. The servants of God can be calm and confident, even with full knowledge of the wicked purposes of

* *Christian World,* vol. vii, p. 132. † *Ibid.,* vol. vi, pp. 305, 359, 454.

their enemies, as they realize "The Lord is our defense; and the Holy One of Israel is our King" (Psa. lxxxix, 18).

The duke in his prophecy only represented the most unworthy element of his nation. America and American principles are better understood and appreciated by England than ever before. We have a hundred friends there to-day for the one that we had in his day, and so also of the wide world; grand men, too, in all ranks of life, who rejoice in our prosperity, and who feel all the stronger in view of the fact that they have such an ally as the United States to stand with them for constitutional freedom (whether monarchical or republican) and evangelical faith, speaking the same grand language, reading the same free Bible, ruled by the same just laws, laboring together to make this world better by the agency of evangelical religion. We can offset the prejudiced duke by one of his own order, the devout Earl of Shaftesbury, when he wrote to Dr. Baird, of New York, declaring, "The union of America with England in all these things of prime importance to the human race is of incalculable value. May God make us to be ever of one mind and one heart for his service and glory!"

All the States of Central and South America have broken away from the yoke of Spain or Portugal, one after another, following the cry for independence proclaimed by Hidalgo in 1811, and have declared for a republican form of government. Mexico became the key to the whole position; she was nearest to us, and, as fast as able, copied our example. The others, bound largely by the medium of a common language, studied and imitated her. Their struggle with dictatorships has resulted in constitutional order more or less perfect. Their concordats are abrogated, in many civil and religious liberty is proclaimed, monasteries and nunneries abolished and their properties secularized for the support of the State and education, the press made free, civil marriage laws passed, and altogether a new life of peace and prosperity has been entered upon under which some of these States have reached an era of order and social welfare which surprises those who visit their territories.

Meanwhile Protestant missions have gone in to offer a purer faith and a Christian education to their youth. This has been accomplished by resolute men in the face of mighty opposition. From Rome came anathemas and excommunications, hurled at them in the name of Almighty God by a power that could not show its right to speak in his name. At home clerical despotism, with all the bitterness it dared to show, fought the new-born freedom, but the rising intelligence of the people saved the precious cause and brought it to its present state of advance.

We select an illustrative instance here from a responsible source, one which will present the very latest aspects of the situation. The government of President Arthur selected a gentleman of known ability to proceed to Central and South America as commissioner and accredited agent of the United States, to examine and inquire thoroughly into the condition of the States of Spanish America and the prospects of trade and commerce with this country, and to furnish reliable information concerning the finances, trade, agriculture, politics, social condition, and necessities of the several States. Mr. William E. Curtis was selected to fulfill this commission. A short time since he returned, and has given us a volume entitled *Capitals of Spanish America*, in which he has concentrated a mass of information, well arranged and illustrated, more complete than can be found in any other work. Mr. Curtis was evidently surprised and delighted to find such enlightened freedom and extending prosperity among these South American States. We present the condition of one State which he visited and found to be in such fearful contrast with all the rest, the lowest of the low, which had deliberately refused the boon that the others had so earnestly sought, and in the possession of which they are so glad and grateful. Yet the fact will show that this sad exception of Ecuador is one fixed exactly according to papal requirement, and just as political Romanism would have it arranged. As our readers study the description they will do well to bear in mind that here is shown the *model* after which

such desperate effort would have been made to mold the future
of Mexico had the French intervention been successful.

That all this miserable condition of things was intended and
provided for by the papacy as their idea of what a State should
be is evident in the terms of the treaty into which this very
State entered, or rather to which its ultramontane President
Moreno committed it, in April, 1863, when he negotiated that
treaty with Cardinal Antonelli, the papal secretary of state.
Three or four paragraphs will show its character as a sample of
her preferences, and will equally show what Rome would have
insisted on had she succeeded in Mexico, and would insist on
every-where if she once gained her hoped-for ascendency in
America. It was expressly stipulated in the case in the pope's
name as follows :

1. The Roman Catholic and apostolic religion is the religion of the republic of Ecuador. Consequently the exercise of any other worship or
the existence of any society condemned by the Church will *not be permitted*
by the republic.

2. The education of the young in all public and private schools shall
be entirely conformed to the doctrines of the (Roman) Catholic religion.
The teachers, the books, the instructions imparted, etc., etc., shall be submitted to the decision of the *bishops*.

3. Government will give its powerful patronage and its support to the
bishops in their resistance to the evil designs of wicked persons, etc.

4. All matrimonial causes, and all those which concern the faith, the
sacraments, the public morals, etc., are placed under the sole jurisdiction
of the *ecclesiastical tribunals*, and the civil magistrates shall be charged to
carry them into execution.

5. The privileges of churches (the ancient right of asylum in consecrated buildings) shall be fully respected.

6. Tithes shall be punctually paid, etc.

The preceding extracts vindicate the deliberate judgment of
Lord Palmerston, for so many years prime minister of England, and who had the widest opportunity to form an opinion
of Romanism in this respect. He left us his conviction in the
following language :

All history tells us that wherever the Romish priesthood have gained a
predominance there the utmost amount of intolerance is invariably the prac-

tice. In countries where they are in the minority they instantly demand not only toleration, but equality, but in countries where they predominate they allow neither toleration nor equality.

But we need not now to go to foreigners to ascertain the real purposes contemplated by the papacy, not only in Mexico and South America, but in this, our own land, as well. The pope may not have intended this to be so plainly uttered just yet in a Protestant country, but as a sample of what is already avowed by Catholic writers, who jump so confidently to their conclusions as to our prospective subjugation when they gain the power of numerical majority, and as an illustration of Lord Palmerston's words, take the following, which appeared some time since in the *Rambler*, a prominent Roman Catholic journal in our own land :

You ask, If the Catholic were lord in the land, and you (Protestants) in the minority, what would he do with you ? That would depend upon circumstances. If it would benefit Catholicism he would tolerate you; if expedient he would imprison you, banish you, fine you, possibly he might even hang you. But be assured of one thing, *he would never tolerate you for the sake of the " glorious principles of civil and religious liberty."* *

Many Protestants suppose, as did the writer in other days, that, whatever might be the record of Romanism in the past, she must have been touched with the tolerant spirit of our age, and that it is a mistake to suppose she is really so false to freedom and so resolutely bent, whenever she gains the power of numbers, on renewing her intolerant course toward those who dissent from her teaching as these utterances of her public writers so often imply. Alas! the language of her highest authorities and her work as we see it here and in Mexico make it impossible longer to hold on to this judgment of charity concerning her real intentions. We have no evidence that as a Church she is changed for the better or would show herself more tolerant and less cruel than she was in the days of old. Romanists can easily be found who favor tolerance, but they do not guide her policy, and could not restrain it if the hour

* *Christian World*, vol. xiv, pp. 299, 301.

and the opportunity which she so much desires should again return to her.

Now, what did Mr. Curtis find in Ecuador as a result of their concordat relations with Rome? We quote a few sentences in reply:

The rule which prevails every-where, that the less a people are under the control of that Church the greater their prosperity, enlightenment, and progress, is illustrated in Ecuador with striking force. One fourth of all the property in Ecuador belongs to the bishop. There is a Catholic church for every one hundred and fifty inhabitants; of the population of the country ten per cent. are priests, monks, or nuns, and two hundred and seventy-two of the three hundred and sixty-five days of the year are observed as feasts or fast days.

The priests control the government in all its branches, dictate its laws and govern their enforcement, and rule the country as absolutely as if the pope were its king. There is not a railroad or stage-coach in the entire country, and until recently there was not a telegraph wire. Laborers get from two to ten dollars a month, and men are paid two dollars and a quarter for carrying one hundred pounds of merchandise on their backs two hundred and eighty-five miles. There is not a wagon in the republic outside of Guayaquil (the port), and not a road over which a wagon could pass. The people know nothing but what the priests tell them; they have no amusements but cock-fights and bull-fights, no literature, no mail routes except from Guayaquil to the capital (Quito). If one tenth of the money that has been expended in building monasteries had been devoted to the construction of cart-roads, Ecuador, which is naturally rich, would be one of the most wealthy nations, in proportion to its area, on the globe.

Although Ecuador is set down in the geographies as a republic, it is simply a popish colony, and the power of the Vatican is nowhere felt so completely as there. . . . So subordinated is the State to the Church that the latter elects the president, the Congress, and the judges. A crucifix sits in the audience chamber of the president and on the desk of the presiding officer of Congress. All the schools are controlled by the Church, and the children know more about the lives of the saints than about the geography of their own country. There is not even a good map of Ecuador. . . . The social and political condition of Ecuador presents a picture of the Dark Ages. There is not a newspaper printed outside of the city of Guayaquil, and the only information the people have of what is going on in the world is gained from strangers who now and then visit the country, and a class of peddlers who make periodical trips, traversing the whole hemisphere from Guatemala to Patagonia.

The ceremony of marriage is not observed to any great extent, for the expense of matrimony is too heavy for the common people to think of paying it. For this the Catholic Church is responsible, and to it can be traced the cause of the illegitimacy of more than half of the population. One fourth of the city of Quito is covered with convents, and every fourth person you meet is a priest or a monk or a nun.

Until the influence of the Romish Church is destroyed, until immigration is invited and secured, Ecuador will be a desert rich in undeveloped resources. With plenty of natural wealth, it has neither peace nor industry, and such a thing as a surplus of any character is unknown. One of the richest of the South American republics and the oldest of them all, it is the poorest and most backward.*

How there could be found people who deliberately prefer this condition of things seems impossible to comprehend. Yet the beneficent changes wrought in other States alarmed the papacy and aroused its determination to force back these States into the condition of Ecuador. For this purpose the French Intervention was attempted in Mexico, to extinguish, if possible, constitutional freedom and evangelical Christianity upon this continent.

Every step toward progress which these now free States made has been fought by the pope. Evidence of this is abundant. We need only quote one as a sample, the case of New Granada. There lies before us the allocution of the pope against that State, dated 27th of September, 1852. Being nearly nine pages long we have room only for the doings which he denounces and his attempted abrogation of them and his threats of punishment. The translation is from the *Tablet*, the Irish Roman Catholic journal. His "holiness" first enumerates the chief actions of the government and legislature of New Granada, which he denounces. They are as follows:

1. The expulsion of the Jesuits and the breaking up of the other orders. 2. The encouragement given to those who had taken the monastic vows to break them and return to the ordinary manner of life. 3. The giving of the appointment of parish priests and the regulation of their salaries to the people of each parish, convened in public meeting. 4. The interference of the government in the question of the revenues of the

* *Capitals of South America*, by W. E. Curtis, p. 306.

archbishop and bishops. 5. The introduction of "free education." 6. The liberty given to all to print and publish their opinions on the subject of religion. 7. And finally the liberty granted to immigrants and to any one else *to profess privately and publicly whatever worship they please.*

And this is all to make him, as he declares, "heavily oppressed," and cause him "bitter grief."

How does he meet the situation? He states that since 1845 he has been complaining and remonstrating with that legislature and government "against these unjust laws" and "nefarious decrees," and had backed up the bishops in their resistance to them; and he condemns the clergy who were willing to accept and obey them, and denounces the proposal of the president "to give our legate his *congé* when he did not neglect to protest in our name against all those wicked and sacrilegious attempts." Then he comes to his denunciation:

We do censure, condemn, and declare utterly null and void all the aforesaid decrees, which have, so much to the contempt of the ecclesiastical authority and of this holy see, been there enacted by the civil power.

He then adds his threat and closes:

We very gravely admonish all those by whose instrumentality and orders they were put forth that they seriously consider the penalties and censures which have been constituted by the apostolical constitutions and the sacred canons of councils against those who violate and profane sacred persons and things and the ecclesiastical power and the right of this apostolic see.*

The legislature and government of New Granada were unmoved by this bitter blast from Rome, and paid it no more attention than the idle wind which passed by them. The president and public men of the State of Honduras were not quite so patient, when about the same time the pope and his secretary of state, Antonelli, tried the same course with them, and on their refusal to be moved one iota from the liberal constitution which they had framed and were following the pope excommunicated the president. When the bull of excommunication arrived the president called a mass-meeting in the public square to hear it

* *Christian World*, vol. iv, pp. 55–63.

read. He had a company of artillery and a cannon placed in front of the crowd, with the muzzle pointed toward Rome and loaded with blank cartridge. When all was ready President Barrundia, standing beside the gun and facing the dignitaries of state, civil and military, drew forth and read aloud every word of the bull. Then, carefully folding it, he placed it in the cannon, had it rammed home, and gave the signal to send it back to Rome!* This was the very spirit of Martin Luther when he burned the pope's bull at Wittenberg. The free and enlightened world applauds the courageous act of the great reformer, as the freemen of South America to-day do that of Barrundia. One of the leading editors of the State struck the key-note of their freedom when, in view of these transactions, he wrote:

We are Catholics and partisans of the absolute emancipation of the Church, because religion is all conscience and needs nothing from force. Its seat is in the heart. What religion needs is what every thing needs—*liberty*, not in licentiousness, but in justice.

When will Rome learn this simple lesson and give up her foolish attempts to override the conscience of mankind?

This is the power whose workings we have to watch with sleepless vigilance as the price of liberty for ourselves and for others—a power unscrupulous, unchanging, and centralized, wielding the false assumption of a divine authority and demanding the absolute subjection of all to its despotic will; its center the Roman curia, its secret police the Jesuits, its army of operations the bishops and priests, sworn to implicit obedience to all its behests, no matter how unpatriotic, illiberal, or unscriptural they may be. Not satisfied with his despotic rule over his own denomination, Pius IX. set his heart upon extending that rule over all the other Churches. He asserted that he was the vicegerent of God upon this earth, without warrant for the claim; still he attempted to force that claim on Mexico, thereby causing the most agonizing conflict of her history. What made this all the more difficult to endure was the fact that he made

* *Christian World*, vol. v, p. 307.

the world believe, for a few weeks at the beginning of his reign, that the spirit of the nineteenth century had reached the Roman curia, and that their war against modern civilization was to cease. The liberal cabinet selected by Pius IX. framed a *statuto* (constitution), which was promised in the pope's name in 1847. The liberal world was taken by storm, men threw up their hats and cheered for "the reforming pope!" "A confederated Christendom" was talked of, with Pius IX. at the head, and universal liberty safe under its protection. Crowded public meetings were held in the cities of our land; one such, on the 29th of November, 1847, in the Broadway Tabernacle, with the mayor of New York in the chair, while the leading men present exulted in "the movement which had placed the head of the most venerable Church in Western Christendom at the front of the great liberal movement in the whole world!" Horace Greeley made one of the addresses, and moved six enthusiastic resolutions, the last of which we here quote:

Resolved, That "peace hath her victories, no less renowned than war," and that the noble attitude of Pius IX., throwing the vast influence of the pontificate into the scale of well-attempted freedom, standing as the advocate of peaceful progress, the prompter of social amelioration, industrial development, and political reform, . . . is the grandest spectacle of our day, full of encouragement and promise to Europe, more grateful to us, and more glorious to himself, than triumphs on a hundred battle-fields! *

Mexico doubtless rejoiced as she heard their jubilations, and supposed her long conflict was ended—that freedom's bright day under the highest religious sanction had dawned at last for her. She could not then have for a moment anticipated a French Intervention and a cruel war, forced upon her within sixteen years, sanctioned by the man who at that moment was raising such hopes of freedom.

Poor Greeley, too! How little he could imagine in that hour that twenty years after he would stand again on that same platform to utter his disappointment at the failure of the hopes he then expressed, to indignantly denounce those who had proved

* *Christian World*, vol. xxii, p. 92.

PIVS IX,
PONTIFEX MAXIMVS
ANNO MDCCCLIX

POPE PIUS IX.,
Who sanctioned and sustained the usurpation of Maximilian.

so false to their pledges of freedom, and to give his sympathy to a real liberty in Italy under the constitutional rule of Victor Emmanuel when the pope's temporal power was in the dust!

This purposed freedom in Rome, under pontifical patronage, was destined to an imperfect development and a short life. It is amusing to read the "faint praise" with which the experiment was greeted by Roman Catholic writers, like Maguire, in his *Rome : Its Rulers and its Institutions.* As we follow him for a little we see that it did not put him into any intoxication of delight, like that exhibited by the advocates of liberty who believed the papacy sincere in its reforming course. Unfortunately for himself, the pope had raised hopes of constitutional freedom in the minds of the liberal party in Italy, but when the constitution, after long delay, appeared it did not give satisfaction. The press of Rome and the liberal leaders began to realize that they were trifled with. The Romans, army and people, resolved not to be cheated out of their right to a liberal constitution, and held Pius IX. to his promises. Their determination was such that the Pope chose to regard himself as in danger for his liberty, if not for his life—an insinuation which they indignantly repelled. Instead of conciliating, he made up his mind to desert them, and thus, he thought, to throw all things into confusion. This was carried into effect on the night of November 24, 1847. Count Spaur, the Bavarian minister, and his wife had their carriage at the palace of the Quirinal, where the pope, disguised in a suit of livery, took his seat on the box beside the coachman, and thus the head of the Catholic world, under the hat of a lackey, rolled away from his palace. They rode all night to Gaeta, where, under the wing of the King of Naples, he was protected during the seventeen months of his absence from Rome. For this secret flight there was no necessity. He had only to keep his promises to his people to win their loving gratitude; but, having decided to disappoint their hopes, and by appealing to the Catholic powers to restore him to his throne by force of arms in case the Romans did not invite his return on his own

10

terms, he could provide for the punishment of the patriotic leaders of the Roman people, who were so obnoxious to him, as well as secure a foreign garrison to keep the people in subjection in the future.

The flight of Pius IX. was welcome news to the Romans, who proceeded at once to organize a constitutional assembly. They closed the Inquisition, re-organized the police, provided educational facilities and other beneficent measures that were greatly needed. A most respectful appeal was made to the pontiff to return and resume his spiritual functions, assuring him of their loyalty to him as the head of the Church, asking only that he recognize the civil liberties which they had established and had determined to maintain. They would concede complete liberty of action in religious matters, and so end peaceably the long contention. But this proposition from the people was indignantly spurned by the pope. Nothing but their absolute submission to the former state of things would satisfy him. Instead of conciliating those whom he professed so much to love, like the "gentle lamb" and "mild dove," as Maguire calls him, he issued an appeal, couched in the harshest language, addressed to the great Catholic powers, demanding their armed assistance to crush his people and their chosen government, to re-instate him on his throne, and to sustain him there. This is the closing sentence of the appeal:

Since Austria, France, Spain, and the kingdom of the Two Sicilies are, by their geographical position, in a situation to be able efficaciously to concur by their armies in re-establishing in the holy see the order which has been destroyed by a band of sectarians, the holy father, relying on the religious feeling of those powerful children of the Church, demands with full confidence their armed intervention to deliver the States of the Church from this band of wretches who by every sort of crime have practiced the most atrocious despotism.*

Louis Napoleon, anxious to bid largely for the support of the priesthood in France, and jealous of the rival power of Austria, regarded up to that time as "the pope's broad shield," promptly

* *Rome: Its Rulers and its Institutions,* by T. J. Maguire, M.P., p. 116.

sent a force of forty thousand men, that after a struggle of two months overcame the heroic defenders of Rome. The Austrian troops meanwhile stamped out all patriotic resistance in northern Italy. The pope may be said to have walked over the mutilated bodies of his subjects to his throne. The survivors published to the world a protest that in vigor of language exceeds any thing ever addressed to any pontiff. This document was prepared by the "Circolo Populare" (the People's Club). It was issued a short time before the city of Rome fell into the hands of Louis Napoleon, and had the widest circulation among the people. In it is expressed with dignity and sincerity an exalted knowledge of justice and right and true religion. We have room for only a few of its vigorous sentences. They thus address Pius IX.:

You say that you have received from God, the Author of peace and charity, the mission to love with parental affection all people and all nations, and to procure for them, as far as lies in you, protection and safety, and not to urge them on to slaughter and death. False words! for they are belied by the solemn fact, confessed by yourself, of your having called against us, and urged on to fratricidal war, Austria, France, Spain, and part of Italy. Who has caused the slaughter at Bologna and Ancona, and the carnage under the walls of Rome? You were adverse to that war which brave citizens fought for the safety of Italy; but O, you are not averse to this one, carried on by vile men for the purpose of replacing you, the most abhorred of sovereigns, on the throne which you deserted, and from which, by the inscrutable decree of divine Providence, rather than by act of ours, you have been deposed! Whose blood waters our land? Whose carcasses cover our fields? Unworthy pontiff! This blood cries for vengeance before the throne of God, and those souls will bring down on you the judgment of the Most High! . . . Who can forgive you your perversions of facts and outrages on persons? Language has not words more black and disdainful than those you employ against us, whose crime is that of having despoiled you of your earthly sovereignty after having exhorted you, in a thousand ways, to carry out true reforms, stable, and such as our wants demanded. It is not the word "republic" we are in love with, but we want a wise, provident, and just government. Now this, call it what you will, is what we have always wanted, and we have a right to it. To this point we tried to urge you, from which the government of the popes had so far receded.

Vindicating their claim to be called Bible Christians, and not "infidels," as he called them for opposing his temporal power, they continue:

We hold the religion of *Christ* dear, because we believe it to be true, saving, and holy. But this religion, which is none other than faith in Christ, by which we are justified before God, and forgiven all sins, can well exist without bishops and priests. This religion of faith, professed by many persons in all parts of the world, constitutes that invisible Church of believers which is universal, whose Head and Pontiff and Priest is, and can only be, *Jesus Christ.* . . .

When you left Rome the Bible entered it. The Bible so long persecuted by the popes, both the Gospel of Christ and the holy letters of the apostles faithfully translated into Italian, are now in the hands of the people, who read them, and there they find neither popery nor pope. . . .

O, senseless we! That we should ever have believed you, ever applauded your feigned promises and ephemeral concessions, to find ourselves now deluded in our hopes and cheated of our happiness! If you appeal to the religion of the canons, we stand by the holy religion of the Gospel; you belie it; we are faithful to God and to his Christ. Yes, we believe in the CHRIST OF GOD, and our faith daily increases in comparing his doctrine with your practice. The more we disbelieve you, the more are we led to see that we ought to believe him. He is the free Saviour of his people, you an oppressor and destroyer. You, who alone might have saved our country and redeemed it from its lost condition, have joined yourself to her enemies to condemn and destroy her.*

These are not the words of "blasphemers of God and religion," nor of "anarchists," nor "red republicans," nor of "demons let loose from hell," as Pius IX. so cruelly and unjustly called them. They were merchants, teachers, business men of intelligence, trusted by those below them in the social scale, whose violence they restrained.

This indignant protest of the heroic defenders of freedom called the attention of the civilized world to the awful vengeance dealt out to the patriots on the restoration of the papal power. When government expostulations had been tried in vain, several public men went to Italy to investigate the truth

* *Christian World*, vol. i, pp. 12–17.

of these reports. From England, among others, went the Hon. W. E. Gladstone and Rev. William Arthur. Their letters and books show what they found.

Mr. Maguire fights very shy of the terrible vengeance taken on the republicans by the government of the pope and the other potentates of Italy on their restoration. He sneers at English opinion, and especially at Mr. Gladstone for aiding to form that opinion, as to the cruelties practiced by the Italian despots in 1849. He assures us that all this is the unwarranted exaggerations of the liberal party, and states that it cannot be true, because "his holiness Pius IX. was as gentle as a lamb and as mild as a dove" (p. 412), and even dares to add that "the King of Naples was one of the most foully libeled of living men." This Romish way of writing history is worthy of Jesuitism itself. The facts form one of the saddest chapters of the modern history of Europe, and received at the time the attention of many competent witnesses. Mr. Arthur gives his authorities for the dreadful facts he presents in his work, *The Modern Jove*. We quote one or two paragraphs:

Under guise of an amnesty the pope excluded from political pardon members of the assembly, general officers, and a multitude besides, and applied the rule with such rigor that among his subjects the word "amnesty" became another name for death, prison, and exile.

No sooner did the French authorities see what cruelties were meditated by the ecclesiastics than they tried to prevent them, but in vain. The Austrians, who held the northern part of his States, were at first and in general ready instruments of the priestly excesses, but even they sometimes turned upon their employers. Gennarelli, in his sad little book, *I Lutti dello Stato Romano*, quotes a case of an Austrian officer who, with his battalion of Croats, had to protect executioners from popular fury, and said that had he to serve such a government he would tear off his uniform and break his sword. In the town of Bologna alone, during the years of restored papal authority, one hundred and eighty-six persons were shot. And as to Faenza and Imola, Gennarelli cites a document in which the government alleges a case where no less than eighty were shot after a single trial, while ten more were sent to the galleys, and thirteen to prison. (P. 108.)

The wonder is that enough to continue the struggle for liberty were left when this savage process had ceased ; and the fact that there were, and to win it, too, shows, as it did in Mexico, how universally and sincerely the people had resolved to be free. God alone knows the price they had to pay in either land to win their freedom. It would be hard to find a patriot people whose heroic endurance of exile, scaffold, and dungeon more appropriately suggests Lowell's lines :

> " Truth forever on the scaffold,
> Wrong forever on the throne.
> Yet that scaffold sways the future,
> And behind the dim unknown
> Standeth God, within the shadow,
> Keeping watch above his own."

One of the most unscrupulous of the officials of the papacy, in carrying out the persecutions and massacres of the defeated liberals, was Monseigneur Bidini, apostolic nuncio. So atrocious was this man's thirst for vengeance that he has been since known and hated through Italy as "the Butcher of Bologna." In view of the character for ferocity which he had acquired there were few governments in Europe that were willing to have him made the medium of communication with them. Yet only two years after these events, and while his cruel notoriety was still so fresh, this was the person chosen by the pope to be sent to America to perform some mission in this country, and then to go to Mexico and Brazil. This seemed to be a studied insult, in complete disregard of our views, for which there could be no excuse. President Polk, in 1847, when sending our first *chargé d'affaires* to Rome, had requested the pontifical court, in the event of their sending any diplomatic agent to this country, to send always a *layman*, not an ecclesiastic— the same thing that the Duke of Wellington had insisted upon before, when it was proposed that England should send an embassador to Rome. Notwithstanding this distinct notification Pius IX. deliberately disregarded the request of our government, and not only selected an ecclesiastic, but one whose hands were stained with the blood of the martyrs of Italian liberty, this Archbishop Bidini, as their chosen emissary to this republic.

Father Gavazzi was here when this ill-omened messenger arrived, and publicly denounced him in one of his lectures. The exiled Italian patriots then in New York heard of his landing, and called a public meeting, where they denounced him from their personal knowledge of his cruel acts against their countrymen, and exhibited his infamous character before the American people. His clerical friends were led to fear for his life, so they kept his whereabouts as secret as possible, and when the hour for his departure arrived he was taken on a tugboat down the Hudson to the ship without passing through the city, and so escaped the vengeance of his countrymen. He had previously been burned in effigy in Cincinnati, Baltimore, and other cities, and his cruelties exposed in many of the leading papers.

In the sorrowful period which now ensued in Italy only one of her sovereigns paid the slightest regard to the constitutions and promises of freedom granted in 1848. The others destroyed their constitutions, resumed their despotic rule, opened the dungeons of the Inquisition, and the cause of freedom soon seemed dead in Italy. The grand exception was Charles Albert, King of Sardinia, who, faithful among the faithless, became the star of hope amid the darkness. Still, what could he do against the despotism of the other six rulers, and the Legion of France upholding the power of the pope? God raised up to help him one of the grandest of men, Count Camillo di Cavour, a man who had traveled and studied the institutions of self-governing countries till the freedom of his native land became his absorbing passion. He believed it was possible to liberate and unite the Italian people. The brave little kingdom of Sardinia had only four millions of subjects, while the reactionary powers had twenty millions, but it began its march of progress by granting liberty to its inhabitants and religious freedom to the Waldenses, who were reduced to about twenty-five thousand souls by the

persecutions that had wasted them for the past six hundred years.
Their gratitude to this constitutional king was unbounded, and
a legion of them was raised that faithfully served in the final
struggle for the unity of Italy.   They bore on their banners
the inscription "The grateful Waldenses to Charles Albert."
The fearful "shadow" over them had been lifted.   All through
the past two hundred and fifty years the prayer of John Milton,
Oliver Cromwell's great secretary, had been in the heart of
evangelical Christendom for them.   The reader will remember how the soul of Cromwell was stirred to indignation by the
accounts of what these people were enduring from the cruelty
of Rome and its allies, and how he interposed for their relief,
and wrote to the Protestant governments of Europe, asking
them to join in their defense.   But Protestantism was then
weak, and power was on the side of the oppressors, and little
could be done.   At that hour Milton wrote his immortal
prayer :

> "Avenge, O, Lord, thy slaughtered saints, whose bones
> Lie scattered on the Alpine mountains cold ;
> Even them who kept thy truth so pure of old,
> When all our fathers worshiped stocks and stones.
> Forget not ; in thy book record their groans,
> Who were thy sheep, and in their ancient fold,
> Slain by the bloody Piedmontese, that rolled
> Mother with infant down the rocks.   Their moans
> The vales redoubled to the hills, and they
> To heaven.   Their martyred blood and ashes sow
> O'er all the Italian fields where still doth sway
> The triple tyrant ; that from these may grow
> An hundred-fold, who, having learned thy way
> Early, may fly the Babylonian woe."

The "bloody Piedmontese" whom he thus so justly characterized were the cruel Duke of Savoy and his troops, urged on to
this awful work by Pope Paul IV., and also Francis I., sovereign
of France, who ordered his soldiers to "extirpate the Waldenses
without mercy."   How wonderful to note now who became the
agents of the Lord's predicted mercy for these people !   First,

the Duke of Savoy's descendant, Charles Albert, and then a successor of Francis I. on the throne of France, Napoleon III., was providentially constrained, by a way that he knew not, and *did not choose*, to close the temporal sovereignty of the pontiff, and to consent that the "States of the Church" should be added to complete Italy's unity! Now the Waldenses worship in Rome, right in view of the Vatican! Milton's prayer has been gloriously answered, to the permanent peace and benefit of all concerned. The papacy still keeps up a tirade against modern civilization and its progress in the hope that the emancipated nations will some day regret their freedom and unite to crush the constitutional security of its former subjects and restore its misrule. Truly this illusion is unique and wonderful!

We have thus passed briefly in review for the better understanding of our main subject the antecedent and contemporary facts by which the events in Mexico are to be understood. No unusual thing, in this sense, was happening to her; she was only suffering from the conspiracy against freedom which had long afflicted the world on the other side of the Atlantic. If she had been able to take a comprehensive view of what was transpiring in Europe, her hope of a blessed solution of her own trials would have been greatly strengthened.

The Roman hierarchy, indignant at the losses which constitutional struggles in Europe had caused, in desperation determined to make good its losses in the New World. To this end all its great resources were ready, and the plans were to be carried out regardless of public opinion or will. Here, then, we find the source of Mexico's latest struggle and recognize those with whom she had to deal.

CHAPTER V.

Desperate efforts of the Mexican clericals—Merits of the conflict—*Coup d'état* of
the church party—Terrorizing policy of Miramon—Violation of British embassy—Republican victories—Benito Juarez, Mexico's "Washington," and his
aids—Perfidy of Louis Napoleon—Intervention—Co-operation of the pope—
"Laws of reform"—Tripartite treaty—Jecker bonds—De Morny—Collapse
of Jecker—"Cinco de Mayo"—Maximilian's call and warning.

SANTA ANNA was recalled in 1853 and appointed president
"for one year, until a constitutional Congress could be convened
and the future provided for." It soon became evident that
the years of his exile had not been employed in learning lessons
friendly to popular government or his country's peace under
republican forms. The record of the past might have saved
the Mexican patriots from the error of supposing that this
"leopard" could change his characteristic "spots." In the
twenty years that had passed since his first inauguration as president he had become as despotic as he had then sworn to be
constitutional.

Hardly was he seated in the presidential chair when he began
to develop his real character. He proceeded to overthrow the
federal republic, and announced himself on December 16, 1853,
as permanent dictator, and assumed the title of "Serene Highness," with power to name his successor! He recalled the
Jesuits, whom the nation had previously expelled, knowing
that they would work out zealously his projects for the church
faction, and finished his desperate course by the crime against
the Constitution of investing, on July 1, 1854, José Gutierrez
de Estrada with powers "to negotiate in Europe for the establishment of a monarchy in Mexico," and this without any
authorization from the nation! This Señor Estrada, as the
agent of the church party, was not new to such business. It

was he who in October, 1840, issued a pamphlet in Mexico advocating the overthrow of the republican institutions and the establishment of a Mexican monarchy. Madame Calderon tells us of the excitement caused by this production. Estrada was compelled to exile himself to escape the vengeance of the government. But he still proved true to his clerical affiliations, and ten years after this authorization by Santa Anna we find him heading the deputation which waited on Maximilian at Miramar, to offer him an imperial crown in Mexico.*

Santa Anna brought about his own overthrow by one more despotic step in abolishing the Institute of Sciences in Oaxaca because of its liberal principles, and was compelled to fly, in August, 1855, to Cuba, and later to St. Thomas. He was tried once again for high treason, sentenced to be hanged, and his property confiscated. President Juarez afterward commuted the sentence to banishment for eight years. This was the end of his power, but not of his disturbing presence in Mexico. We shall hear from him again, in an aspect of deception which illustrated still more fully the vileness of his character.

The overthrow of Santa Anna carried down once more the unscrupulous church party and swept away the plan of Tacubaya, under which they acted. Estrada was not able to bring his royal prince to aid in time, and the nation was aroused to a sense of this new conspiracy against its freedom. These various "plans" were found to contain one fatal defect which the growing liberty party now resolved to remedy. This was the attempt to build a free State without its foundation-stone. All the constitutions framed under the various "plans" retained the papal concordat as an item of the social compact. From 1822 to this time (1854) this excluded religious liberty. The highest of all liberty being denied, the remainder was not worth dying for. At last the true republican idea was embraced, the concordat abolished, and religious freedom was to be incorporated into a constitution under which the nation should find permanent peace.

* *Mexico and the United States*, p. 276. *The Fall of Maximilian's Empire*, Schroeder.

General Alvarez, a true patriot, but aged and infirm, was elected president, and called Benito Juarez to his cabinet as secretary for the departments of justice, ecclesiastical affairs, and public instruction. Soon afterward there was issued a proclamation for the election of delegates to a national Congress, "for the purpose of reconstructing the nation under the form of a popular representative democratic republic." On the 22d of November, 1855, the celebrated law for the administration of justice, known as the "Law of Juarez," was proclaimed. This grand law abolished the whole system of class legislation, and was deeply resented by the clerical party. The Congress devoted a whole year to the task of framing a Constitution based on this law, and on the 3d of February, 1857, it "issued in the name of God, and by the authority of the Mexican people," the magnificent Constitution of which Mr. Seward said that he regarded it as the best instrument of its kind in the world. It may be found in Abbot's *Mexico and the United States*, p. 283.

President Alvarez having been obliged to resign on account of increasing infirmities, General Comonfort was elected to the office. The implacable and still powerful church party pronounced against the Constitution. We present the leading principles of each of the parties in question, so that what they were fighting for may be made clear to the reader.

The clerical platform was as follows:

SYNOPSIS OF THE PLAN OF TACUBAYA PROCLAIMED BY ZULOAGA.

1. The inviolability of all church property and church revenues and the re-establishment of former exactions.
2. The re-establishment of the *fueros*, or special rights of the church and of the army. (Under these *fueros* the military and clergy were responsible only to their own tribunals, and not to the law of the land.)
3. The restoration of the Roman Catholic religion as *the sole and exclusive* religion of Mexico.
4. The censorship of the press.
5. The exclusive system with regard to foreign immigration, confining it solely to immigrants from Catholic countries.

6. The overthrow of the Constitution of 1857, and the establishment of an irresponsible central dictatorship, subservient solely to the Church.

7. If possible, the restoration of a monarchy in Mexico, or the establishment of a European protectorate.

In contradistinction to this was the platform of the Republican party, as follows:

SYNOPSIS OF THE LIBERAL CONSTITUTION OF 1857.

1. The establishment of a constitutional federal government in the place of a military dictatorship.

2. Freedom and protection to slaves that enter the national territory.

3. *Freedom of religion.*

4. Freedom of the press.

5. The nationalization of the $200,000,000 of property held by the clergy, from which, and other sources, the Church derives an annual income of not less than $20,000,000.

6. The subordination of the army to the civil power and the abolition of military and ecclesiastical *fueros*, or special tribunals.

7. The negotiation of commercial treaties of the fullest scope and liberal character, including reciprocity of trade on our frontiers.

8. The colonization of Mexico by the full opening of every part of the country to immigration, and the encouragement of foreign enterprise in every branch of industry, particularly in mining and in works of internal improvement.*

The resources of wealth wielded by the church party were yet too strong for freedom, and Comonfort was compelled to retire in 1858. However, Juarez was soon elected to the presidency. Before he could assume the reins of government the clericals, led by the papal nuncio, Clementi, called the "Junta de Notables" (an aristocratic council of twenty-eight persons of their own choice), and sustained by a small body of the military, annulled the grand Constitution over which the whole country was rejoicing and proclaimed the plan of Tacubaya in its stead. They elected Zuloaga as their president, while the constitutional president was compelled to leave the capital and carry on his government at Guanajuato or Vera Cruz, protected by the loyal portion of the army, and being recognized and sus-

* *Mexico in 1861–62, by Dr. C. Lempriere, p. 37. London, 1862.*

tained by all the States of the Mexican Union save two, which were under the control of the clerical troops. Though this clerical government held only the cities of Mexico and Puebla and the country immediately surrounding them, they managed by their large financial resources to hold their position for three years. How the usurpation was accomplished and how it retained its hold of the capital for such a length of time needs explanations. Of all the despotic acts of the clerical party this was the most daring. Four men were chiefly used for the purpose, Gabriac, who represented France, Señor del Barrio, the Guatemalan minister, Señor Pacheco, from Spain, and Louis Clementi, the nuncio of the pope. The latter was the ruling spirit and inspired the others with the idea that it was the will of the pope, and of Almighty God through him, and was their positive duty, to render their service to the pontiff and the cause of religion. So firm was the stand which they took, though concealing the religious motive as well as they could, that the other foreign ministers stupidly allowed themselves to be led to recognize the usurpation of Zuloaga. This prolonged the situation, which otherwise could only have lasted for a few months. The clericals improved the opportunity to send embassadors to foreign courts, Almonte, the most detested of their agents, being sent as representative to the French court, where he was soon to plan, with Napoleon, so much suffering for his native land. These agents represented only a pronunciamento of traitors, not the lawful government of Mexico. President Juarez meanwhile issued protests against the legitimacy of their actions, the nation became thoroughly aroused, while the facts began to find their way to foreign governments, so that one after another the embassadors of England, Prussia, and the United States were ordered away from the capital, and appeared at Vera Cruz to recognize President Juarez, our own representative, Mr. McLane, being the first to do so.

The downfall of these traitors was approaching. The Republican army, ably led by such generals as Ortega and Uruaga, was augmenting and increasingly victorious.

The clericals were not long in discovering that Zuloaga was not exactly the man to do their work. Their purposes required an instrument with less conscience and more despotism. Zuloaga was displaced and General Miguel Miramon was named by the junta as their president, on January 31, 1859. The character of this new instrument of papal power, as well as of Marquez, whom he made commander-in-chief, was eminently worthy of the party which sanctioned and approved of their conduct, both then and some years later, under Maximilian, when they repeated, only on a larger scale, these same outrages on the laws of war and of common humanity. In illustration of this we here quote an order of Miramon to the general-in-chief, issued after the battle of Tacubaya (in which the Republican troops were victorious), when the church president resolved that he would terrorize Mexico by authorizing assassination of all those who would lift their hands to help her into the possession of constitutional freedom :

MEXICO, *April* 11, 1861.

In the afternoon of to-day and under your excellency's most strict responsibility, your excellency will give the order for all the prisoners holding the grade of officers and chiefs to be shot, informing me of the number which have fallen under this lot. MIRAMON.

Marquez at once followed this out by a proclamation to the nation itself, as follows :

LEONARDO MARQUEZ TO THE PEOPLE OF MEXICO.

Know ye, that in virtue of the faculties with which I am invested, I have resolved to publish the following decree :

1. Benito Juarez, and all who have obeyed him or recognized his government, are traitors to their country, as well as all who have aided him by any means, secretly or indirectly, no matter how insignificantly.

2. All persons coming under the heads of the preceding article shall be shot immediately on their apprehension, without further investigation than the identification of their persons. MARQUEZ.*

This atrocious attempt to terrorize a whole people into obedience to a body of despots is the most awful fact up to this

* *Mexico in* 1861–62, by C. Lempriere, p. 127.

date in Mexican history. The clericals knew that the masses of the people were overwhelmingly against them, yet they authorized these two men to work out their will, becoming guilty of the blood of their countrymen in order to serve those who professed to be ministers of God! Nor was this all of which this pair of traitors proved themselves to be capable. At the close of 1860 there was in deposit in the British Legation in the city of Mexico the sum of $660,000, which President Juarez had paid in on account of the English bond-holders' debt. It was under the seal of the British embassador, who was then absent. Miramon and Marquez, who were on the eve of being thrust from the capital by the advancing Republican army, forcibly entered the legation, broke the seals, and carried off the money. The British government exonerated the government of Juarez and the Mexican people from blame for the outrage, but Mexico had to pay the amount over again notwithstanding.

There was one government, however, which was in no haste to be undeceived, and which had ulterior ends to be served. This vile Miramon faction had negotiated a treaty through its agent at Paris, Juan N. Almonte, which conferred advantages and recognized claims before refused by every liberal government of Mexico, and this to a very large amount. The constitutional government protested against this *Almonte* treaty as "unjust in its essence, foreign to the usage of nations in the principles it established, illegal in the manner in which it was negotiated, and contrary to the rights of the country." But it furnished Napoleon III. with just such a weapon as he wanted, and he gladly took its infamous author under his special protection and resolved on a war whose injustice will be recognized as long as modern history is studied by honest men, and can never be forgotten by Mexico.

As to how matters seemed to strike an intelligent stranger visiting the country at the time, we may quote a sentence from the work of Dr. Lempriere, fellow of St. John's College, Oxford, whose indignation was aroused to find that his own government was so completely deceived by the artful policy of the cabal then holding the city of Mexico. He writes thus:

And yet at present England seems moving as the tool of such an unmitigated scoundrel as Miramon—a man whom, if there existed an extradition treaty, we should have insisted on being hung; Gabriac (the ultramontane French representative), the fosterer of this man's murderous rule, and Pacheco, both of whom have been hooted out of the country with well-merited and universal execration. These are the men who are moving the strings at Paris, with Almonte their able embassador. The clergy of France are in accord with their distressed and exiled brethren; but who can explain the action of England? [He means in recognizing such a usurpation as the true government of Mexico.] We are aiding a power and establishing a religious dominion which is abhorrent to the mind of every honest Englishman.*

He adds this note on Gabriac:

In the papers of the Archbishop of Mexico (captured by the Liberals) was found a recommendation of this man to the prayers and favor of the pope for the valuable services he had rendered the clerical party in the revolution of Mexico, and the recognition of Miramon, their champion.

Another proof of the papacy being the life and soul of these reactionary measures against popular freedom, as much so as it had been against those of Italy and other lands already liberated from its despotism.

During Miramon's absence at the head of his army the demoralization in the city of Mexico was such that a document was drawn up and signed by the members of the diplomatic corps still remaining at the capital, with the exception of the Guatemalan minister and the nuncio, declaring that "there was no government existing at the capital." On the 23d of December, 1860, Miramon returned to the city, escorted by only two or three aids, having been completely routed the day previous at Calpulalpam. The ministers of France and Spain tried to make terms for him with the advancing General Ortega, but he would not listen to them. So Miramon fled secretly, taking with him what remained of the English bond-holders' money, which he had stolen eight days before from the legation. The

* *Mexico in 1861-62*, p. 9.

11

advanced portion of the constitutional army reached Mexico
city the next day—Christmas day—and the government of
Juarez was peacefully established in the National Palace on the
11th of January, 1861.

There was one more struggle to be endured ere the clerical
party should submit to popular rule, and this the most deadly
of all. The Spanish element here dropped from sight and
was replaced by the French, or rather by the French emperor,
for France would not have been guilty of such wrong against
a feeble nation; but for the following six years she had to
see her sons and her resources employed to assassinate freedom, the very form of freedom that she preferred above all
others.

The compromised clerical and military traitors fled from Mexico, fearing the vengeance of the Republican government. It
is significant that they went directly to Paris, to the man who
was already known as the protector of all such, and by whose
army they were to be escorted back within a year to renew the
cruel struggle against Mexican liberty.

Three of the compromised diplomatic representatives resolved to remain, perhaps not aware that their records were so
well known to Juarez. They were Pacheco, del Barrio, and
Clementi. Four days after the re-establishment of the government in the capital they were ordered to leave the country
forthwith. Señor Ocampo, the secretary for foreign affairs, prepared a circular, stating the reasons for the action, which was
sent to every legation where Mexico had a representative.
What he said concerning the reasons for Clementi's expulsion
we will quote in full:

Don Louis Clementi has held in this country the mission of nuncio
from his holiness the pope. His disposition, and the general tone of the
Roman Church which he has represented, has caused him to figure
throughout the civil war as a partisan of the seditious clergy of the
republic, who, to the greatest degree, have stained with blood the past
revolution in this country, under the pretext of religion.

Now that the Mexican republic has, in the exercise of its sovereign power, declared religious liberty, and the absolute independence of each other of Church and State, the official representative of the Roman Church can have no mission whatever to the general government of the republic.

OCAMPO.*

It is sad to add of this worthy minister Ocampo, one of the most disinterested patriots of the land, that within three years, when Maximilian was emperor and the clericals had induced him to employ Miramon and Marquez as generals, they took the first opportunity to be revenged. He had retired from public life and was living in his private residence in the country, when Miramon came upon him with his army and brutally murdered him, after torturing him for two days. The full account is given in the *Libro Rojo*.

Let us contemplate the man, the most remarkable in every respect that Mexico has yet produced, *Benito Juarez*, one of Montezuma's race, without a drop of Spanish blood in his veins, often affectionately styled in Mexico "our little Indian," being small in stature. We call attention to his portrait on the frontispiece of this work, taken from a life-size painting which hangs in the place of honor in the "Hall of Embassadors," in the National Palace, which is regarded as the best in existence of this patriot, whom Castelar called "the saviour of the honor of his country." Juarez was born in 1806, in the little Indian village of San Pablo Guelatao, twenty miles north-east of the city of Oaxaca. His early years were passed in the quiet of the little hamlet, serving as shepherd for his uncle's flocks. His parents having died, leaving him in care of relatives, at the age of twelve he went to a sister living in Oaxaca, where for the first time he began to learn Spanish and to study under the care of a worthy citizen named Perez, who recognized the ability of the lad. Another kind merchant, Señor Diego Chavez, encouraged him to enter the seminary of Oaxaca, from which he graduated with honors. A friendly Franciscan monk urged him to enter the priesthood, but his liberal ideas inclined him to a political career, and therefore he pursued the law course in the

* *Mexico* in 1861–62, p. 9.

Institute of Sciences, being admitted to the bar in 1834. Before this he had become somewhat prominent in his advocacy of liberal ideas and reforms, and suffered imprisonment during one of the terms when the Conservative party was in power. In 1842 he was elected chief-justice of his native State, and when the Governor of Oaxaca resigned, being unable to quell a revolution raised by the clericals on account of a proposition to despoil them of some of their possessions in order to defend the State from the invasion of the American army in 1847, Juarez was placed in power, and for the ensuing five years governed most acceptably, bringing the finances of the State to a better condition, encouraging reforms, and making the State the most prosperous of the Mexican Union.

In 1853 he was exiled by Santa Anna, on account of his liberal views, and took up his residence in New Orleans, where he lived in great poverty, but gaining strength for the future conflict from the study of our institutions and our leaders. Washington and Bolivar were his heroes. Two years later he joined Álvarez in a revolution against Santa Anna's despotic rule, and on its success he was again brought into power as minister of justice under President Álvarez. His first act was to abolish the special military and clerical courts, which had so long removed these two classes from the power of the national law. In 1858 he became president, and we shall follow him as we note the events of the country's history.

His family life was of the happiest nature. No shadow of injustice or wrong dims the luster of his name. In his various prominent positions many opportunities must have presented themselves for him to gain wealth at the expense of the nation, but he was superior to such temptations and died a comparatively poor man.

How he impressed a stranger is admirably given in the description of Colonel G. S. Church, of the United States, who visited him at Chihuahua during the French intervention:

Pushing aside the curtains from the door of an interior room a quiet, unassuming man advances to meet you. A courteous greeting, a frank grasp of the hand, and a cordial invitation to be seated place you at once at your ease, and you prepare to study the Indian before you. He is, perhaps, five feet five inches in height, thick set, and with a broad, full chest, which gives him a powerful vitality. A bold rounded and high forehead, very slightly receding from a vertical line, eyes large and swimming in liquid blackness, finely cut eyebrows, arched and curving far back, a goodly development of practical as well as theoretical brain. While at rest his Indian features do not show the power behind them; but once kindled to action the brain illuminates every one of them, and the black eyes flash a peculiar light, as if to give more forcible expression to his language. A quiet, unyielding determination and a firm reliance upon self are the impressions you gain of him upon acquaintance. You converse upon politics, and you find that your ideas are not more thoroughly republican than his; you speak of war, and his military knowledge meets you half-way; you turn to political economy and find that you propose nothing that he has not analyzed, and you finally leave him with the impression that you have met one of the ablest men that Mexico has produced.*

Such was the man on whom had already fallen the heaviest burden of responsibility and care for his country's freedom that had probably ever rested on a patriot's heart. How well and conscientiously he bore it, and to what victory he carried it, this record will soon show. If our space had permitted it would have been a pleasure to have presented a view of the noble men who stood so faithfully by him to the last through that "great fight of afflictions," and who were, in the mercy of God, spared to share his triumph. Prominent among these was Matias Romero, his worthy and distinguished representative at Washington, who so faithfully and laboriously sustained his duties as embassador of Mexico. Few have any adequate idea of the toil demanded from one filling the position of Mexican representative during the events of the Intervention. Señor Romero had not only the usual diplomatic duties resting upon him, but had also to be on the alert to collect the archives of the governments of England, France, Spain, Austria, and the Holy See in regard to the Mexican Empire, so called, and to make this information available for his government and also for the Presi-

* *Historical and Political Review of Mexico*, by Col. G. S. Church.

dent of the United States. It was necessary to have the truth concerning Mexico published in order to counteract the false statements of the press agents of the empire ; to purchase arms and munitions of war and charter steamers to convey them to ports where they could be safely entered ; to print Mexican bonds and negotiate them in the market, and to make contracts for other purposes as well as being the medium of intercourse to and from the outside world for all matters, postal and other-wise. Señor Romero has been honored almost ever since by his grateful country, by keeping him in his important position.

The cabinet of Juarez also deserve mention for their loyalty during the dark period from 1862 to 1867. We can but name these patriots : Sebastian Lerdo de Tejada, secretary of state ; José Maria Yglesias, minister of the interior ; Ignacio Mejia, minister of war ; and Ignacio Mariscal, minister of justice. And the brave military chiefs who served their country with such valor, Zaragoza, Escobedo, Porfirio Diaz, Salazar, Arteaga, Treviño, Corona, and others, deserve honorable mention for their services to the cause of freedom in Mexico.

Before proceeding with our narrative let us consider the man who was to be for the ensuing five years the controlling impulse of all the wrong which liberty was to suffer from his " Intervention." This picture here given well expresses the sinister character of the man whom Mexico especially has rea-son to hold in abhorrence through all her future life. What a record has he left behind for the world to study ! We abridge a few sentences from Hugo's summary of his earlier life : Charles Louis Napoleon was born in Paris, on the 20th of April, 1808, the son of Hortense de Beauharnais and Louis Napoleon, then King of Holland, and brother of Napoleon I. This youth commenced his varied career by scheming in his own interest for the overthrow of the French monarchy, on the 30th of Oc-tober, 1836, at Strasburg, being then twenty-eight years of age. This abortive attempt was pardoned by King Louis Philippe, with the understanding that Louis Napoleon was to exile himself to the United States. But before two years had expired he

LOUIS NAPOLEON,
Who devised and carried out the "Intervention" in Mexico.

violated his parole and returned from America to Switzerland. Finding that the French government was made uneasy by his return, he wrote assuring them " that he lived almost alone in the house where his mother died, and that his firm desire was to remain quiet." They supposed he meant what he said, but his characteristic duplicity manifested itself when on the 20th of August, 1840—only two years after giving his solemn pledge to the government—he landed at Boulogne at the head of sixty followers (disguised as French soldiers). He carried a gilt eagle on the top of a flag-staff, with a live eagle in a cage, and a large supply of proclamations pronouncing for an empire. As he and his curious following advanced up the street he flung money to the passers-by, and, elevating his hat on the point of his sword, cried out, " Vive l'Empereur ! " Meeting with no favorable response, he fled, but was captured and condemned to imprisonment for life in the fortress of Ham, from which, disguised as a working mason, he escaped six years afterward and took refuge in England.

In 1848 the French monarchy fell and a republic was proclaimed. Professing to lay aside his imperial aspirations, he returned to France and offered himself as a representative of the people in the Constitutional Assembly. When elected he made a display of his pretended democratic sentiments, saying, " All my life shall be consecrated to the strengthening of the republic." Though some were suspicious of him he was elected president. On the 20th of December he took the oath, and as the president of the Assembly uttered the formula, " In the presence of God, and before the French people, I swear to remain faithful to the democratic republic, one and indivisible, and to fulfill all the duties which the Constitution imposes upon me," Louis Napoleon raised his right hand and said, " I swear it." He then voluntarily added :

The suffages of the nation and the oath which I have just taken command my future conduct. My duty is traced. I will fulfill it as a man of honor. I will see enemies of the country in all those who would try to change by illegal means what France entire has established.

The president of the Assembly replied, "We call God and man to witness the oath which has just been taken."

They expected he would be true to this pledge. The Constitution, which he swore he would maintain, contained among other articles these :

Article 36. The representatives of the people are inviolable.

Article 37. They cannot be arrested on a criminal charge save in case of flagrant misdemeanor, nor prosecuted except after the Assembly has permitted.

Article 68. Every measure by which the president of the republic dissolves the National Assembly, or places obstacles in the way of the execution of its decrees, is a crime of high treason. By this sole act the president is suspended from his functions.

On December 2, 1851, less than three years after the memorable oath was taken, he proclaimed, "The National Assembly is dissolved ; the first military division is placed in a state of siege ; the council of state is dissolved."

To this terrible record of the highest treason against a whole nation by this perjured adventurer the historian adds the following dreadful record, in which one would fain hope that there may be some exaggeration, as the account was written so close to the events—only a few weeks after—and under the fearful pressure of that *coup d'état*. But it must be confessed that the judgment of charity thus intimated finds little confirmation of its hope in the subsequent career of this man either in France, Rome, or, above all, in Mexico. The historian adds :

At the same time Paris learned that fifteen of the "inviolable" representatives of the people had been arrested in their homes during the night by order of Louis Napoleon. In the days following he seized the executive power, made an attempt on the legislative power, drove away the Assembly, expelled the high court of justice, took twenty-five millions from the bank, gorged the army with gold, raked Paris with grape-shot, and terrorized France. He proscribed eighty-four of the representatives of the people, decreed despotism in fifty-eight articles under the title of a constitution; garroted the republic, made the sword of France a gag in the mouth of liberty, transported to Africa and Cayenne ten thousand Democrats, exiled forty thousand Republicans, placed in all souls grief and on all foreheads blushes.*

* *The Destroyer of the Second Republic,* by Victor Hugo, 1852, p. 29, etc.

How significant it is that this violent change from a free republic to a despotic empire was quickly indorsed by the hierarchy of Rome and the pope, and that neither is on record as having uttered one word of protest against the overthrow of the government of the people or the acts of treason by which it was consummated! It is equally significant that the first person to congratulate him on the complete success of his move was the Countess Montijo, who was already known as being under Jesuit influence, intensely bigoted, and to whom he was soon afterward married. The church party could now rejoice that they had an emperor and that he was suitably mated for their purposes. Victor Hugo seems justified in his assertion that "Louis Napoleon had on his side the clergy, from the highest to the lowest, in the *coup d'état*."

Almonte, the embassador of the clerical party of Mexico, found in Napoleon a ready listener to his wicked statements concerning Mexico, that it was "monarchical to the core," only held back from expressing its preferences by a faction of Republicans "without character, who were stained by crimes and oppressions of the worst kind," and that it would be a highly meritorious and Christian act for some power to intervene to free Mexico from her oppressors, and give her an opportunity to express her preferences, which, he said, "she would do promptly and gratefully." Louis Napoleon was eager for just such a chance, now outlined as desirable. We have already seen what his apologist, the Abbé Domenech, admitted as to the ultimate object of Napoleon's intervention in Mexican affairs, and how he fondly anticipated that the results would so redound to his fame as to be afterward regarded as "the crowning event of the nineteenth century," and Mexico was but the stepping-stone to this consummation. He was already being dispossessed of the idea that he could emulate his uncle's fame and become the dictator of Europe, to give away thrones and dominions. Probably he imagined he could gain in the New World what was eluding his grasp in the Old. He knew he could use the papacy in aid of his purpose, by having an under-

standing with the pope, and that he could calculate on Spanish
aid in view of the compensation he could render her in South
America. We find both these influences co-operating with him
in the project. The intervention in Mexico was to be an entering
wedge to split up the democracy of America and found a monarchical system upon its ruins. Similar work south of Mexico
would have been comparatively easy. With our United States
divided by civil war, and the presence of an aristocratic element in the Confederacy, the bribe of a restored slavocracy
might have had an immense influence in reconciling the Southern States to a monarchical system, which could have been mild
at first, and less constitutional later. How long could the North
have held her own under such circumstances? With her millions of Romanists acting as a unit under priestly guidance, and
a doubtful papal immigration (and the reader will remember
that immigration, avowed by the Duke of Richmond, is hinted
at by Domenech as part of Napoleon's plan) pouring in upon us,
soon gaining the "balance of power," then, alas! might soon
have come a long farewell to freedom and republican government on this continent.

But there is a divine providence in human affairs, however
much such men as Napoleon choose to ignore it, and we were
under its blessed care.

On his restoration to Mexico city President Juarez set himself zealously to establish order and carry out the enactments of
the Congress, especially in regard to the financial condition of
the country. When he and his cabinet reached the capital they
found the treasury empty, so the continuation of the seculariza-
tion and sale of the unused church property became a necessity.
The hierarchy had previously been requested to consider the
situation and to relinquish a portion of their large possessions
that they did not require, but without avail. Even the Abbé
Domenech admits that they were blind to refuse such a compromise. The sales, though slow at first, brought into the public
treasury within a year the sum of $5,000,000,* and confirmed

* *La Corte de Roma y el Emperador Maximiliano.* Mexico, 1870.

the purpose of the Liberals to thus utilize a portion of this vast property.

The pope issued his expostulations and sustained the Mexican bishops in their resistance to the law until two of them—the Bishops of Puebla and of Guadalajara—were exiled by the government for rebellious interference. As a last resource the pope issued an *allocution* declaring, " We condemn, disavow, and declare absolutely *null and void* and of no effect all the decrees above mentioned, and all the acts which the civil power in Mexico has done, in contempt of the ecclesiastical authority of the holy see." He then expresses " the deep grief of his soul" over these principles, and closes by threatening the " penalties and censures" which he holds against "these usurpers of the rights of the holy see." He utters a similar jeremiad against South America, as "following the sad example of the Liberals of Mexico." *

The leaders of Mexico, instead of heeding the pope's nullification, shrugged their shoulders and went on with the good work of building up the welfare of the nation. Mexico and South America were not doing a deed unknown in any other nation, as the papal lamentation might lead one to believe, but they were doing what England, France, Italy, Portugal, Germany, and nearly all the other States of Christendom had already done. Of the nationalization of ecclesiastical property, and abolition of monastic institutions, European history is full, from Magna Charta and King John down to our days in Italy. Mackenzie puts the facts in regard to France :

The possessions of the Church, amounting to one third of all the soil of France, were seized. Henceforth the priests were to be paid their painfully reduced salaries by the State. The Church held property valued at £80,000,000 ($400,000,000), and yielding an annual revenue of over £3,000,000 ($15,000,000), all of which was appropriated by the State in its necessity in the period when it abolished feudalism and privilege and laid the foundations of French freedom. The nation afterward safeguarded her rights and limited the interference of the pope and the

* *Christian World*, vol. xiv, p. 195.

Church in matters of state by a dictated concordat, which is to-day her
defense against ecclesiastical aggressions.   (P. 5.)

And in the same way Magna Charta, wrested by the liberty-
loving and sturdy barons of England from that papal tyrant
and coward, King John, proved the sure foundation of English
freedom, notwithstanding the thunders of excommunication
which Pope Innocent III. hurled against the barons and their
Charta, and his foolish attempt to hand over the English kingdom to Philip of France, as well as absolving John from all
obligation of fidelity to the solemn signature which he had
affixed to the great document.

No wonder that when the French troops and their officers
reached Mexico, in 1864, and heard the complaints of the church
party against the Republicans on these grounds, they were
amazed, knowing well, as they did, that their own country had
done the very same things with the papal Church and its over-
grown wealth and monastic orders, and in doing so had laid the
foundations of the liberties and greatness of France.   It was
equally a matter of surprise to the Abbé Domenech, and for
the same reasons.   Mexico and South America could thus
quote a score of precedents to justify their actions in all that
they did, and yet the pope in this allocution bitterly denounced
Mexico as if her government and legislative action were unprecedented and unjust.

It is surprising how legally the statesmen of Mexico moved
in their measures to build up the condition of their country
on right foundations.   Even in this very matter, where to the
superficial observer they might seem to be depending alone
on power, they kept within the clear limits of the accepted
usages and law which govern such cases.   There is probably
no higher authority on the "Law of Nations" than Emerich
Vattel, of Switzerland, and no commentator on English law
superior to Sir William Blackstone.   Both of these jurists
lay down rules which vindicate the actions of the popular
government of Mexico in the demands which they made on
the vast ecclesiastical property.   Blackstone says:

The priests would have engulfed all the real estate of England. It took centuries to protect and perfect the nation against their rapacity and schemes to avoid the statutes.

And Vattel covers the whole question arising out of this condition of affairs in the following rule:

Far from the goods of the Church being exempted because they are consecrated to God, it is for that very reason that they should be the first taken for the welfare of the State. There is nothing more agreeable to the common Father of men than to preserve a nation from destruction. As God has no need of property the consecration of goods to him is their devotion to such purposes as are pleasant to him. Besides, the property of the Church, by the confession of the clergy themselves, is chiefly destined for the poor; and when the State is in want it is, doubtless, the first pauper and the worthiest of succor.

To carry out the provision and purposes of the national Constitution and guard the liberties which it guarantees, enactments of the legislature, called "Laws of Reform," were issued. We will here enumerate the leading items of these laws, issued by the secretary of state:

The complete separation of Church and State.

Congress cannot pass laws establishing or prohibiting any religion.

The free exercise of religious services. The State will not give official recognition to any religious festivals, save the Sabbath, as a day of rest:

Religious services are to be held only within the place of worship.

Clerical vestments are forbidden in the streets.

Religious processions are forbidden.

The use of church-bells is restricted to calling the people to religious work.

Pulpit discourses advising disobedience to the law, or injury to any one, are strictly forbidden. Worship in churches shall be public only.

Gifts of real estate to religious institutions are unlawful, with the sole exception of edifices designed exclusively to the purposes of the institution.

The State does not recognize monastic orders nor permit their establishment.

The association of Sisters of Charity is suppressed in the republic, and Jesuits are expelled and may not return.

Matrimony is a civil contract and to be duly registered. The religious service may be added.

Cemeteries are under civil inspection and open for the burial of all classes and creeds.

No one can sign away their liberty by contract or religious vow.

Education in the public schools is free and compulsory.

This synopsis of the " Laws of Reform " represents the action of the Mexican Congress on the 12th of February, 1857, with the amendments of the same of September, 1873, and the circular issued by the Interior Department January 15, 1877.

In view of the conspiracy to overthrow the republic and to establish a monarchy a special law was passed in 1862, making a capital crime of

Invitations given by Mexicans, or by foreigners resident in the republic, to subjects of other powers, to invade the national territory or change the form of government the republic has adopted, whatever the pretext set up.

Yet within three months after the enactment of this law Almonte and his associates left Paris for Mexico and were received with honor by the French military chiefs at Vera Cruz, given the protection of their flag and an escort of two thousand cavalry, thus violating the statutes of the land, which they pretended they had come in a friendly spirit to establish.

The pretense under which that army and the forces of England and Spain were sent to Mexico was the "tripartite treaty," reached at the convention of London, and signed by the three powers on the 31st of October, 1861, for the accomplishment of common objects in Mexico. The necessity for such a convention had been well worked up by the representative of Napoleon in Mexico, M. Saligny, who all through, like Shylock, mercilessly insisted upon having his " pound of flesh," no matter how much blood came with it. In the unsettled condition of Mexico by the intrigues and pronunciamentos of the clerical party during these years, society was disturbed and wrongs were perpetrated, by forced loans, highway robbery, and otherwise; and foreigners shared in these imposts, Frenchmen among them, of course. Saligny trumped up a heavy list of these inflictions against the Republican government and demanded heavy indemnities for each case. While admitting some of them the government declared the majority were without foundation, and asked for the *proofs*, which Saligny could not furnish. He resented all attempts to require evidence of his French claims, and his master backed him up in his demands.

Let it also be remembered that these forced loans and other criminalities were not inflicted by the Republican party, but by their bitter foes during the brief terms in which from time to time they held power, and yet that all of these were saddled upon the Republican government when restored, which had to pay these exactions, as in the case where Miramon robbed the British Legation of the $600,000. Another item of the claim was made out of the debts due to foreigners who had lent Mexico money in her emergencies, at enormous rates of interest, and these debts she did not deny, save when fictitious claims were added to them, as in the case of the "Jecker bonds." The Mexican government, on its restoration to power, finding the treasury empty, and being unable to raise money sufficient, postponed payment of the interest on outside debts for two years, promising then to resume payment. In the business world such a concession is constantly made by creditors toward those who only want 'time' to enable them to recover, especially when the parties thus favored have hitherto met their obligations faithfully. But Mexico, on which now rested the duty of self-preservation, which in a nation is certainly for the time being superior to the obligation to pay debts, was now to realize no mercy from hard-hearted men who took her by the throat, saying, "Pay me what thou owest!" though she pleaded, "Have patience with me, and I will pay thee all." M. Saligny had circulated the false and cruel impression that she *could* but would not. Hence England and Spain were led blindfolded into "the London Convention," only to be undeceived a year after, when their commissioners reached Mexico and ascertained the truth from interviews with Señor Doblado, President Juarez's secretary of state. England and Spain

12

freely gave Mexico the time she required, and their claims were recognized to be paid, principal and interest.

As we examine this unworthy transaction there is revealed an unexampled rascality. Government documents furnished by Mexico present the facts of her indebtedness with detailed statements of what had been paid these three nations, and what she still owed to each when they invaded her soil. Apart from the Jecker claim, the diplomatic correspondence shows, quoting a dispatch of Sir Charles Wyke that was laid before Parliament, "the French have only a small debt of $190,856 to recover, which is being paid off by twenty-five per cent. of the import duties levied at Vera Cruz." The first thing that Saligny did when he left his legation at the capital and came down to meet the French force, to guide its action, was to advise the French commander to seize the custom-house and appropriate its income to meet the French claims, so that it is likely that almost all had been paid ere Sir Charles wrote his dispatch. Saligny contended, however, that the claims of the "Jecker bonds" should be added to the French debt, and the Mexican government had to submit. After a full investigation they decided that all that could be honestly claimed by France for the debt, the indemnities due to French subjects for losses during the revolutions, for interest, and the Jecker bonds was $2,859,917. So her debts to the three nations were shown to be, "to British subjects, $69,311,657; to Spanish subjects, $9,461,986, and to the French the smallest sum of all, $2,859,-917." France was then the nation which had the least motive to make war on Mexico. Napoleon's object was not merely the settlement of the claim, but he sought a pretext for a quarrel with Mexico for the accomplishment of ulterior purposes. When the English and Spanish commissioners understood this they withdrew from the country, leaving Saligny to push the outrageously magnified Jecker bonds, which Napoleon was confident they could force to payment.

M. Jecker was a Swiss speculator who went to Mexico and assumed the role of a banker during the period when Miramon and the clericals held the capital. The ready money of the party running low, Jecker made the most of the opportunity. He could furnish $750,000 cash, and securities amounting, apparently, to $740,000 more, in all $1,490,428. "For this amount the reactionary government issued paper to the value of $15,-000,000, at six per cent. annually, and fundable in eight or ten years." A large part of the issue was made available "for the value on their face at the custom-houses in Mexico, in the proportion of a fifth of their exhibits, M. Jecker to pay the bearer interest at three per centum." *

Merchants who bought up these bonds were soon to realize how Miramon had deceived them when they began to present them for duties. The constitutional president, on learning of their issue, had proclaimed them illegal and worthless, and not a custom-house in Mexico would accept them. Merchants turned to the French Legation, on the ground that France had recognized the Miramon party as the government of Mexico, and a plot was raised to include these bonds as part of the French claims against the Juarez government and to demand payment for the full amount on their face. Just then it was discovered that Jecker was not a French subject, and therefore his bonds could not legally be included in French claims; but the rogues were not to be defeated, and an effort was made to naturalize him and leave the date of the nefarious deed in the background. Before the naturalization papers could arrive from France two packets of secret correspondence between Jecker and his representatives in Paris fell into the hands of the Republican troops, were forwarded to the president, and the villainous conspiracy was revealed. They stated, among other things, how the conspirators were manufacturing public opinion in Europe, how much they were afraid of the coming of Pacheco, the embassador of Juarez, who would be sure to expose their baseness, of their efforts to get the naturalization papers to Jecker, and how they "showed your letters to his majesty," and speak of their intercourse with "the duke,"

* *Diplomatic Correspondence of the United States*, 1863, pp. 239, 249.

called in one place "the new duke," which soon identified the
person intended, who was so deeply interested in the success of
the Jecker claims.

Who was this person so high at court, thus mysteriously
named as "near the throne," who had so much at stake in these
fraudulent transactions? Only a few knew when the dispatches were written, but recently it has been given to the
world. The new duke referred to was the Count de Morny,
illegitimate half-brother of the French emperor. When a
child he was given into the custody of a Frenchman by name of
de Morny, who had his home in the West Indies. His mother
left him 40,000 francs, which was intrusted to the guardian,
who squandered it in gambling. When the young man became of age he was penniless, but returned to France and entered the army, developing soon the sharp points of his character.
He and Louis Napoleon had never yet met, but Napoleon
heard of him as a suitable instrument for his purposes in the
coup d'état which he was then contemplating. He was brought
to Paris and proved just the conscienceless personage such as
Napoleon wanted to aid in this great crime against the republic. When he had proclaimed himself emperor the traitors
who shared in the iniquitous plan were rewarded, De Morny's
share being money, which he much coveted, and the life-presi-
dency of the Corps Legislatif. A more mercenary man never
held office. His extravagance earned for him the title of "the
Magnificent Spendthrift." It is asserted that "his great crime
was in taking money from all sides, all parties, all men." While
president of the Corps Legislatif he was "known to receive a
yearly subsidy from the Viceroy of Egypt for certain reasons."
Napoleon made him a duke while Miramon was the clerical
party's President of Mexico, and when the chance arose to
make a few millions out of these infamous Jecker bonds this
unprincipled man demeaned himself still further by stooping
to unite with Jecker and Miramon to organize the scheme to
float these worthless bonds and to force their payment in full
on Mexico, while his half-brother seized upon them as an ad-

ditional pretext to carry out his ulterior purposes in America. They were worthy of each other in the wicked use they made of power.*

When our civil war broke out the French emperor deemed that the time had come for the development of his purposes in America. The convention of London was arranged, and the allied fleet arrived at Vera Cruz in December, 1861. There was some surprise felt on finding that England had no soldiers, only seven hundred marines as a guard of honor for her representative, and Spain but a few soldiers, while France had nearly seven thousand men fully prepared for aggressive movements. The Spanish commissioner was General Prim, the English, Sir Charles Wyke, and the French, M. E. Jurien. They opened negotiations with the government of President Juarez, professing solemnly over their respective signatures that the object of their coming was entirely pacific, without any intention of interference with the form of government preferred by the nation, but they were there only as " lookers-on, to preside at the grand spectacle of your regeneration, guaranteed by order and liberty." They then gently intimate that they also seek " satisfaction for outrages inflicted, and sacred obligations that have not been discharged," but assert that the other is the higher object of their coming.

To this President Juarez replied that, while obliged to them for their interest in the welfare of the country, he was not conscious that Mexico needed any intervention for the regulation of her affairs, being competent to manage for herself; but in regard to any claims, he was willing to hear and consider them, and that they could appoint commissioners on their part, who should be met by others from him, and the cases be considered. He did more; for on the commissioners informing him that their men were suffering from sickness on account of the heat and climate, and would soon be liable to the yellow fever, so

* *Diplomatic Correspondence of the United States*, 1863, part i, p. 239, etc. *The Cosmopolitan*, May, 1890. *Christian World*, vol. xvii, p. 72. *Diplomatic Correspondence Presented to Parliament*, 1862, pp. 602–614.

common in Vera Cruz during the heated term, and requesting
his permission to move up to the mountain region where they
would be exempt, the president kindly granted this concession as soon as the allies would agree upon its conditions. This
led without delay to what is called "the Convention of Soledad"
(twenty-six miles from Vera Cruz), where the commissioners proceeded and were met by the secretary of state. A conference
was agreed to, to be held at Orizaba, up in the mountains and
eighty-two miles from Vera Cruz, where it was comfortable
and healthy, and during the negotiations the troops might be
brought up and allowed to occupy the towns of Cordova, Orizaba, and Tehuacan. The fourth article stipulated:

That it may not be believed, even remotely, that the allies have signed
those preliminaries in order to procure the passage of the fortified positions garrisoned by the Mexican army, it is stipulated that, in the unhappy
event of the rupture of negotiations, the forces of the allies shall evacuate
the aforesaid towns and situate themselves in the line which is before
said fortifications on the way to Vera Cruz.

The fifth article provided that in these unfortunate circumstances "the hospitals that the allies may have shall remain
under the safe-guard of the Mexican nation."

These fortifications were places of great natural strength and
could easily be defended by even a small force. The president
could not then dream that any of the persons whom he had
thus treated with such candor and kindness would prove unworthy or unfaithful to this fourth article, after having accepted
and signed it.

As the negotiations progressed the bad faith of the French
began its development and introduced confusion, and at last
involved defeat of the entire effort. The first of these was the
announcement that General Miramon and staff were on the expected English mail steamer with the intention of renewing the
civil war which had only just died out after the three years'
bloody struggle. It was also ascertained that a party of church
troops, with horse and munitions, were awaiting him above to
enable him to penetrate into the interior. The commissioners

discussed the situation, and the majority were for preventing
him from landing, while the English Commodore Dunlop declared he would "arrest him for having robbed the British
Legation if he lands while our flag is flying here." It was
very significant that Saligny "earnestly protested in the name
of his government against any such thing being attempted."
Nor could he be moved by the consideration urged by the
British and Spanish commissioners, that to allow Miramon to
land, and thus invade the country with an expedition of his
own, would utterly disgust the Liberal government with whom
they were treating and lead it and the nation to infer that the
allied commissioners must be in collusion with that traitor to permit him to land where their flags were flying. So Dunlop, notwithstanding Saligny's protest, two days after, when the packet
arrived, had Miramon arrested and returned to Havana by
the next steamer, and the difficulty ended for a time.

The English and Spanish claims for indemnity were accepted
by the Mexican commissioners without any difficulty. They
were recognized and placed on file to be discharged as soon as
possible. But when the French claims were presented the
commissioners were simply amazed, and especially when the
"Jecker bonds" were introduced and full recognition demanded for them. No wonder that the English and Spanish
commissioners were astounded when demand was made by Saligny for their recognition to the full amount of the $15,000,000!
In common honesty the government of Juarez did not owe
Jecker a single dollar. When Miramon fled from the city on
the approach of the national troops, and President Juarez had
arrived, he was soon after called on by Jecker, who claimed
to be under the protection of the French Legation. Under
the supposition that the president was intimidated by the Intervention and would yield any thing, Jecker made a demand
for the payment of the bonds issued by the fugitive clerical
president on the plea that "one government must be held
responsible for the acts and obligations of the other." This
Juarez refused to do. A parallel case would have been orig-

inated had Jefferson Davis after the battle of Bull Run entered Washington, and while he remained there in the absence of Mr. Lincoln had issued bonds to French subjects and gone off with the money received from them, and Napoleon on the return of Mr. Lincoln had sent a force to the United States to demand the payment of said bonds. The Jecker claims were originated by one who was a rebel against the constitutional government, which had not ceased to exist during the three years, and ought not therefore to be held responsible for the acts of an unlawful party.

For the sake of peace, and in order to get rid of the hostile visitors, the Mexican government was disposed to concede the original sum of $750,000, with five per cent. interest, but repudiated any further claims on that ground. The English and Spanish commissioners positively declined to be parties to pass up such claims to the Mexican president, and reported the facts to their respective governments, and were sustained in their course. The next item in the French demands was for reclamations for injuries and impositions suffered by French subjects on various occasions during past years; for them a round sum of $12,000,000 was claimed. No detailed statements were presented, no names of persons or dates of events or extent of wrong or injury in each case were forthcoming, and when these were inquired for the French minister replied that his government had made a general estimate to cover all the cases, and that he regarded that as entirely sufficient. The English and Spanish commissioners, after having submitted the items in their claims which they were to urge on the Mexican government, felt that they could not be parties to include a demand like this without vouchers of any kind. They then proposed to M. Saligny to grant to the Mexican government the right to examine into the justice of such claims through the medium of a mixed commission, to which Mexico was ready to consent; but even this reasonable proposition was declined by M. Saligny. Mexico must pay what France demanded, "trusting to her high sense of honor to demand only what was right." The ulterior object of

France was by this made manifest. Up to this hour the French government on repeated occasions had declared that it went to Mexico "to obtain satisfaction for its demands, and nothing more." The French representative signed the agreement in the treaty of London and of Soledad, "not to interfere in the interior affairs of Mexico." In the address of Napoleon's secretary of state to the French Parliament he used these words:

France can do no more than she has already—that is, to repeat the assurance that she does not propose to intervene in any manner with the internal affairs of Mexico; that her sole object is to obtain payment of her claims and reparation of the injuries that had been done her. . . . But to compel them by force, never!

Honest men have only certain terms to characterize professions like these when they contrast so widely with the conduct pursued. It is worthy of note that while the convention was sitting ships of the French navy were visiting the leading ports of Mexico, trying to induce them to "pronounce" in favor of the plan of Almonte (the agent of the church party) and monarchy, as well as sheltering traitors like Miramon, Marquez, and others who were ready, when this convention should break up, to commence their efforts to overthrow the Republican government preferred by the nation and erect on its ruins an imperial throne!

To proceed further was impossible; the convention of Soledad terminated. The English and Spanish representatives duly informed the Mexican government, and retired with their military escort from Mexico, sending on the facts to their respective governments, which approved their action. The French representative alone remained and transferred to the French general and his army the obligation to proceed without delay to execute the will of their imperial master, and ordered up the additional troops that had arrived. Saligny was asked if he really did not intend to observe the distinct condition into which they had all entered, in case the negotiations were broken off, to retire their troops "to the line below the fortifications" on the Cumbres before beginning their operations. Not he! He well knew he served a master who would freely condone the base treachery of thus violating his own signature. He had an immense advantage for his purpose, and was going to retain it, no matter how all honorable soldiers, or the whole world itself, might stamp it with infamy as an almost unprecedented violation of diplomatic and military honor! The French emperor gained what he wanted, the power to act alone, on his own terms, in forcing his demands, at the bayonet's point, on an enemy whose generosity he violated, while he demanded full payment of fictitious claims, and then drove him from the seat of authority to which the nation had elected him in order to place upon it a stranger whom he had already selected for that purpose!

In addition to a full account of the convention so disastrously ended Sir C. Wyke and General Prim declared to their governments that their observation and inquiries in Mexico "had fully satisfied them that a monarchy was not desired by any one in Mexico save a few Conservatives and the church party."

The church party embraces all that is bigoted and fanatical in the country, and is therefore retrogressive in policy, and at variance with the spirit of the age, and is detested by a great majority of the people, who are in favor of a liberal policy. (P. 723.)

It is not usual for the secretary of state of a great nation to take the responsibility of expressing himself so bluntly concerning the measures of a neighboring sovereign and his government as Lord John Russell did at this time concerning the whole question under review here. Writing to his embassador at Paris, who he expected would report the sentiments of his government to the French secretary of state, Lord Russell says:

It is hardly possible that claims so excessive as that of $12,000,000 in the lump, without an account, and that of $15,000,000 for $750,000 actually received, can have been put forward with an expectation that they would be complied with. . . . I stated to Mr. Flahault (the French embassador at London) that what we could not agree to, and must keep clear of, was the putting forward of claims merely for the sake of making a quarrel. That was a course we could not adopt ourselves nor defend in others. . . . The principle of non-intervention having been always maintained by the

English government, our force was withdrawn and our flag hauled down upon the express determination of Admiral de la Gravière and M. Saligny to march to Mexico for the purpose of overthrowing the government of President Juarez.*

General Prim in his address to the Cortes held exactly the same position.

Having gained their point of being left alone in Mexico, being heavily re-enforced, ultimately up to forty-five thousand men, and with the full intention of forcing the payment of both these enormous claims, and in addition resolved to make Mexico " pay the expense of the war, which on her side was not provoked, nor declared by the other," as Señor Romero phrased it, the march toward Mexico city was begun. Before the allied commissioners had left Saligny made an unexpected proposal. He had evidently become alarmed at the effect which his enormous demands would have on public opinion in Europe when the reasons for the breaking up of the convention were made known ; so he offered to abandon the Jecker claims if the other two commissioners would indorse the claim for $12,000,000, which, being entirely without evidence, they would not do. Saligny then withdrew his proposal and referred the matter to Napoleon.

Late in September, 1862, the Republican forces operating between Vera Cruz and the city of Mexico intercepted another packet of letters addressed to M. Jecker by his friends in Paris. They were sent to President Juarez, and were found even more nefarious than the previous ones captured. The president sent them to Señor Romero, who laid them before the government at Washington, and they were sent to Congress. A few sentences will show their purport, and who was operating influentially behind the scenes in this abominable business, and also give a clearer view of the objects of these enemies of freedom and justice. One tells Jecker, among other things, " Your letter of July 16 has been presented entire before the eyes of his Maj-

* Diplomatic Correspondence Presented to Parliament, 1862, part iii, pp. 242. 720, 801.

esty, as has been done with the previous ones when *their tenor has permitted.*" Another of this band of sharpers writes:

Affairs are taking a better aspect for us. For a decision has been come to to colonize. Forty-five thousand men are to be sent out. . . . Our friends think the bonds will be admitted in Mexico. I will divulge nothing though I see every thing has been prohibited since the disgusting correspondence of Sir C. Wyke has been submitted to Parliament. That diplomate has been your adversary and deadly enemy. . . . Feeling itself almost anticipated, and closely watched by Wyke, the French government lets nothing transpire with reference to its projects of protectorate, colonization, etc. Not less than eighteen generals go out with the expeditionary corps, for which reason it must be very considerable. . . . The expedition will have relation also to the affairs of the United States.

Jecker's father in another letter says:

I have not deceived you in repeating to you now for more than a year that there would be colonization, a throne, protectorate, etc. I believe, also, these forces have in view to restrain *the United States,* drunk with pride and vain boasting. . . . In Paris, for the present, it is better not to wake the cat that sleeps. Wyke has been our real enemy, Juarez should burn a long candle for him. . . . With forty-five thousand men submission will follow, and even a pressure will be brought to bear upon the United States, the position of which is not without its influence on what passes. . . . With reference to the organization of the government (in Mexico), Maximilian was nothing more than a pilot balloon without any importance. Who will be placed to govern under the tutelage of France I cannot say. . . . C—— (who has just returned from Mexico) says: " The reactionaries fear the entire and full recognition of the bonds, because it would burden the treasury. The Liberals execrate them, and the French believe the calumnies employed to depreciate them, so that I can truly say that I have not encountered any one in Mexico but *Saligny* who sustains them." *

These are merely samples. The "new duke" figures constantly, and they boast of the able men whom they employ to manufacture public opinion in France and Europe to favor the bonds and to sustain Saligny's policy, yet (up to September 3) the naturalization papers for Jecker had not reached him, and the French government was thus zealously engaged in behalf of a wretched swindler who was not even a French subject!

* *Diplomatic Correspondence of the United States,* No. 54, pp. 375–387.

Having sold his bonds at a large advance, Jecker had obligated himself to pay interest at three per cent. until they were redeemed at the treasury or custom-houses of Mexico for their face. So long as Juarez held power nothing could be realized on them. The interest had to be paid promptly to keep up the credit of the bonds, and Jecker was ruined before aid could reach him. President Juarez (early in October) ordered the arrest and banishment of Jecker and his crew from the country, and thus ended their dreams of enormous wealth at Mexico's expense.

The expulsion of Jecker and the contents of the intercepted letters were not long in reaching the English government, and soon after found their place in the London *Times*. Telegrams to Paris of what was coming created quite a commotion among "those personages who occupy high positions in the court of the Tuileries near the imperial throne." It was in vain the next morning to prohibit the entrance of *The Times* into Paris as they attempted. Many had obtained the news, and Jules Favre arose in the Chamber of Deputies to question M. Billant, who was known to be the mouth-piece and defender of the emperor. The questions were scorching, such as a minister has rarely had to face in Parliament. The worst could not be spoken, but men understood the meaning of the courageous deputy as he denounced those who had so despicably traded with the character of France in a foreign land, while the Duke de Morny sat presiding over the Assembly! No wonder that Jecker had boasted in the past that Napoleon was bound to sustain him and his bonds because of the hold he had upon his character and of those who stood with him.

The Mexican government had come to understand that France was not to blame for her sufferings, and attributed them solely to the emperor. An incident which showed President Juarez's feeling on the subject occurred at a reception given in his honor at Chihuahua, when an indiscreet admirer spread the French flag on the ground in front of the door with the intent that the president should tread on it. The moment that Juarez saw it

he turned, went around it, and requested that it be lifted up.
When remonstrated with for declining to dishonor the flag that
was invading their country he answered: "No, that flag represents France, against which we have no cause of complaint.
We distinguish between the French people and their emperor,
and when all is over France will yet do Mexico justice. Let
us honor that flag."

On the way to the city of Mexico the French troops under
General Laurency were met near Puebla by a force of Republicans under General Zaragoza, and there, under the shadow of
the snow-capped volcanoes, Popocatepetl and Ixtaccihuatl, they
suffered the humiliation of defeat by Mexico's poorly equipped
soldiers. The heroes of Solferino, who had known no defeat
since Waterloo, were driven back to Orizaba with serious loss.
It was not because of any special superiority of numbers or facilities of the ground occupied by the Mexicans in the struggle.
Under God it was won by the vigor which comes to those who
fight for their homes, their country, and the freedom which
they love. This triumph filled Mexico with exultation and
hope, and the day, the fifth of May, "Cinco de Mayo,"
is yearly celebrated. The French troops waited at Orizaba
for re-enforcements before renewing their march against Mexico. The chagrin of Napoleon may be imagined, and his pride
urged him to send forward more than adequate resources,
with a consequent increase of expense which he confidently
expected that Mexico should pay, and which claim was embodied in the convention between himself and Maximilian, as
we shall see.

This check and its results consumed several months of time,
and enabled President Juarez and the Congress more fully
to make their final arrangements for the preservation of the
government and the defense of the nation against its implacable enemy. At Miramar and Rome matters were being pushed
forward in regard to the departure of the Archduke of Austria
for Mexico as soon as the French should clear his way to the
capital. Already he had accepted the crown proffered him,

not by "the people of Mexico," as he was untruthfully assured, but by the exiles and traitors who hung around the French court, and by the "Assembly of Notables," so called, who mysteriously kept up from the Mexican capital communications with these enemies of their country's freedom. Maximilian apparently tried to believe their assurances of the sentiments of their country—that he would find his path "strewn with flowers from Vera Cruz to the throne in the 'Halls of Montezuma,' and that all opposition would drop into the dust within a few weeks of his arrival," and "the united nation would gather around him with enthusiasm as their beloved sovereign." Yet, after all these assurances, he seemed to hesitate, and stipulated that a general vote of the people should be obtained, that he might have the assurance that not a class only, but the nation itself, was really calling him to be their sovereign. This hesitancy was not causeless. It was the result of a warning that he had received by a trusty messenger from President Juarez, in regard to the danger to which his advisers were luring him for their own purposes. Happy had it been for him had he heeded that warning. It appeared on his trial and aided in his condemnation. The Conservative faction assured him that the popular vote which he desired would most certainly be promptly taken. If Maximilian had not been weak-minded and so disposed to yield to undue influence he would have known that such a vote was impossible in view of the fact that the Republican forces were controlling more than two thirds of the nation, and that less than one third was held by French bayonets, and that only in places where the latter held sway could such a vote be taken, and that even then it would be utterly unreliable as an expression of the popular will.

Among those surrounding the archduke was Señor Gutierrez de Estrada, president of the delegates of the "Council of Notables," which was an assembly of aristocratic aspirants, composed of persons whose families formerly bore titles before the republic superseded them, while the rest of the council was made up of "priests, friars, and military officers in the service of the bishops." They anticipated a titled aristocracy as a suitable setting for an imperial throne in Mexico, and this would have required territorial endowments, a law of primogeniture and entail for its due dignity, while the Church was to "raise her mitered fronts in court and Parliament," and Mexico was to bear the financial burdens of those Old World pomps and decorations. Some of the doings became known, and liberals, even in Austria, made themselves merry over the situation and the ridiculous aspects of the matter. Among these questions were proposed : "What relation has the young prince to Mexico, that he should be made emperor ?" "By what title will he reign over a country at the other end of the world ?" while others offered the advice that "Maximilian should study the Spanish, in order to be able to converse with his subjects!"

John Lothrop Motley was at that time the United States embassador at the court of Austria, and was personally acquainted with the archduke and his views. As an American he was frequently asked his opinion of this curious affair in its different aspects. We place before the reader what he says upon the subject in his correspondence, as follows :

VIENNA, *September* 22, 1863.

In this capital the great interest just now is about the new Mexican emperor. The Archduke Maximilian is next brother to the Emperor of Austria, and about thirty years of age. He has been a kind of lord high admiral, an office which, in the present condition of the imperial navy, may be supposed to be not a very onerous one. He was Governor-General of Lombardy until that kingdom was ceded to Victor Emmanuel, and he is considered a somewhat restless and ambitious youth. . . . It is, I believe, unquestionable that the archduke is most desirous to go forth on this adventure. It is equally certain that the step is exceedingly unpopular in Austria. That a prince of the House of Hapsburg should become the satrap of the Bonaparte dynasty, and should sit on an American throne, which could not exist a moment but for French bayonets and French ships, is most galling to all classes of Austrians. The intrigue is a most embarrassing one to the government. If the fatal gift is refused, Louis Napoleon, of course, takes it highly in dudgeon. If it is accepted, Austria takes a kind of millstone around her neck in the shape of gratitude for something she didn't want, and some day she will be expected to pay for it in something she had rather not give. The deputation of the so-called "Notables" is expected here this week, and then the conditions will be laid down on which Maximilian will consent to lie in the bed of roses of Montezuma and Iturbide. The matter is a very serious and menacing one to us.

He adds, under the same date, to Oliver W. Holmes, and in allusion to the drought then prevailing in Austria, the significant words :

There is no glory in the grass nor verdure in any thing. In fact, we have nothing green here but the Archduke Maximilian, who firmly believes that he is going forth to Mexico to establish an American empire, and that it is his divine mission to destroy the dragon of democracy and re-establish the true Church, the right divine, and all sorts of games. Poor young man!

Speaking of Maximilian's characteristic and church notions, Mr. Motley adds what might have been expected as a result of the training which he received under the bigoted influence of his mother, the Archduchess Sophia :

Maximilian adores bull-fights, rather regrets the Inquisition, and considers the Duke of Alva every thing noble and chivalrous and the most abused of men. It would do your heart good to hear his invocation to that deeply injured shade, and his denunciations of the ignorant and vulgar Protestants who have defamed him. . . . You can imagine the rest.*

How completely Maximilian was in the hands of the wily French emperor may be seen in the terms of the treaty which he was required to sign before he left for Mexico. How any man with his eyes open could be induced to bow his neck to accept such a heavy load of financial obligations is incomprehensible. Not merely did it include the cost of the intervention from first to last, but also the claims rejected at Soledad, and which could be made to cover, surreptitiously, even the Jecker bonds. Besides these it was necessary to provide for his imperial salary, the civil list, and all the national expenses, military and naval. Very adroitly the proposed loan of £8,000,000 sterling at ten per cent. interest, about to be floated, professedly

* The Correspondence of J. L. Motley, vol. ii, p. 138.

to put Maximilian in funds to begin his administration, was arranged so that fifty-four million francs were at once to be paid
to the French emperor on account, and twelve million francs
as an installment of the indemnities due to Frenchmen! Poor
Maximilian, this treaty was to prove one of the millstones that
was to sink his empire! He signed it because he was misin-
formed and deceived as to the professedly great resources of the
land he thought he was invited to govern!

CHAPTER VI.

Why Maximilian failed—Warnings in Austrian history—Francis Joseph—Papal denunciation—Denying a grave—Juarez and Congress—Juarez and Lincoln —South American interest—Netherland League—Position of the United States—Marshal's disagreement with the archbishop—Impossible task—Empire without foundation—Abbé Domenech—Career for the Latin race—Grant —Failure of efforts—Nuncio—Pope's expostulation—Clericals in politics— Confidential letter of Carlota—Denial of papal authority.

MAXIMILIAN had his personal warnings as to the serious risks in which such a course as he was now entering upon might involve him. He had seen this illustrated under his own eyes during the previous five years, and to what risks and humiliation attempts to do the papal will and ignore popular rights had brought his brother the emperor, until at last, driven to desperation by the pope's demands, Francis Joseph had to fling these demands to the winds and break with the papacy in order to save his crown and kingdom. He thus made Austria constitutionally free, and gave Roman Catholic Europe an example which she has been swift to follow in ridding herself of the burden of political Romanism. Many concordats were smashed when it was seen that Austria, so long subservient, could no longer exist in the nineteenth century hampered with one. This had recently occurred under Maximilian's observation, and was the more emphatic as he was obliged to relinquish his viceroyalty of Lombardy and yield up that territory to Victor Emmanuel for the unification of Italy, as demanded by her people, who scorned Austria's claim to rule longer any part of their land. This prince leaves all this scene of rectified wrong in the interests of a nation's liberty, as if he had learned no lesson from it to cross the ocean and impose a foreign sovereignty on a free nation, and all this in order to do the will of a crafty pope and

his clergy, and through the agency of.an army of foreigners
sent by an unscrupulous sovereign.

The Austrian nation had long been regarded as "the broad
shield of papacy," and had been trusted accordingly. In all
emergencies of the pontiff a word was sufficient to bring the
armies of Austria to his aid. Freedom was thus repeatedly
crushed and despotism sustained. In her pride and self-confidence
she aspired to dominate Germany, and watched with jealous eyes
the rising greatness of Prussia. Meanwhile she was closely
observed by Louis Napoleon, who coveted her peculiar position
as patron of the papacy, and aspired to fill the place of "the
eldest son of the Church." To gain this point he was ready to
aid Victor Emmanuel to drive Austria out of Italy. The hour
desired came in 1859, and the terrible overthrow of Magenta
and Solferino spread the gloom and despair of defeat throughout the Austrian empire. Four years previously Francis
Joseph had completed with the pope a concordat, every item
of which had been dictated by the clericals, and under the protection of which Austria considered herself safe. The pope's
allocution, issued only six weeks later, intended to strengthen
the concordat, wrought exactly the other way. As a sample
of how the papacy can pour its adulation upon those who stoop
so low as the Austrian emperor did to take this yoke upon him,
it is very monitory.

Thanks to the infinite bounty of God, and to the piety of our most dear
son in Jesus Christ, Francis Joseph, Emperor and Apostolic King of
Austria, what we desired has come to pass—in this completed concordat
—and has been regularly and solemnly confirmed. . . . We offer up great
thanksgivings to the Father of mercies and God of all consolation, who
has given a wise and enlightened heart to our most dear son in Jesus
Christ, Francis Joseph, Emperor and Apostolic King of Austria.

All this gush of joy soon proved a delusion, and this "dear
son " had a rude awakening when, crushed on the battle-field,
he found no hand to help him. Hurrying back to Vienna, he
took counsel with the best men of his diversified empire. They
advised him to break with the papacy, to cast off the concordat,

and to unify his empire by granting civil and religious freedom. Acting upon this advice, the emperor adopted a constitutional course which saved Austria. Under the guidance of Count von Beust (a Protestant statesman, called to be premier) the nation began to enjoy freedom and peace. Nearly all that Kossuth and his compatriots had unsuccessfully struggled to obtain more than a score of years before was conceded, and the empire was at last united in civil and religious freedom, guaranteed to them by their enlightened sovereign and the excellent constitution which he had signed. While the States around were rejoicing with the Austrians in their freedom and the peace that had come with it, there was one power which surveyed the scene with envious eyes and cursed it, not merely " in their hearts," but in the bitterest language, and that too, in the name of Almighty God, whose holy providence had led these millions out of such long-time tribulation into the happiest condition their country had ever known. That power was the papacy.

An allocution full of wrath was pronounced by the pope. How outspoken and violent it was may be judged by our readers from an epitome of it expressed in his own words. He denounces them for having not only abrogated the concordat with him, but for having, in place of it, dared to pass " the following odious and abominable laws : "

1. Laws establishing liberty for all opinions, liberty of the press, and liberty of faith and worship.
2. Laws granting to the members of all denominations the right of establishing schools and colleges.
3. Laws permitting the intermarriage, on terms of religious equality, of Catholics and Protestants.
4. Laws permitting civil marriage.
5. Laws permitting the burial of Protestants in Romish lands where Protestants have no cemeteries of their own in which to bury.
6. Laws establishing public schools for secular education that shall be free from the control of the Romish priesthood.

The pope denounces the above laws and declares them "contrary to the doctrines, rights, and authority of the

Catholic religion;" and adds, "Let it be understood that the
Roman Catholic Church declares such laws as these, wherever
they may be enacted, to be *null and void.*" * He closes his
lengthy and excited allocution by reminding all who had act, hand,
or part in the framing or enactment of those laws that they had
made themselves amenable to "the censures and spiritual punish-
ments" which it was in his power to inflict upon them! To this
un-Christlike tirade Baron von Beust, the premier, calmly replied through the embassador of Austria at Rome, informing the
pope and his curia that they were not going to be moved in the
slightest degree from the beneficent course they had deliberately
chosen for themselves as freemen; nor have they been moved
from that day to this. The people and the press of Austria
have stood by their government loyally, and the clergy have not
dared to institute any resistance to the national will.

If there be any thing in a man's relation to his fellow-creat-
ures that is most detestable in the estimation of heathen and
Mohammedan people, it is the very course here pursued by the
pope of Rome, when he utters his shameful protest against the
humanity of the Austrians in allowing a dead Protestant a
place to rest in peace. Yet here is a man ready to shed his
tears because the Austrians had that much common humanity
left. That unreasoning fanatics of his Church should now and
then so far forget themselves as thus to insult the dead of
other Christian denominations is a small offense compared to
this. Here is a man professing to be the chief priest of Christianity, publicly taking this awful stand before all the world, and
this, too, in our tolerant age, as the avowed and settled policy
and principle of his Church every-where, that she holds the
power to inflict this last indignity upon the man, the woman,
or the babe that dies where his religion has temporal sway!
We may well thank Heaven that Romanism controls only a
limited portion of our race, and also that of those she yet controls there are not five States to-day that would do her bidding
on this question, while even this number is growing less.

* *Christian World*, vol. xix, pp. 312–314.

Maximilian was going to a country where such wicked intolerance was carried out not so many years ago, while in Europe it was common enough, in papal lands, in the days of our fathers. The readers of Dr. Young's *Night Thoughts* will recall his terrible experience in Spain. Dr. Young, as a last hope for recovery, took his gifted daughter to try the effect of that climate upon the consumption that was wasting her away. She continued to fail and soon died. He went out to make arrangements for her burial and was horrified to learn from the undertaker that no grave could be claimed for her, she having been a "heretic!" Dr. Young inquired of the man what then was he to do. A shrug of the shoulders was the only answer. Money could not bribe him to attempt it, even privately, for fear of the priests; so that Dr. Young returned to his dead almost distracted. The account runs that a kind-hearted gentleman came to advise with him, and they arranged to make up the body into the smallest parcel possible, and after midnight, when all had retired, they bore the precious burden between them, and, leaving the road, found a plowed field, where they dug such a grave as they were able and laid the loved one to her rest. The doctor has memorialized the event in his *Night Thoughts:*

> "While nature yearned blind superstition raved,
> That mourned the dead, and this denied a grave."

Surely here is evidence in the pope's own words, as well as the facts of history, justifying the sad conclusion that Romanism is unchangeable, that the cruelty she has inflicted upon humanity, living and dead, she would repeat if she only had the power again to exercise it, and that therefore she cannot be trusted.

Napoleon's increased army now advanced to open the way for the Austrian archduke, and the Mexican president and Congress, unable to offer an adequate resistance, were compelled to retire from Mexico city. The Congress dispersed, but before doing so they invested the president with what is called in

Mexico "ample faculties," giving him their unlimited confidence, and the use of all the available resources of the nation in the great task of carrying on the conflict for the freedom of Mexico. Thirty days after the return of peace the Congress was to convene and receive the report of the use made of this power. How wonderful the scene when the legislature transferred its authority to the discretion of this incorruptible patriot! The sublime faith and devotion to the cause embodied in the Constitution which he drew up in 1857 displayed by this distinguished man is a most remarkable fact in the history of freedom. With the army of a foreign despot threatening his capital and his navy bombarding the coast cities to force a foreign monarch on the nation; with domestic treason, led by men called ministers of the Most High; with forces scattered, few in number and deficient in resources; with foes to misrepresent the truth in other lands and with none to help, yet this good Republican president faints not. There is only one man with whom to compare him—Lincoln; and they are worthy to be associated in honor together.

The address of Bishop Simpson, able, affectionate, and excellent as it was, at the funeral of our martyred president, contained nothing more notable than the quotation that the orator made from one of Mr. Lincoln's speeches, uttered in 1859 (four years before these events in Mexico), in which, speaking of the slave power, he said : "Broken by it, I, too, may be; bow to it, I never will. The probability that we may fail in the struggle ought not to deter us from the support of a cause which I deem to be just, and it shall not deter me. If ever I feel the soul within me elevate and expand to those dimensions not wholly unworthy of its Almighty architect, it is when I contemplate the cause of my country, deserted by all the world besides, and I, standing up boldly and alone, and hurling defiance at her victorious oppressors. Here, without contemplating consequences, before high Heaven and in the face of the world, I swear eternal fidelity to the just cause, as I deem it, of the land of my life, my liberty, and my love." No inspiration finer than this breathes in any of Mr. Lincoln's utterances. It almost seems as if an intimation of his life and death were given to him at the moment, as if à glimpse into his own and his country's future had been vouchsafed to his excited vision.*

* Holland's *Life of Lincoln*, p. 534.

Every word here could have been adopted by Juarez as his own in his struggle with clerical despotism. How wonderful the providence that raised up *two* such men, living and acting side by side, taking the same risks for the same cause, enduring this during the same eventful decade, 1860 to 1870, thinking not of themselves, but of that " vision of their country's future," by that God-given glimpse vouchsafed to each of them, now so fully realized by their grateful countrymen and by those who love liberty in every land !

Juarez and his cabinet sought safety in the Northern States of the republic while they were developing the resources of their country and preparing their plan of resistance in the hope of ultimate victory over all this wrong. The States of Central and South America took the alarm to heart very seriously. They hastened to communicate with the Mexican president, to assure him of their detestation of Louis Napoleon's treason to freedom, and that they held the cause of Mexico as their cause, and it should have their abundant sympathy, while they would forever honor the man who so worthily bore the banner of constitutional freedom for the New World, as he was doing. We have not room for their utterances which came to cheer Juarez in that anxious hour, and can only briefly refer to them. The president of Peru, in his address to the Congress at Lima, closed with these stirring words :

No; the republics of the New World, from Hudson's Bay to Tierra del Fuego, are and will be free, independent, and sovereign; because such is their will—it accords with their democratic instincts and most profound convictions; and because in America monarchy is an impossibility. Mexico responds with her friendship and sympathy to that which Peru displays and demonstrates for her.

The Argentine Republic, Chili, Bolivia, Nicaragua, the United States of Colombia, and others followed, adding their protest against the French invasion. Under all the circumstances they regarded our own United States as within the circle of danger should Mexico fall before the remorseless power which had already its grip upon her life, and which led the venerable Masquera, then President of New Granada, to say to his own Congress, "If the United States fails *we all go under*." Well he might say so, in view of the fact (among many other things then taking form) that when Peru proposed that "league for mutual protection," and it was being discussed, it was credibly reported that the minister of Napoleon at Bogota remarked to the minister of Ecuador that "*France* would not *allow* such a league to be formed!"* So the pressure first was to fall on Mexico, but the others correctly understood that that was but the entering wedge to more destructive results, and that thus Mexico was not merely struggling for the rights and freedom "which affect all America," as the address of the United States of Colombia declared, but on a broader and higher scale even than this, as Abbott remarks, like Washington and the founders of our republic "she was struggling not for herself and America alone, but was in a sense fighting FREEDOM's BATTLE for all mankind and for posterity."

The eyes of the world were already drawn toward Mexico, and true lovers of constitutional liberty on the other side of the Atlantic were yielding their sympathy and prayers for her success in the unequal conflict. In a document drawn up by the "Netherlands League," a Democratic association at the very home of Carlota, were the following expressions, sent to President Juarez by Señor Romero:

We address you as the only legal representative of the Mexican nations, to congratulate you on your persevering resistance against a foreign usurper, who is trying to rob the Mexicans of their liberty and independence. . . . The sixteen hundred young men who left Belgium for Mexico were made to believe that they were going solely to serve as a guard to the so-called Empress of Mexico, daughter of the King of the Belgians, and these men, thus deceived, continued to enlist without reflecting that they were going to uphold principles of tyranny and oppression. The people of Belgium are lovers of liberty, and the independence they want for themselves they desire for other nations.

* *Christian World*, vol. xvi, 1865, p. 136.

The hour had now come for the United States to take their position so as to justify their future course, whatever that might be. Mr. Seward wrote on the 7th of April, 1864, to our minister at Paris, for the information of the French government:

A resolution passed the House of Representatives by a unanimous vote, which declares the opposition of that body to a recognition of a monarchy in Mexico. He adds in his letter to the minister these decisive words: "I remain now firm as heretofore in the opinion that the destinies of the American continent are not to be permanently controlled by any political arrangement that can be made in the capitals of Europe."

At the same time, in response to a dispatch in which Napoleon assumed great frankness, while really concealing his purpose toward Mexico, Mr. Seward stated our position:

While I appreciate the frankness and the good-will which the emperor's government manifests in thus communicating its views and purposes on the subject, it nevertheless remains my duty to say that this government has long recognized and does continue to recognize the constitutional government of the United States of Mexico as the sovereign authority in that country, and the president, Benito Juarez, as its chief. This government at the same time recognizes the condition of war existing in Mexico between that country and France. We maintain absolute neutrality between the belligerents.*

Our present duty was done when President Lincoln laid before Congress, a few days after, the views of the administration in regard to Mexico, expressed with his usual candor. Napoleon might dissemble as he chose, but henceforth he knew what to expect from the United States in regard to Mexico.

As President Juarez passed out of the northern end of the valley of Anahuac the vanguard of the French despot entered at the southern, coming to dictate in the New World what style of government he would allow here, and what measure of civil and religious liberty we must give up, and what we might retain, conformably to papal dictation!

The president fixed his government at San Luis Potosi, Chihuahua, and El Paso alternately. So well was he served by his faithful people that, though the clerical faction would have given "large money" to any one who would have betrayed him into their hands (and they would probably have given him but a short shrift), yet he was preserved from all plots, to carry on his great work, until his cause was triumphant in Mexico.

After his departure from the capital, and until the Austrian archduke should arrive, an interregnum government was arranged by a regency of three persons, of whom Archbishop Labastida was one. This domineering prelate was in his element, and soon tried to introduce reactionary and repressive measures. He could not wait till the prince arrived and had the opportunity to approve what was now done in his name. The insolent course of this ecclesiastic soon brought him into conflict with Marshal Neigre, who commanded the French forces. The archbishop was not disposed to relax one iota of the Church's claims on the confiscated property, but demanded that the sales should be declared "null and void," though they had been effected legally under the preceding regimen; but he cared nothing for the laws of the Congress, and considered a simple decree of the regency sufficient to restore all the properties, no matter whose interests were violated. The marshal expostulated, and reminded the prelate that such action did not become him who had so lately been sheltered at the French court and had been brought back under the protection of the French flag. He considered the archbishop's course so compromising and premature that he raised the question whether an appeal to the pope "against this retrograde spirit of the higher Mexican clergy would not be successful and the archbishop suppressed."

The heavier storm, however, came when the marshal requested the archbishop to indicate which of the unused churches at the capital might be taken as a place of worship for such of his soldiers as were Protestants. His own government made such provision, and furnished chaplains for them, and they expected the same privilege in Mexico. The wrath of the archbishop was extreme when the marshal preferred his reasonable request, without dreaming of being refused. What followed we will state in the language of Chevalier, a French writer, who, though a Romanist, seems to have been as much surprised at the prelate's violence and intolerance as was the marshal:

The Archbishop of Mexico, forgetting not only what he owed to France, but also the services that the French Intervention was rendering to Mexico and to Catholicism, was eager to create a sensation. He resigned his functions as a member of the provisional government, he issued a protest, and a little later he distributed papers among the faithful, in which, according to the terms of a letter addressed to this high church dignitary by General Neigre, "appeal was made to the most detestable passions against the army of his majesty the emperor." The circumstances of the case were such that the general thought it his duty to address these severe words to the archbishop. . . . "Tell that party, monseigneur, that we are watching them and are aware of their plots. Tell them that though it is always repugnant to us to employ violent measures of repression we shall yet, should circumstances make the painful duty incumbent, know how to thrust back the real enemies of Mexico into the obscurity from which they dare to issue their diatribes." *

Alas! General Neigre forgot he was not in enlightened Europe, but in Mexico, so long oppressed, and that this wicked prelate was trying to drag the nation back into the darkness from which she had so lately emerged, and that in doing this he was obeying the will of the pontiff, to whom they dreamed of appealing against his acts. What a lesson unfolds itself in this interference of the marshal and its results as to the burden which had so long oppressed Mexico!

All things being now ready, Maximilian went to Rome to receive the papal benediction. Pius IX. was flattered by this act. It recalled the customs of the Middle Ages, and the most was made of the example; but it has had no imitators, and how much good the pontifical benediction did this "crowned adventurer," as some one then called him, we shall see. Maximilian received the full assurance of "perpetuity to his dynasty," and the "blessing of Heaven upon his enterprise" from the pontiff, who claimed that, as God's vicegerent, he was the only authority on earth which could originate a new dynasty by "divine right" and transmit to it Heaven's indorsement. The entire clerical

* *Mexico, Ancient and Modern,* by M. Chevalier, 1864, p. 10.

party seconded this assurance. How grim this appears now, and
what a fearful mistake this " infallible " man made in regard to
this new Catholic empire and its perpetuity ! Pius IX. did a
large amount of blessing and cursing in his time. Some curious
lists were made up to illustrate how often and how completely
Providence reversed his benedictions and his anathemas until
men became so indifferent that they neither desired the one nor
feared the other, and especially after the overwhelming disaster
that followed his benediction upon Maximilian and his empire !
Of God alone, as the omniscient Judge of men, can the words of
the heathen king of Moab to Balaam be true : " I know that
he whom thou blessest is blessed, and he whom thou cursest is
cursed." The exercise of these prerogatives God has never conferred on mortal man, not even on this one who set up his claim
to be "supreme judge of Christendom ! "

Even though thus fortified there is evidence that Maximilian
was not quite assured that his empire would be altogether safe.
Before leaving Miramar he exacted a guarantee from Louis Napoleon, pledging the power of France to " keep the new throne
secure." What power on this continent could Maximilian be anxious about save the United States? Already Napoleon's minister,
M. Billant, had begun in the French Parliament to dilate on the
benefits which his master's policy was to confer upon this hemisphere. He intimated that when the emperor had succeeded in
giving "a good government" to Mexico he might then extend
his benevolence "over the other *disorderly republics* of the New
World." And it was noted that M. Billant in this connection
made no exception of the United States.* Señor Romero, the
Mexican embassador, had full evidence in his possession for his
belief that Napoleon had unfriendly intentions against our
country. This he placed before Mr. Seward and President Lincoln. When our hands were tied on account of our civil war
Napoleon hastened the Intervention in Mexico, and undoubtedly
stood prepared to utilize his chances, whatever they might be,
to our disadvantage.

* *Diplomatic Correspondence of the United States*, 1863, pp. 63, 310, 444.

MAXIMILIAN, ARCHDUKE OF AUSTRIA,
For three years, by usurpation, "Emperor" of Mexico.

The church party made great preparations to receive Maximilian and Carlota at Vera Cruz, and on the 12th of June, 1864, they made their formal entry into the city of Mexico, and were escorted with great pomp to the cathedral, where they were enthroned. The great building was decorated, and under the direction of Archbishop Labastida all that was possible was done to show popular jubilation. Mr. Flint gives a very full account of what was said and done, and evidently leaves nothing out in his zeal to mark their welcome to the capital and to create the impression that Maximilian was received in a great blaze of popularity. How much of this was spontaneous and outside of clerical manipulation this partisan does not state, but the further part of this narrative will show.

We here present this now imperial couple to our readers. The pictures are from photographs taken at Trieste, when on their way to sail for Mexico.

The prince, or emperor, as we must now begin to call him, came well equipped to set up a gorgeous court before the Mexicans. Among other costly articles he had brought a gaudy state carriage, so rich with gold trimmings, plate-glass, and other trappings, after the old French style, that it was a load for four horses to draw, and is reported to have cost $47,000. Tourists go to see this curiosity, and also rooms full, until lately, of furniture and other luxurious articles, all bearing the imperial monogram. Few of them came into use and some were never unpacked! Sad reminders of vanities and glories provided at an immense cost! Colonel Evans gives five pages to an enumeration of these frivolities with which the poor emperor provided himself, which those curious in such matters can consult. What intensifies the foolishness of the prince who was thus led to emulate the court spendors of Napoleon III. was the fact that they were provided with borrowed money, much of which was never paid, and never will be! Maximilian himself was comparatively poor, and had only a small patrimony. These thousands thus vaingloriously squandered in advance could have been taken only from that ill-starred Mexican Loan in Europe

14

into which Napoleon had led him. Thus Maximilian lands in the country which he invades at the head of a foreign army, and, before he can realize a dollar from taxation or from her customs, fastens round her neck bonds which demand millions for their discharge, but for not one cent of which could the poor suffering nation be fairly and honestly held accountable in any court on earth. Nor is this all, nor even the worst of the financial wretchedness he brings to load her down in helplessness and long years of future misery. How is his costly court and administration and this reckless war he wages to be sustained by her?

This question was thoroughly examined by a competent Mexican statist, Señor Francisco Zarco, of Saltillo. The entire paper lies before us, but we have only room for his exhibit for the yearly demand and his conclusion upon it. After showing that the new empire had to begin its life with a debt of its own of $26,580,000 he comes to the question of the *annual expense* sanctioned (including interest on the $40,000,000 of the loan taken in Paris, Brussels, Hamburg, and Amsterdam), and develops the following table as the result to be met when the first year ends:

International obligations	$12,781,000
Interest on the home debt	1,200,000
The emperor's salary	1,500,000
Appropriation for the empress	100,000
Expenses of the imperial household	100,000
Worship and clergy, at least	5,000,000
The army, 40,000 men, same pay as French	8,000,000
Civil list, pensions, rewards, annuities, and secret service fund	8,000,000
A total annual expense of	$36,681,000

While Maximilian is perfecting this prodigious invention the empire would have to suffer a deficit of $20,681,000 in the second year of its establishment, as the revenue could not be more then than $16,000,000 annually, considering the state of war and other serious obstacles. How was this deficiency, threatening to increase, too, from year to year, to be supplied? That is the question. It is the death of the empire in its cradle!

CARLOTA, ARCHDUCHESS OF AUSTRIA,
and "Empress" of Mexico.

Señor Zarco pauses here to realize how Prince Maximilian, with his eyes open, could have been led into such a hopeless and helpless enterprise as this; and then, recalling the archduke's amazing confidence in the pope's blessings and in Napoleon's deceptive assurance that he " was going to seat him on piles of gold and silver instead of on a throne," Zarco laconically winds up his review of the doubtful situation with this remark :

> The pope's precious blessings may do well for eternal life, or help to make a passage through purgatory shorter, but nobody ever made a pot-pie out of them. . . . Sad will be the archduke's waking, when his frolic is over, and, looking for the promised "piles of gold and silver," sees only his poor wife's dressing-table.*

In confirmation of the accuracy of Señor Zarco's estimate it is well to note that the same ground was gone over in the following year by Mr. Middleton, secretary of the British Legation in Mexico, fully sustaining what Señor Zarco had anticipated.† No wonder that Louis Napoleon's minister of finance declined to make France responsible for so much, or that Francis Joseph refused to have part in such transactions, or that so early there arose the talk of "taking material guarantees," or even the proposals for " the sale of the border States of the empire, with the Juarists thrown in as chattels." Who could be the purchasers? The United States did not desire an extension of territory ; the Confederate States could not afford such luxuries, and France was not in condition to claim Sonora or Tehuantepec, much as she desired them, in satisfaction of the Miramar contract!

Sad and distracting as all this was there lay before the unfortunate emperor a more difficult duty to his employers, through which he was expected to go without shrinking so as to carry it to its full consummation. The clericals had laid out the work, and the pope had accepted the arrangement. Maximilian had no alternative, nor was he to be allowed any *modification* of

---

* *Diplomatic Correspondence of the United States*, 1864, p. 573. *La Accion*, June 18, 1864.

† *Papers Relating to Foreign Affairs of the United States*, 1866, part ii.

its execution. Those whose work he was to do laughed at his modern notions of a "limited monarchy" and "constitutional sovereignty." "The allocution of the holy father" against Mexico (already presented to our readers) was placed before him as his guide. It bitterly condemns the laws passed under the famous Constitution drafted by Juarez, and declares all the acts done under it to be "condemned, disallowed, and absolutely null and void, and of no effect!" The people, the Congress, and the government are sternly required to bow down before the demands of the pope and to surrender all that they had won, under the threat of "the penalties and censures of the holy see." Maximilian was to build up by its terms a model Romish State for this continent! At first he tried to conciliate the hierarchy, choosing the members of his cabinet from among the Conservatives, and endeavored to subjugate the national affairs to the papal will.

Let us now turn our attention to the broader facts of the Intervention now so fully launched in Mexico. It had more than armies in the field and navies on the ocean for the accomplishment of its purposes. It had its trained writers and pamphleteers, for the manufacturing of public opinion, stationed in New York and in the leading cities of Europe. All that related to the Intervention was put in the most flattering aspects, and the republic was misrepresented in a detestable manner, calculated to bring down the curse of "the God of truth" upon those who sought their objects by such means. The man who occupied a prominent position among the calumniators of the republic, and the special eulogist of the empire, has already been introduced to our readers. The Abbé Emmanuel Domenech bore the title of "Senior Director of the Press of the Cabinet of his Majesty the Emperor Maximilian," and was so appointed by Napoleon for very special service. He thus occupied a position between two thrones, was informed concerning all that passed, and had immense influence in molding public opinion in Europe in regard to the Mexican question. His whole heart was given to the work of representing unfavorably the character of the Mexican Liberals and to building up on this continent the European system of government, with its civil and religious despotism. In his volume, *Mexico As It Is,* he distinctly avows that the object of Napoleon in the Intervention was to checkmate the United States. Our transformation was to be accomplished by overthrowing the Monroe doctrine, and by "giving to the Latin race a career on this continent." That career was to change the republics of Central and South America into monarchies, and thus open the way to monarchize us. We will quote his words:

> If monarchy should be successfully introduced into the Spanish republics, in ten years the United States would themselves declare a dictatorship, which is a kind of republican monarchy adopted by degenerate or too revolutionary republics. (P. 226.)

He next asserts that the settled policy of the United States was to appropriate Mexico as their own, and then the rest of the continent. He adds:

> In starting with the principle, which is now a fact, that the American continent is the common property of the human race, and not of the shattered union of a single race, without title or right, at least to Spanish America and the Latin race, mother of all civilization, it evidently follows that the principle of the protection of Europe, at least in the seventeen republican States of South America, belongs to us (the French) and to all the powers of the Old World. We must protect the Latin race, and in order to protect it we must first take possession of the point menaced by the United States. (P. 230.)

This is the policy indicated by Napoleon's words on another occasion, when he said, "My object is to assure the preponderance of France over the Latin races, and to augment the influence of those races in America." * Domenech then adds:

> It would have been good policy to have recognized the Southern Confederacy, in order to make the work of intervention more speedy. (P. 240.)

While several times too he declares:

> The Intervention was a grand and glorious undertaking, which promised to be for France *the crowning glory of the reign of Napoleon III.,* and

* Mackenzie, p. 53.

for Europe and the world *the grandest enterprise of the nineteenth century.* (P. 223.)

These assertions were written after the utter failure of the Intervention, when the French had left Mexico, and this "Senior Director of the Press of the Cabinet of his Majesty the Emperor of Mexico" was trying to account for the overthrow of all these grand plans of his master, and felt so exasperated against Mr. Seward's diplomacy and the moral support which the United States had given to Mexico in her struggle. He knew far more than he chooses to tell us; but as he sits there, so disappointed and so disconsolate, with the ruins of their "empire" around him, the Confederacy collapsed and the United States right before him now more powerful and glorious than ever, we can well enough understand what he means when he writes this closing paragraph and says:

Behind the Mexican expedition there was *more* than an empire to found, a nation to save, markets to create, thousands of millions to develop; there was a world tributary to France, happy to submit to our sympathetic influence, to receive their supplies from us, and to ascribe to us their resurrection to the political and social life of civilized people. (P. 242.)

Yes, indeed, behind the Mexican expedition there was *more* to be accomplished than he here enumerates. He does not state what or how much more, but it is no longer difficult to surmise the rest, after these admissions of this deeply disappointed priest and the side lights that we now have from so many other quarters. The wicked conspiracy stands clearly revealed.

How blind to the teachings of history must have been this man! The Latin and the Teutonic races had been struggling for supremacy for generations on the European continent, and such battle-fields as Sadowa and Gravelotte had given the ascendency to Teuton civilization, and that of Sedan soon after consummated the great change. Three hundred years ago the Latin race held the wealth of the world in its possession, with

all that that wealth could command, and the fairest and most
fruitful realms of earth as its own, to show what it could do
for humanity. Refusing the blessings conferred by the Reformation and the open Bible, it bowed to papal despotism, and
now the result shows Italy, Spain, Mexico, and South America
far behind Protestant nations in enterprise, intelligence, industry, and virtue!

Yet this enemy of constitutional freedom was vain enough
to imagine that he could dazzle the world by holding up the
ignis fatuus of "Latin civilization" as something to be preferred
to Protestant and Christian freedom at the close of the nineteenth century. His folly provoked extensive examinations into
national statistics covering such questions as those of illiteracy,
crime, legitimacy, and prosperity, which were tabulated and
published, presenting comparisons as to the respective results of
the two systems of civilization. These various exhibits lie before us, but leaving those which present the sad results of Latin
civilization in regard to all the other points, we take up the
one that deals with *illiteracy* and present it for the consideration
of our readers. Eight countries of each civilization, aggregat-
ing each other closely in population, etc., are here compared.*
What a lesson do these tables teach!

ILLITERACY OF LATIN AND TEUTONIC POPULATIONS.

ROMAN CATHOLIC COUNTRIES. LATIN.	Population.	Per cent. of Catholics.	Per cent. of illiteracy.	PROTESTANT COUNTRIES.	Population.	Per cent. of Protestants.	Per cent. of illiteracy.
Venezuela.........	2,075,245	90.0	90.00	Victoria..........	1,009,753	73.0	.035
Austria-Hungary..	39,224,511	67.6	32.00	Sweden	4,682,769	99.0	.30
France.............	38,218,903	78.5	25.00	Switzerland........	2,846,102	59.0	.30
Brazil.............	12,922,375	99.0	84.00	Netherlands........	4,336,012	66.0	10.50
Spain	16,958,178	99.0	60.00	Germany..........	46,852,680	62.6	1.27
Portugal...........	4,708,178	99.0	82.00	Denmark..........	1,980,259	99.0	.36
Belgium...........	5,520,009	99.0	42.00	Great Britain......	30,066,646	93.3	11.00
Italy..............	28,459,628	99.0	61.94	United States......	57,928,609	86.4	9.40
Total.........	148,087,027			Total.........	149,702,820		
Average	....	91.4	59.64	Average	....	79.78	4.156

*From *Indian Witness*, 1890.

These figures, being fairly compared, teach very important lessons, especially at this time.   They show:

Sixty illiterates out of every one hundred is Rome's average where she has a fair chance.   Four illiterates out of every one hundred is the Protestant record, using round numbers in both cases.   That is, the Roman group turns out fourteen thousand three hundred and forty-three times as many ignoramuses as the Protestant group.   There is no doubt she has many profoundly learned men in her fold.   But Romish influence on popular education, where she is unhindered, is the influence of the upas-tree. It blights and kills.   Study the two Americas, North and South.   The one is under a pall of mental and spiritual darkness.   The other basks in the rays that shine from the common school and an open Bible.*

A study of the above table and the exhibits from which it was compiled draws out also three significant facts, as follows, on which our readers can reflect :   •

Fact number one: In Rome there are one pope, thirty cardinals, thirty-five bishops, one thousand four hundred and sixty-nine priests, two thousand two hundred and fifteen nuns, and three thousand monks.   Fact number two: In Rome over one hundred thousand of the population can neither read nor write.   Fact number three: The Romish Church says it is in favor of education, and wants us to allow it to have its own way in this matter, as it has had in Italy, Mexico, and elsewhere.

To leave the United States any longer unchecked all men would soon believe, as we do, in the charter of human rights, and millions would accept along with this the inspiring soul of our Anglo-Saxon civilization—the original and procuring elements of our elevation in the public school, the open Bible, and the evangelical creed.   To see this great country, with a territory larger than all Europe, grow up on such foundations as these, with the almost certainty within sixty years more of having a population, mostly Protestant, equal in number to the present population of Europe, standing then peerless in unity, influence, and power among the nations of the earth, remodeling the world by its high example, was a prospect that the papacy and the despotism of the Old World could not endure!   Hence

* William Wheeler, in *Pittsburg Christian Advocate.*

their hatred, their desperation, and their efforts for the over-throw of the United States as their ultimate object. General Grant so regarded it, and few men were more far-sighted than he. He was not deceived by the fact that Mexico was at first placed in the foreground, as if that were *all* that was aimed at. In the last pages that he ever wrote, when dying at Mount McGregor, this subject engaged his thoughts. He says:

> Under pretense of protecting their citizens these nations seized upon Mexico as a foot-hold for establishing a European monarchy upon our con-tinent, thus threatening our peace at home. I, myself, regarded this as a direct act of war against the United States by the powers engaged, and supposed as a matter of course that the United States would treat it as such when their hands were free to strike.*

Maximilian, having chosen his cabinet from among the Con-servatives, gave himself to the consolidation of his empire. But no man ever undertook to found an empire amid such dif-ficulties. Nor was this due to the fact that a state of war sur-rounded him, carried on by troops that were not under his control; nor was the chief obstacle the lack of funds for neces-sary expenses, nor in the conviction that the nation failed to come to his standard. All these and other discouragements loomed up before him, but the chief trouble he found in the heart and purpose of Archbishop Labastida in Mexico and the pontiff in Rome.

The archduke had been promised during his visit to the Vatican that he should receive the constant benediction of the holy father, and that a nuncio would soon be sent who would be his confidential adviser. Month after month went by, and no nuncio came, though Maximilian's embassador at Rome con-stantly urged the emperor's desires and expectations. He was left to the guidance of the hierarchy in Mexico (as was no doubt intended). They made their demands, backed up the allocution of the holy father for the *reversal* of all that the nation had done in the interest of self-government. This mediæval docu-

* *Personal Memoirs of U. S. Grant*, vol. ii, p. 545.

ment had been ignored by the Republican leaders, but Maximilian was now expected to carry out its entire provisions.

Chevalier, as a French Romanist, was amazed to find this allocution demanding of Mexico what the pope would not dare require of France or of any other European country, as they had all in succession done exactly as Mexico had done. It seemed to him that the pope was speaking with "a double voice" in thus condemning Mexico for what he allowed unrebuked in larger countries. What this distinguished writer expresses of his astonishment in finding the papacy taking this stand in the New World, and attempting to found a monarchy on doctrines rejected by the intelligence and conscience of all the old States of Christendom, so as to force into acceptance a type of political Romanism three hundred years behind date, gives the true interpretation to the events now opening before us. It explains why Maximilian failed, and how deliberately wicked were those who sent him to this continent to do such work, that they might spread by force their system of absolutism over lands already enlightened and free!

Maximilian soon realized the injustice of the demands of the allocution, and refused to carry out its decrees concerning religious intolerance, the recall of the Jesuits, and the restoration of clerical estates sold under former laws. To reverse this would cause a greater revolution than the one which had brought it about, the number of titles having multiplied into the thousands, and the nation would not justify the attempt. His cabinet stood with him in this resolution. Finally, by decree, on December 27, 1864, he ordered the continuation of the sales of the former ecclesiastical property. It now became the turn of the clericals to become alarmed, and they eagerly looked for the nuncio to head off the liberal tendencies of their emperor. In this matter and the consequences which resulted it was necessary to have evidence ready for every statement, as so many contradictory representations were made. The writer realized this need so imperatively that he returned to Mexico and spent several months looking for reliable information, and was fortunate in finding what was required. When the empire collapsed its archives fell into the hands of the republican government, and were made available. The *Official Daily Journal*, with voluminous correspondence, pamphlets, and books, explained what could not be otherwise understood. Some of these volumes contain the very information necessary at this point, and especially the one entitled *La Corte de Roma y el Emperador Maximiliano*. It furnishes the documents which passed between the two courts, and, besides, contains confidential letters written by Maximilian and Carlota, which shed full light upon the sad situation and the pressure brought to bear upon the unfortunate emperor to compel him to do the will of the pope and his curia; how Archbishop Labastida and the nuncio used their influence, almost to the point of torture, till at last, maddened by the persistent goading, Maximilian threw off their hold and broke with them, but too late either to save his empire or life, or the reason of the empress!

We first present the leading portion of the pope's letter, or protest, to Maximilian, dated October 18, 1864, which was expected to spur him to the duty before him. It reads:

SIRE: When in the month of April last, before assuming the reins of the new empire of Mexico, your majesty arrived at this capital in order to worship at the tomb of the holy apostles and to receive our apostolic benediction, we informed you of the deep sorrow which filled our soul by reason of the lamentable state into which the social disorders during the past few years have reduced all that concerns religion in the Mexican nation.

Before that time more than once we had made known our complaints in public and solemn acts, protesting against the iniquitous law called "The Law of Reform," which attacked the most inviolable rights of the Church and outraged the authority of its pastors, against the seizure of the ecclesiastical property, the dissipation of the sacred patrimony, and the unjust suppression of the religious orders.

For these reasons your majesty must have well understood how happy we were to see—thanks to the establishment of a new empire—the dawn of pacific and prosperous days for the Church in Mexico; a joy that was increased when we saw called to the throne a prince of a Catholic family, and one who has given so many proofs of religious zeal and piety. Equally intense was the joy of the worthy Mexican bishops who had the happiness of being the first to pay their sincere homage to the sovereign-elect of their country, and of hearing from his own lips the most complete assurances of his firm resolution to redress the wrongs done to the Church and to reorganize the disturbed elements of civil and religious administration. . . .

Under such auspices we have been waiting day by day the acts of the new empire, persuaded that the Church, outraged with so much impunity by the revolution, would receive prompt and just redress, whether by the revocation of the laws which had reduced it to such a state of oppression and servitude, or by the promulgation of others adapted to the suppression of the disastrous effects of an injurious administration. . . .

Ah, sire, in the name of that faith and piety which are the ornaments of your august family; in the name of the Church, whose supreme chief and pastor God has constituted us, in the name of Almighty God, who has chosen you to rule over so Catholic a nation with the sole purpose of healing her ills, and of restoring the honor of his holy religion, we earnestly conjure you to put your hands to the work, and laying aside every human consideration, and guided solely by an enlightened wisdom and your Christian feelings, dry up the tears of so interesting a portion of the Catholic family, and by such worthy conduct merit the blessings of Jesus Christ, the prince of pastors.

With this purpose, and in compliance with your own wishes, we send you our representative. . . .

We have instructed him to ask at once from your majesty, and in our name, the *revocation* of the unjust laws which for so long a time have oppressed the Church.

Your majesty is well aware that, in order effectively to repair the evils occasioned by the revolution, and to bring back as soon as possible happy days for the Church, the Catholic religion must, above all things, continue to be the glory and the mainstay of the Mexican nation, *to the exclusion of every other dissenting worship;* that the bishops must be perfectly free in the exercise of their pastoral ministry; that the religious orders should be re-established or reorganized, that no person may obtain the faculty of teaching false and subversive tenets; that instruction, whether public or private, should be directed and watched over by the ecclesiastical authority; and that, in short, the chains may be broken which up to the present time have held the Church in a state of dependence and subject to the arbitrary rule of civil government. . . . And, besides, you will give a striking example to the other governments of the republics in America, in which similar very lamentable vicissitudes have tried the Church; and, lastly, you will labor effectually to consolidate your throne, to the glory and prosperity of your imperial family.

Confidently hoping to see these most ardent desires of our heart, we send to your majesty and to your august spouse our apostolic benediction.

Given at Rome, in our Apostolic Palace of the Vatican, 18th Oct., 1864.

PIUS IX.*

The nuncio, Monseigneur Meglia, bearing the above letter duly arrived and was received with all the honors usually accorded to a messenger from the "holy see," and the anxious emperor hoped with his aid to arrive at some satisfactory arrangement notwithstanding the dubious character of the pope's communication.

On the day after the nuncio's arrival an interview was accorded, but Maximilian was surprised to find him quite noncommittal. It soon became manifest that his policy was one of passive resistance. He allowed Maximilian to do the talking, and when requested to represent the pope's views of the situation and of how the various *difficulties* were to be met and overcome, he would fall back on his phrase that he "had no instructions," the pope's epistle was enough, and marked the duty expected of Maximilian. No matter what were the barriers in the way of reversing the acts of the nation which the emperor pointed out, this was the invariable answer. The terms of the pontiff were not to be discounted; it was these or nothing. Maximilian soon realized that this policy of the nuncio was disrespectful and embarrassing to the last degree. So, hoping to develop some concession, he took these two propositions from his programme and handed them to the nuncio for his consideration:

First. The Mexican government tolerates all forms of worship which were formerly forbidden by the laws of the country, but concedes its especial protection to the Catholic, Apostolic and Roman, as the religion of the State.

---

* *History of the French Intervention in Mexico*, by E. Lefèvre, official documents taken from the archives of Maximilian, vol. ii, p. 16, etc. Brussels and London, 1869. *Appleton's Annual Cyclopedia*, 1865, p. 749, etc.

Second. The public treasury shall provide for the expenses of public worship, and shall pay its ministers in the same way and in the same proportion and under the same title as the other servants of the state.

The next morning the nuncio sent to Señor Escudero, the minister of justice, his conclusions upon them. We need only quote that on liberty of worship; he says:

Touching some of the points of this proposition, I have disapproved the first, on the tolerance of worship (other than Catholic), as *contrary to the doctrines of the Church*, and the desire of the Mexican nation, which is all Catholic.*

Just at this time Marshal Bazaine arrived in Mexico, and on understanding the situation at once took sides with the emperor and against the demands of the nuncio and hierarchy in the interest of the nation's right and peace. Maximilian seems to have exhausted all his patience in trying to bring this haughty ecclesiastic to a reasonable course, but in vain. The members of his ministry then tried, but they too failed. Last of all, the empress resolved to see what her negotiation with him could do to effect a settlement which the nation might be led to endure. Yet, after subjecting herself to his lordly manner, she too had to give up the effort. The emperor's advisers urged him to send an embassy, accompanied by two special councilors, to place the difficulties before the pope, in hope of a better understanding. The result showed that this effort was of no avail to turn the Roman curia from their purpose to force Maximilian to act according to the lines laid down in the allocution.

One more effort was made by the ministry to bring the nuncio to some reasonable ground, but it was equally unsuccessful. We present the closing paragraph of his reply, where our readers will be amazed to read the new and pompous title he confers upon the pontiff (italics ours):

I take the liberty to request that you will beg his majesty, who is devotedly attached to the holy father, to abstain from taking any steps contrary to the Church and its laws, that he may not add to the sorrow of

* *La Corte de Roma y el Emperador Maximiliano*, p. 52.

a pontiff so good, and who has suffered so much, and that he await the oracle of *His Beatitude*, which can only redound to the glory of religion and to the true welfare of his majesty the emperor.*

Tired out with the long delay and resistance of the nuncio, Maximilian resolved to act for himself and the nation, and proclaim a constitutional system for his empire, as the only chance of its establishment. So on the 27th of December, 1864, he wrote to his secretary of state:

In order to overcome the difficulties which have arisen regarding the so-called "Laws of Reform," we have purposed to adopt a means which, while it shall satisfy the just demands of the country, shall have for its object the re-establishment for all the inhabitants of the empire of tranquillity of mind and peace of conscience. To this end we endeavored when in Rome to open negotiations with the holy father as the universal chief of the Catholic Church.

The apostolic nuncio has come to Mexico, but, to our great surprise, has declared that he is not provided with instructions to negotiate. The difficult situation, prolonged now for six months, no longer admits of delay. It must soon be brought to a conclusion. Consequently we charge you to propose to us immediately measures whose object shall be:

Justice to all without respect to persons.

The legitimate interests created by the laws of reform to be guaranteed without hinderance to the measures necessary to be taken to repair the injustice and excuses to which said laws have given occasion.

The support of divine worship and the safeguard of religion to be provided for.

And, lastly, the sacraments and the other functions of the ecclesiastical ministry to be exercised throughout the empire free of charge.

In order to this you will submit to us at once a plan for the revision of the operation regarding mortmain property conveyed to the clergy.

Finally, you will be guided by the most ample principles of religious toleration, without losing from sight that the religion of the State is the Catholic, Apostolic Roman.   MAXIMILIAN.†

This outline of the emperor's policy startled the clerical faction, who had all along bitterly fought these very same liberal ideas when put forward by Juarez and the Republican party. The bishops sent a protest, bitterly condemning his action.

* *La Corte de Roma*, p. 53.   † *Ibid.*
15

Though it lies before us we can only quote one sentence show-ing its character. They say, "With regard to religious toler-ance we can see nothing that renders it, not to say urgent, but even excusable."

Cardinal Antonelli again wrote in the same strain, warning Maximilian not to fail to recognize his "*true interests and the real purpose of the mission*" which God had confided to him by obedience to the course marked out for him by the pontiff.

The manifesto of the bishops drew forth a reply from Maxi-milian that fell like a thunder-bolt in their camp. Boldly does he dare before the nation to tell them that their previous assertion of never having occupied themselves in politics is *un-true*, that they have resisted the State, producing revolutions and securing for themselves temporal possessions to the neglect and injury of their flocks. Even Juarez could hardly have lectured these guilty prelates more harshly than does this im-perial manifesto. He says:

You state that the Mexican Church has never taken part in political events. Would to God it had been so! But unhappy proofs exist which demonstrate clearly that even the dignitaries of the Church have flung themselves into the revolutions, and that a portion of the clergy have ex-hibited a very active resistance against the State. Confess, my well-esteemed prelates, that the Mexican Church, by a lamentable fatality, has mingled too much in politics and in affairs of temporal possessions, neg-lecting, in consequence, the Catholic instructions of its flocks. Yes; the Mexican people are pious and good, but they are not yet, for the most part, Catholic, in the true sense of the holy gospels, and it is not their fault. They need to be instructed, to receive the sacraments as the Gos-pel ordains, gratuitously. But Mexico will be Catholic, I assure you. Suspect, if you will, my Catholicism; Europe has long known my senti-ments; the holy father knows my thought. The Churches of Germany and of Jerusalem, that are to the Archbishop of Mexico as to me, bear wit-ness for me on that point. But, just and good Catholic as I am, I will be also a just and liberal prince. Receive the expression of my affection.

MAXIMILIAN.*

Maximilian was left by this with a very limited clerical sup-port. They put him in a position where no man with a con-

* *Christian World*, vol. xvi, 1865, p. 158.

science could succeed, and then fell away because he could not do what they demanded. What was said at Rome is reported by the well-informed editor of these confidential letters:

We know by the mouth of persons to whom Pope Pius IX. said it, not long since, that he considered the Mexican empire as a thing that could not last long. He said: "Maximilian commits many errors in Mexico. He cannot hold himself up. He should lean solely on the clergy and be governed by them alone. But on the contrary he asks things which cannot be granted to him, because they are contrary to his own interests." *

No wonder that, thus surrounded with uncertainty and gloom and clerical intolerance, the following sad and confidential letter to a friend was wrung from the heart of the Empress Carlota. It was written early in January, 1865, and gives the inside view of matters. She writes:

Your kind letter, I repeat, has caused me a double pleasure, because it is at once a proof of your remembrance and of the friendship which ever unites us. To speak frankly, we need friendship just now, because the situation is far from improving. I do not know if you are aware that the holy father, who has a merry disposition, says often of himself that he is "jettatore" (playful). So it is a fact that since his envoy set foot on our soil we have had nothing but disappointments, and can only expect soon to have many more. The clergy, wounded to death by the letter of December 27, are not easily appeased; all the old abuses elude the efforts of the emperor to remedy. We have here, perchance, not fanaticism, but such a dull and painful tenacity that I believe it impossible for the members now forming the clergy ever to form anew. What shall be done with them? That is the question. . . . It is a month now since we entered upon a serious crisis. If we pass through it victoriously the future of the Mexican empire is assured; if not, I know not what may come about. For the first six months every one pronounced the government perfect; now, touch any thing, interfere in the least, and you are cursed. . . .

The army is decreasing, and with it the material forces of the government. What is needed is soldiers. The Austrians and Belgians are very well in time of calm, but let the tempest come, and we see only red trousers (French). I believe it is going to be very difficult for us to pass through the first vital crisis unless the country is more extensively occupied

* *La Corte de Roma*, p. 89.

than at present. Every thing is greatly scattered, and it seems to me that instead of withdrawing in the least, it is necessary to increase. . . .

In case of need we can retire, as Juarez did, to a distant province, or return to the place from whence we came; but France must triumph, first, because she is France, and, second, because her honor is at stake.*

The nuncio's last effort was to address a communication to the emperor so dictatorial in character that the ministry resented it and informed the nuncio that he was presuming to interfere with matters which had not been submitted to him, which the government reserved for its own action. The minister of justice bravely stated to him:

Those who allow themselves to be carried away by an extravagant zeal and push the papacy beyond its limits and despoil it of its character forget the severe lessons of history.

And against the nuncio's efforts to subjugate the emperor to the will of the pope they say:

Maximilian, a citizen and member of the Christian communion, bows with respect and submission before the spiritual authority of the common father of the faithful; but Maximilian, the emperor and representative of the Mexican sovereignty, does not recognize any power on earth superior to his own. Consequently I cannot accept the thought which possibly may have escaped your excellency, in exalting the sovereignty and independence of the Roman pontiff, to the effect that the emperor should obey him as his subject. Allow me to respectfully suggest to you that said word is most improper.

The emperor and the pope have both received directly from God their full and absolute power, each within his respective limits. Between equals there can be no subjection. This Bossuet himself also says, and it is a precept taught by an authority superior to his, that of the divine code of Christianity.

We must now observe what Providence had been doing outside in aid of the cause of liberty in Mexico by restraining the enemies of that cause, who were so anxious to weaken the influence of the United States, so as to hinder her efforts to help Mexico.

* *La Corte de Roma,* p. 24.

CHAPTER VII.

THE sympathy of the Confederate States with the French
Intervention was a matter of anxiety to our government.
That sympathy became active along the line of the Rio
Grande when it resisted the republican force under General
Negrete and tried to intercept the bearers of dispatches between President Juarez and his minister at Washington, thus
acting as allies of the French emperor. Jefferson Davis tells
us of how much value they were to him and his cause. Napoleon ardently desired to recognize the Confederacy, and
urged the British government to join him in such recognition.
Mr. Davis says:

> Napoleon was anxious to go beyond this, and so was the pope of Rome,
> and they only. . . . Napoleon's efforts looking toward the breaking of
> our blockade met with refusal from England, the country whose artisans
> were the chief sufferers by the cotton famine.*

How hard Mr. Davis tried to induce the Emperor of the
French to authorize the construction of war-vessels for the
Confederate navy, in order to prey upon the commerce of the
United States, is well known to the readers of the work of Mr.
J. Bigelow, our minister to France in 1862–68.†

* *Rise and Fall of the Confederate Government*, by J. Davis, p. 618.
† *France and the Confederate Navy*, by J. Bigelow.

Far more important for us and for Mexico was the position taken by England in the question of recognition. Had she thrown her influence against us, long years might have been added to the sad struggle, or the North, for the sake of peace, might have allowed the South to go. This might not have ended the ' contest or saved republicanism in Mexico, but it might have compelled us, as Motley wrote,

To build a Chinese wall of custom-houses and forts across the widest part of the American continent, from the Atlantic to the Pacific, and keep an army of three hundred thousand men perpetually on foot, and a navy to match, in order to watch the nation on the other side of that wall and fight it every half-dozen years or so, together with its European allies. The present war, even if it lasts ten years longer, is cheaper in blood and money than the adoption of such a system.*

There were special difficulties in the way of England's complete understanding of our cause. The tory class was jealous of our democratic views and of our growing power, and was willing to see us weakened and divided. In regard to the position actually taken by the English government it is satisfactory to have the assurance which has lately appeared over the signature of Hon. W. E. Gladstone. He writes:

As a member of the cabinet of Lord Palmerston, and now nearly its sole surviving member, I can state that it never at any time dealt with the subject of recognizing the Southern States in your great civil war, excepting when it learned the proposition of the Emperor Napoleon III., and declined to entertain that proposition without qualification, delay, or dissent. . . . You will, I am sure, be glad to learn that there is no foundation for a charge which, had it been true, might have aided in keeping alive angry sentiments happily gone by.

This is decisive, coming, as it does, from the highest authority.

Among the leading journals of England, also, there were some which could rise above the superficial aspect of matters and do justice to the United States in their anticipation of the inevitable results, and this, too, as early as 1863. The London

* *Correspondence of J. L. Motley*, vol. ii, p. 77.

Morning Advertiser closed one of its able articles in the following strain:

It strikes us there is no doubt whatever that, in due season, Napoleon will have to meet the United States, for they will again be united, in the field of mortal conflict, to defend his right to interpose in a continent severed from his own empire by rolling oceans. It will be to no purpose to plead that a consul was insulted, or that a French merchant was maltreated. These are things for which it is easy to provide a remedy. Such things furnish no reasonable ground for the transfer of an army and the invasion of a country. In the event of such a war, which we take to be absolutely certain, Napoleon will find that his present glory is purchased with a fearful reversion. It will be found that the United States is at once training both troops and generals, and that, should the day arrive when they resolve to hurl the French into the Pacific, and to undo their work in Mexico, it will be found that they are once more confronted, in effect, with the steel of England—that of England's sons—and it will then behoove the emperor, should he not have changed his lodgings at the Tuileries long before, to mind what he is about.

The North was not alert in placing its cause before Europe; the agents of the Confederacy were more than a year in advance, manufacturing opinion favorable to the Confederacy, before our government realized the importance of having our cause rightly understood there. Our friends were at first denied a hearing in many leading cities. The biography of Henry Ward Beecher is interesting on this theme. He, among others, went to England determined to be heard, that the British public might be undeceived. After careful study he decided that the friends of the North were to be found among the middle class and the laboring people, with a few of the upper classes, the queen and prince consort, the Quakers, and religious folk generally.

In some of the meetings which he was to address, in Manchester and Liverpool especially, the mob would howl so that it was almost impossible to speak. When a lull occurred Mr. Beecher would throw in a few words, the beginning of some incident or story, till finally the pauses became longer as their attention was gained, and the very disturbers were soon found applauding the sentiments he uttered. His biographer gives us an account of what proved to be the greatest of his triumphs in changing, within two hours, prejudiced and mistaken foes of the North into its cordial friends and well-wishers.

This event occurred at Manchester on the 9th of October, 1863, in the Free Trade Hall, an immense room capable of holding from five to six thousand people. It was full. The great crowd at last consented to be quiet and hear Mr. Beecher for his cause. As he went on he realized that he was gaining all the time on their good-will.

Toward the close of his address a telegram was passed up to the chairman of the meeting, who read it, and then rose and said a word to Mr. Beecher, who paused, and the chairman then said to the audience, "I hold in my hand, just received, a telegram from London stating that her majesty has to-night caused the 'Broad Arrow' to be placed on the rams in Mr. Laird's ship-yard at Birkenhead." This meant a stoppage of those ships which were being built by Messrs. Laird for Confederate cruisers. The effect was startling. The whole audience rose to its feet and cheered and waved their hats, while women waved their handkerchiefs and wept. A howling mob was transformed into a friendly crowd, while hundreds hurried to the platform to shake hands with the eloquent defender of the North.*

The last page ever written by Mr. Beecher was on this subject. He had been requested by *The Century Magazine* to prepare an article on his English tour in 1863. On the morning after his death the unfinished article was found in his desk, the closing words of which were:

A more pathetic example of the heroism of the poor was never exhibited than in the case of the Lancashire weavers. They saw their industries wasting, their bread grew scarce, even their poverty became poorer, nor was there any sign upon the horizon that this cloud would soon pass away, and yet they held fast in their integrity; and, believing the cause of the North was the cause of the day-laborer the world over, they patiently bore famine and distress with fortitude until the day dawned. No other men among all English-speaking people gave a testimony of the love of liberty so heroic and so pathetic as the weavers of Lancashire.

* *Biography of H. W. Beecher*, p. 410.

Early in the year 1863 these working-men of Manchester sent Mr. Lincoln a letter, to which he gave a grateful and cordial reply. They, although greatly suffering in consequence of the war, sent him their sympathy; and in his reply he said to them:

It has been often and studiously represented that the attempt to overthrow this government, which was built upon the foundation of human rights, and to substitute for it one which should rest exclusively upon the basis of human slavery, was likely to obtain the favor of Europe. Through the action of our disloyal citizens the working-men of Europe have been subjected to severe trial for the purpose of forcing their sanction to that attempt.

Under these circumstances I cannot but regard your decisive utterances upon the question as an instance of sublime Christian heroism, which has not been surpassed in any age or in any country. I do not doubt that the sentiments you have expressed will be sustained by your great nation; and on the other hand I have no hesitation in assuring you that they will excite admiration, esteem, and the most reciprocal feelings of friendship among the American people.*

The attitude of the papacy during our civil war was a source of anxiety to our government and to thoughtful men. Individual exceptions there were, undoubtedly, but the general trend of the Roman Church was unfriendly. As if by a subtle instinct the lowest member discerned that he could have no interest in preventing the power of this nation from being crippled, or its prestige as the great Protestant republic destroyed. Their vote was generally thrown against the war, as the enemies of our country at home and abroad desired. For a contrast look at the various Protestant sects of our land, and see how loyally they rallied to the help of our government to the last hour of the conflict. There is a reason for this marked distinction; our downfall would have been the failure of Protestantism at its culminating point. It is a curious thing to compare the stern refusal of the Romish authorities in Mexico to permit the Protestant soldiers of the Intervention to have the use of a place of worship in which to hold divine service in the

* Holland's *Life of Lincoln*, p. 419.

city of Mexico with what so recently had happened in Rome.
Since 1850 Americans in the "Eternal City" had been in the
habit of meeting for a simple religious service on the Lord's
day in a private house.   Major-General Cass, our embassador
to Rome, and Mr. King, our consul, supported the service.   Even
singing was sometimes omitted to avoid giving the intolerants
a motive to complain.   But it became known that the service
was held, and a demand was made for its suppression.   The influence of our embassador with the papal government postponed
this for a time.   Rev. G. H. Hastings was pastor of the little
congregation.   When word reached this country that such a
service was held in Rome the bigoted Roman Catholic papers,
instead of advising that the service should have the same liberty
so fully granted to their Church in the United States, flamed up
and professed to be horrified at the idea of a Protestant service
in Rome!   The editor of the *Freeman's Journal*, the organ of
Archbishop Hughes in New York, wrote an article misrepre-
senting the service, which was in English, for English-speaking
people exclusively, and then adds: "Mr. Hastings can do
nothing, as the very first convert he should make he would be
kicked out of Rome, though Mr. Cass should bundle up his
traps and follow him." *   This written under the Stars and
Stripes of our glorious freedom!   "Kicked out of Rome!"   As
though liberty of conscience was not as dear in Rome as in
New York or London!   Yet if Cardinal Wiseman converted
an Englishman, who talked of "kicking" him out of London?
or Archbishop Hughes out of New York if he converted an
American?   Yet in this spirit of intolerance Pius IX. ordered
the suppression of the little Protestant service!   The "pious"
pope of the nineteenth century proved less tolerant than the
infamous Nero of the first.   The emperor of pagan Rome
allowed Paul to preach undisturbed in his "hired house" for
years, and "to receive all who came unto him," preaching and
teaching with all confidence, "no man forbidding him."   Even
the personal troops of the emperor were the objects of his

* *Christian World*, vol. ii, p. 203.

ministry—"the whole pretorian guard" (Phil. i, 3, Rev. Ver.) and "saints in Cæsar's household" sent their salutation to Christians every-where. No wonder that God so soon after ended this worse than pagan bigotry by wresting from the papal grasp the power which it so misused. Mr. Hastings had the right to re-open his services, and Victor Emmanuel provided that no man should "kick him out of Rome" for making a convert, but would have rather rejoiced had he made ten thousand in the city!

Ere this happened General Cass, returning home, was elected to the Senate of the United States from Michigan. The question of Romish intolerance toward the living and the dead came up, and he made a grand speech on the right of Americans to freedom of religious worship and Christian burial wherever they may be, and the question was referred to the Committee on Foreign Relations. A few weeks later, when Congress was taking the vote on supply, some one moved that the legation at Rome be left without an appropriation, which ended it, and thus another of the temporal dignities of Pius IX. passed away. This "sovereign," occupying such a precarious throne, was desperately anxious to exert his influence in our conflict, that he might "ride on the whirlwind and direct the storm" according to his own interests. The measure he tried first was by directing a pastoral to his archbishops of New York and New Orleans, authorizing them in his name to convey his wishes as "the administrator of the vicegerent work of Him who is the Author of Peace" to our "chief rulers and people." With their subordinate bishops as commissioners of the pontiff of Christendom they were to undertake to settle our national troubles by the utterance of platitudes from one who was not invited to interfere at such a time, when the appeal had been made to the Lord God of Hosts, to give the victory to the side which he espoused. There was a well-known cause for the war, but the pope did not touch it nor state the remedy—"to break every yoke and let the oppressed go free!" He did not send his commissioners with that message to Jefferson

Davis and so end the war by extinguishing its cause, if they would but obey him. No, the papal commissioners were to expostulate with Washington and the Northern people, not with Richmond and the South.

Remembering that Abraham Lincoln and the Congress are pointed at, let us note a few sentences from this papal pastoral :

Apply all your study and exertion, with *the people and their chief rulers*, to *restore forthwith* the desired tranquillity and peace.

Neither omit to *admonish* and exhort *the people and their supreme rulers even in our name*.

We are confident that they would *comply with our paternal admonitions*.

We have no hesitation, venerable brothers, but that, calling to your aid the services of your associate bishops, you would abundantly satisfy these our wishes, and by *your wise and prudent efforts bring a matter of such moment to a happy termination.**

How flattering must have been the self-conceit that could imagine that the "name," "authority," and "paternal admonitions" of this curious old man could "restore forthwith the desired tranquillity and peace!" Think of how Stanton and Seward would have listened to such an admonition to "bring a matter of such moment to a happy termination!" Or imagine the president's face if he had listened to these commissioners of Pius IX.! What a refreshing "admonition" would have been sent back "in the name of" Abraham Lincoln, importing that Italian priests should mind their own affairs and rectify their own great wrongs against civil and religious liberty, with some allusions to the unchristian treatment of Mr. Hastings at Rome, in the closing of the American chapel, with the ending of the legation at Rome thrown in as a clincher!

The archbishops did not deliver this message to those to whom it was nominally addressed, but it was given out to those who are not mentioned, and wrought its purpose by drying up the patriotism of many who took their politics as well as their religion from Rome, and had, it is feared, its effect in the draft riots in New York, and their attendant horrors a few months

* *Christian World*, vol. xiv, p. 357.

later.   Americans are not likely to forget Archbishop Hughes's
address to the lawless crowd while those ruins were still
smoking.

Instead of taking warning by the issue of this intermeddling,
the pontiff adopted a more open measure to aid the side he
favored.   Deeply disappointed that Napoleon could not be induced to go forward alone and recognize the Confederacy,
Jefferson Davis had been urging the pope to take the initiative
under the idea that the Catholic powers would follow his lead,
as they had done in generations past.   It is evident from the
letter that we are about to present that Davis was informed of
the communications sent to the archbishops, by copies sent to
himself.   On the 23d of September Davis wrote direct to the
pope, humbly thanking him for interfering on *their* side.   It
was sent by the hand of his agent, Colonel A. D. Mann, of Virginia, who in a dispatch to the Confederate secretary of state
gives an account of the interview with Pius IX.   Colonel Mann
informs his chief that the pope, in referring to "the rulers of
the other peoples of America," spoke of them as "Lincoln &
Co.," *and then furnished his recognition and reply, as follows:

LETTER OF PIUS IX. TO JEFFERSON DAVIS.

ILLUSTRIOUS AND HONORABLE PRESIDENT: We have just received
with all suitable welcome the persons sent by you to place in our hands
your letter dated 23d of September last.   Not slight was the pleasure we
experienced when we learned, from these persons and the letter, with what
feelings of joy and gratitude you were animated, illustrious and honorable
president, as soon as you were informed of our letters to our venerable
brothers, John, Archbishop of New York, and John, Archbishop of New
Orleans, dated the 18th of October of last year, and in which we have
with all our strength excited and exhorted those venerable brothers that
in their episcopal piety and solicitude they should endeavor with the
most ardent zeal, and in our name, to bring about the end of the fatal
civil war which has broken out in those countries, in order that the American people may obtain peace and concord and dwell charitably together.
It is particularly agreeable to us to see that you, illustrious and honorable
president, and your people are animated with the same desire of peace and

* *The Century Magazine*, May, 1891.

tranquillity which we have in our letters inculcated upon our venerable
brothers. May it please God at the same time to make the other peoples
of America and their rulers, reflecting seriously how terrible is civil war,
and what calamities it engenders, listen to the inspirations of a calmer
spirit and adopt resolutely the part of peace. As for us, we shall not
cease to offer up the most fervent prayers to God Almighty that he may
pour out upon all the people of America the spirit of peace and charity,
and that he will stop the great evils which afflict them. We at the same
time beseech the God of mercy and pity to shed abroad upon you the light
of his grace and attach you to us by a perfect friendship.

Given at Rome at St. Peter's the 3d day of December, 1863, of our
Pontificate 18.   Pius IX.*

Who that reads the above letter and his pastoral to his bishops
can doubt that the writer had already taken his side in the dis-
pute? His influence was thrown in favor of the South and
made official by his *recognition* of the slave-holding Confederacy and its illustrious and honorable president! The pope
was the only sovereign power that did recognize it. Expecting
that the Catholic nations would follow his lead, he looked around
to see France join his position, but she did not, nor Spain or
Austria. Having no navy to give effect to his recognition, he
had the mortification of knowing that his act was practically
worth nothing to the South, while it revealed his real preference
and position to the North and to the world at large.

On the 8th of December, 1864, the pope issued the *encyclical*
and *syllabus* (before referred to) addressed to all " patriarchs,
primates, archbishops, and bishops in connection with the
apostolic see throughout the world." They reiterate his denunciations of the errors and heresies of modern civilization,
and in virtue of his " apostolic authority" reprobate and condemn eighty " prominent errors," the holding of which (according to Pius IX.) cut off every one maintaining any of them
from Heaven's grace or hope of mercy. The errors enumerated
are not all that men hold or commit, but are those which assail
principles which the papacy regards as dangerous to itself and
the claims of its domination over mankind. The enlightened

* *Appleton's Annual Cyclopedia*, 1863, vol. iii, p. 830.

reader, when he examines this list, will be amazed to find that some of these "errors," so bitterly denounced, are cherished items of his religious and political creed, held by millions of the most intelligent men and women in this world, for the maintenance of which they would yield up life; such as "the right of private judgment," "religious liberty," "freedom of worship" for all, and our "public school system." There are some other "errors" mentioned, "errors" which Protestants would denounce as firmly as he does, such as infidel socialism, divorce, or denial of divine rule in human affairs; but, unlike him, we would not condemn nor persecute men for their opinions, but leave them to the just judgment of God.

These fanatical documents may be found in full in *The Papacy and the Civil Power*, Thompson, Harpers, p. 721, and also in *Rome and the Newest Fashions in Religion*, W. E. Gladstone, Harpers, p. 109.

To give a general idea of the character of this encyclical, we copy here, from an able summary which appeared at the time, some of its leading points, where the pope condemns in the most unequivocal manner the foundation principles upon which our government rests, and which Mexico and the South American States had imitated, and against which he calls up the millions of his followers in this land to unite for their overthrow:

1. The Catholic Church ought freely to exercise until the end of time a "*salutary force*, not only with regard to each individual man, but with regard to nations, peoples, and their rulers."

2. The best condition of society is that in which the power of the laity is compelled to inflict the penalties of law upon violators of the Catholic religion.

3. The opinion that "liberty of conscience and of worship is the right of every man," is not only "an erroneous opinion, very hurtful to the safety of the Catholic Church and of souls," but is also "delirium."

4. Liberty of speech and the press is "the liberty of perdition."

5. The judgments of the holy see, even when they do not speak of points of faith and morals, claim acquiescence and obedience, under pain of sin and loss of the Catholic profession.

6. It is false to say "that every man is free to embrace and profess the religion he shall believe true," or that those who "embrace and profess any religion may obtain eternal salvation."

7. The "Church has the power of *availing herself of force*, or of direct or indirect temporal power."

8. In a legal conflict "between the ecclesiastical and civil powers" the ecclesiastical "ought to prevail."

9. It is a false and pernicious doctrine that "public schools should be open without distinction to all children of the people and free from all ecclesiastical authority."

10. It is false to say that the "principle of non-intervention must be proclaimed and observed."

11. It "is necessary *in the present day* that the Catholic religion shall be held as the only religion of the State, to the exclusion of all other modes of worship." *

Protestants in general regarded the appearance of this remarkable document from the Vatican as a matter for thanksgiving. The liberalism of our times had led many people to suppose that Romanism had really altered for the better, and that while many of its writers still kept up occasionally the role of intolerance the papacy itself had abandoned its denunciations of the evangelical faith and its followers. But the appearance of this portentous paper and the signature at the end settled that fond notion for all the future. Kind-hearted, tolerant people awoke from their dream and felt pained to be obliged to admit that here was evidence to which they could no longer close their eyes, furnishing a complete refutation of all apologies that had been made in times past respecting that semi-religious political power, the Roman hierarchy.

Young Italy indignantly burned the document in the cities and villages, the press almost universally condemned it. Many ridiculed it as "post-dated by about three hundred years," and asserted that its author must have imagined himself living in the fifteenth century. Notwithstanding the liberal concordat that gives France special protection, Louis Napoleon was more indignant than any other ruler, as it helped to spoil his own

* *The Christian Advocate*, New York, 1865.

work in Mexico and arrested its progress. He took measures to make the pope realize his annoyance. So the convention between him and Victor Emmanuel was made closer in regard to withdrawing his troops from Rome, and leaving the pope to the care of his own people. More important still, an imperial decree appointed Prince Jerome Bonaparte vice-president of the privy council, and, in case of the emperor's death, regent of the empire, thus changing the regency from the Empress Eugénie (who was regarded as wholly at the pope's service through her confessor) and conferring it upon one who had ever been opposed to French patronage of the papacy, and who, as son-in-law to Victor Emmanuel, could be counted upon to favor the unity of Italy. This act was a terrible blow to the pope. This attempt of his to overthrow the leading, priceless privileges of modern civilization proved too much for even Roman Catholic nations, while free Protestant countries viewed it with contempt. There was the true ring of freedom in the speeches made in the parliaments of Italy, France, and other nations, rejecting the papal demand. The same was true of the legislatures of South America, and Mr. Bingham's grand utterance in the Congress of the United States will be long remembered. We quote a few sentences:

The syllabus is an attempt to fetter the freedom of conscience; it is an attempt to fetter the freedom of speech; it is an attempt to strike down the rising antagonism against every despotism on the face of the earth in the form of representative government, foremost among which is America, the child and hope of the earth's old age. . . . Do not the gentlemen know that the foremost of all the men reared in the faith of the Church of Rome . . . uttered the word while under the ban of Charles V., Leo X., and Henry VIII., which speaks to-day all over Christendom? I refer to the Augustine monk who found out for himself and repeated to mankind the great central fact which to-day possesses the enlightened mind of the nineteenth century, that no mitered head may, in "the grace of God," or of divine right, interpose his dark shadow between man and his Maker. Under the omnipotent power of that utterance every tyrant, whether in Rome or out of it, holds to-day the reins of power with a tremulous and unsteady hand, and the day is not far distant when the very throne of his power

16

shall turn to dust and ashes before the consuming breath of the enlightened public opinion of the civilized world, which declares for free government, free churches, free schools, free Bibles, and free men.*

Thus was God opening a door of hope to Mexico even by the
jealousies and self-seeking of their common enemy, and at the
same time preparing the way for their overthrow and for her
own deliverance.

This papal effort was a failure as far as even Maximilian was
concerned. Following the example of the other Roman Catholic governments in Europe, we find him and his cabinet forbidding the publication of the encyclical or any papal documents
without imperial sanction previously obtained. This involved
another collision with the clergy. The situation in the United
States, where the North was gaining victories and power, and
the attitude of the French Parliament and press had now begun
to add seriously to Maximilian's anxieties. Favre and Thiers
were friends of Mexican freedom, and resisted the emperor's
policy as far as they dare, while the following extract from one
of the leading French papers will show the public feeling:

It is a sad thing to say, but we fear for our cash-boxes that peace may
be made in the United States. The largest thorn we have in our foot is,
incontestably, the Mexican affair, which trammels our finances and causes
lively apprehension for the future. The equilibrium of our budget will
feel for a long time, we think, the Mexican expedition.

Maximilian had been trying to attract some of the Mexican
Republicans to his cause, but they quietly repelled his advances.
He now again took up the idea, which he had broached the year
before to Baron de Pont, of Brussels, that an interview with
President Juarez, if it could possibly be brought about, would
greatly facilitate "in smoothing the difficulties and enlightening
him (Juarez) on the views of the archduke for the good of the
country he is called to rule over!" This ridiculous proposal
Maximilian now carried out, guaranteeing to "Señor Juarez"
a safe conduct to any locality he might designate where the

meeting could take place, and was even foolish enough to intimate motives of personal aggrandizement to induce the president to consent to such a consultation! This incorruptible
ruler answered the letter of Maximilian with dignity, as the
republican chief of his nation. We quote its closing passages:

It is impossible for me to accede to this call; my official occupation
will not admit of it. But if in the exercise of my public functions I could
accept such an invitation, the public faith, the word and honor of an
agent of Napoleon, the perjured, would not be sufficient—of a man whose
safety reposes in the hands of Mexican traitors, and of a man who at this
moment represents the cause of one of the parties who signed the treaty
of Soledad. . . .

I had previously noted when the traitors of my country presented
themselves as commissioners at Miramar with the view of tendering
to you the crown of Mexico—sustained only by the treacherous proceedings of ten towns of the nation—that you had not seen in all these
proceedings any thing more than a ridiculous farce unworthy totally
of being seriously considered by an honorable and intelligent man.
You replied to these frauds by demanding the will of the nation, freely
expressed, as the result of its unanimous vote. Why, therefore, should
I not be surprised to see you come upon the Mexican soil when no
measures have been adopted concerning the conditions exacted? Why
should I now not be astonished when I find you accepting the deceits
of the traitors, adopting their language, decorating and placing in your
service bandits like Marquez and Herran, and surrounding yourself with
that low class of Mexican people? I have, frankly speaking, been greatly
deceived.

You tell me that peace will result from the conference we may have,
and with it the happiness of the Mexican people, and that the empire will
hereafter, by placing me in an important position, have the benefit to be
derived from my knowledge and the support of my patriotism. It is
true, sir, contemporaneous history registers the names of great traitors
who have proved false to their oaths, their promises, and their words,
who have betrayed their former history and every thing that is sacred to
the man of honor; that in all their betrayals of all human relations the
traitor has been guided by the infamous ambition of rule and the vile desires of pandering to his own passions and vices; but the present incumbent in the presidency of the republic, *who rose from the obscure masses of
the people*, shall bow poor and full of misery, if in the arcana of Providence
it is decreed that he shall so succumb, but complying with his oaths, and

thus meeting the hopes of the nation over which he presides, he will thus satisfy the inspirations of his conscience.*

What a lesson of uprightness and honor is here presented before a proud descendant of Charles V. by a humble republican of the Aztec race? This letter was published in the various state journals of the governments of South America, and became the subject of warm eulogies in their congresses.

In a proclamation of great courage the President of Mexico once more rallied the nation to put forth its best efforts to complete the work of their deliverance, closing with the words:

We have generous co-laborers within and without the republic who with their pens, their influence, and their money are aiding us, and they offer up earnest prayers for the salvation of our country. Redouble, then, your efforts.

Mr. Seward, conscious of the firmer ground occupied by the government of the United States, on the 16th of December, 1865, sent the following to our embassador at Paris:

It is the president's purpose that France should be respectfully informed upon two points, namely:
1st. That the United States earnestly desire to continue and to cultivate sincere friendship with France.
2d. That this policy would be brought into jeopardy unless France could deem it consistent with her interest and honor to desist from the prosecution of armed intervention in Mexico to overthrow the republican government existing there and to establish upon its ruins the foreign monarchy which has been attempted in the capital of the country. . . .
We should think it wrong, as well as unwise, on the part of the United States to attempt to subvert by force monarchical governments in Europe, for the purpose of replacing them with republican institutions. It seems to us equally objectionable that European States should forcibly interfere in States situated on this continent to overthrow republican institutions and replace them with monarchies or empires.
Having thus frankly stated our position, I leave the question for the consideration of France, sincerely hoping that that great nation may find it compatible with its best interests and high honor to withdraw from its aggressive attitude in Mexico within some convenient and reasonable

* *Official Journal of the Mexican Government*, Chihuahua, July 29, 1865.

time, and thus leave that people of the country to the free enjoyment of the system of republican government they have established for themselves, and of their adhesion to which they have given what seems to the United States to be decisive and conclusive as well as touching proofs.*

There was some cunning maneuvering to extract a promise from our government that his work in Mexico should be respected after the withdrawal of his forces (which was not conceded) before Napoleon fixed the date for the evacuation of Mexico by his troops. The deplorable condition of the Mexican empire was already revealed by Maximilian himself in the following confidential letter to a friend:

CHAPULTEPEC, *June,* 1865.

It is needful to confess frankly that our military situation is as *bad* as it can be. Guanajuato and Guadalajara are threatened. The city of Morelia is surrounded by enemies. Acapulco is lost, and provides, by its excellent position, an ever-open road to feed the war and supply the enemy with men and arms. There is no news from the North, so that the situation is, I suspect, very bad, worse than it was last autumn.

Precious time has been lost, the public treasury is ruined, confidence is disturbed, and all because they have been made to believe in Paris that the war has been gloriously concluded and immense territories, vaster than France itself, have been tranquillized. A large number of troops, believing these absolutely false rumors, have withdrawn, thinking that by so doing they would overcome opposition. An insufficient number of soldiers remains. On the other hand, we have been obliged to spend enormous sums on the bad auxiliary troops, and so this poor country has to pay French troops and hordes of natives troops who only cause disaster; and in recompense for these huge pecuniary sacrifices we see the principal cities of the country, the centers of wealth, threatened by daring soldiers who are generally known as and called "*thieves,*" but who manifest a remarkable military talent and take immediate advantage of the many weaknesses of our position. . . .

Speaking of Morelia reminds me of the promises made to me last year. They talked then, as now, about the rainy season, and said every thing would be over in the winter. A thousand promises were made to the unhappy towns, and though a whole year has gone by we find ourselves in just as deplorable a position as then.   MAXIMILIAN. †

* *Diplomatic Correspondence of the United States,* 1865, p. 451.
† *La Corte de Roma,* p. 27.

The contrast between the sad revelations of this letter and the roseate reports being published by clerical journals and such authors as Domenech, Flint, Elton, and others is most striking! The French troops openly boasted that they " were trampling the Monroe doctrine of the Washington government into the mud of Mexico under their horses' hoofs! " They did not report the increased number of towns where patriotic meetings were being held, nor that resources of trained men and munitions of war were being added to the republican army, nor that they themselves were being slowly driven back toward the capital. Nor did they report the facts that proved indisputably that, apart from the clerical party and compromised traitors, monarchy had no following in Mexico, and that its only prospect for a standing was in foreign soldiers and foreign money. Take a simple incident in illustration. Chihuahua, the largest city of north-west Mexico, was two or three times captured by the French, to prevent Juarez from having his government there. When military necessity obliged them to give it up it was at once re-occupied by a republican force and the president and his cabinet returned. On one occasion during the French occupation Señor J. Escobar, who had filled various responsible offices and had been secretary of legation at Washington (in 1861–63), attempted with others to celebrate the 16th of September in honor of Hidalgo. He was arrested, imprisoned, and made to sweep the streets with the common prisoners of the city. But the ladies and children turned out *en masse* and strewed flowers along his way as he performed his humiliating task.

Just at this time there was developed that feature of vacillation in Maximilian's character which resulted in acts so relentless and cruel that the world was horrified when the facts came out, and which have left his name covered with an infamy which will last as long as the French Intervention is remembered. Whether he made up his mind to pursue this terrorizing course of his own volition, or whether he was urged to it by the advice of other wicked spirits around him (such as Miramon and Marquez), has not been made clear. But he assumed the terrible responsibility, and so far as the human eye can now see the " sin lieth at his door " alone. God and man hold him accountable. Finding that he could not overcome the republican forces by fair fight, he concluded to deny them every right of war or belligerency, and advertised them as brigands to whom no mercy should be shown when captured. He was weak enough to suppose that decrees to this effect would paralyze their patriotism as they fought for their country's freedom against the rule of a foreigner. His first move to accomplish this purpose was to deny that they had a flag or a government to follow. Therefore, on the 2d of October, 1865, he issued a decree to the nation asserting positively that President Juarez had been driven out of Mexico and taken shelter in the United States; that this fact left them without a leader and turned them into bandits, whose assassination was therefore lawful and imperative in the interest of order as well as of the imperial government!

This decree was a *falsehood.* President Juarez never left the territory of Mexico for an hour while carrying on his government. He was then at Paso del Norte, and remained there till the 17th of the following June, when he and his cabinet removed to Chihuahua, two hundred and forty miles nearer to the capital.

Next morning (October 3) Maximilian issued another decree, known ever since and will be known in the future of Mexican history as " the Black Decree." It was drawn with great artfulness, so as to catch not merely the officers and men of the republican army, but also all who sympathized with them, or who afforded them the least help or comfort or information in the conflict. We here present, almost in full, the text of this inhuman decree :

We, Maximilian, Emperor of Mexico, by the advice of our council of ministers and of our council of state, do decree as follows:

Article I.—All persons belonging to armed bands or societies not legally authorized, whether of a political nature or not, whatever be the number of those forming the band, or its organization, character, or denomination, shall be tried by a court-martial, and, if found guilty, if only of the act of belonging to such a band, they shall be condemned to capital punishment, which shall be executed within the twenty-four hours next ensuing after the declaration of the sentence.

Article II.—Persons belonging to the band described in the foregoing article, when caught using arms, shall be tried by the *commandants* of the force making the capture, who, within twenty-four hours after such apprehension, shall cause the offense to be verbally investigated, hearing the offender in his own defense. A record of such investigation shall be written down, terminating with the sentence, which shall be capital punishment should the offender be found guilty, if even solely of the fact of belonging to the band. The commanding officer shall cause the sentence to be executed within twenty-four hours, allowing the culprit to receive spiritual consolation, and *after* execution of the sentence the said officer shall forward a record of the proceedings to the minister of war.

Article XIII.—The sentences of death rendered for the crimes described in this decree shall be executed within the periods stated, and *no petitions for pardon will be received.*

Article XV.—The government reserves the right to declare when the provisions of this decree shall cease.

Given at the palace in Mexico, October 3, 1865.   MAXIMILIAN.

To show how this barbarous decree worked we will refer to the first case that occurred under it. Only ten days after the signing of this decree the fortunes of war in the State of Michoacan threw into the power of Colonel R. Mendez several hundred republican troops. Among these were officers of the highest rank, such as Generals Arteaga and Salazar, six colonels, and a number of subordinate officers. They were surprised and taken prisoners in the town of Santa Anna Amatlan. They all belonged to the regular army and were gentlemen of education and profession, and had fought for the independence of their country from the time that the French entered Mexico. Arteaga, who had been twice Governor of the State of Queretaro, had reached the highest rank in the military service and was in command of the Army of the Center. He was a patriot without blemish, and enjoyed among friends and foes the highest reputation for honor and humanity. They were informed of the decree signed ten days before, and told that within twenty-four hours they would be executed!

But even Mendez, one of the most heartless of traitors, as his record shows, seems to have shrunk for the moment from thus immolating fellow-countrymen like these. He postponed the execution and wrote at once to Mexico to inquire from the emperor if this was really the purport of the decree, and whether he would be justified in sacrificing them according to its terms. Appended to this dispatch was a note by the officer next in command to Mendez, C. D. Barres, as follows. Speaking of the surprise in which the party were captured, he says:

This achievement, one of the most glorious of the campaign, does the greatest honor to Colonel Mendez and simplifies the task of pacificating Michoacan. Arteaga, without being a skillful general, is an honest and sincere man, who has distinguished himself more than once in his career by traits of humanity. Justice to the conquered.

This honorable indorsement appended to the dispatch of Mendez went before Maximilian and his military advisers for their action.

During the seven days that elapsed before the reply could reach Mendez every effort was made by French, Belgian, and Austrian soldiers who had been taken prisoners and humanely treated and exchanged by the forces commanded by Arteaga. Two hundred and fourteen of them, then within reach, signed a protest against the execution, and another communication by them was sent in haste to Maximilian. All in vain. On the 21st the reply arrived, a mandate from Maximilian through the imperial minister of war, that "*they were all to be shot, and directing Mendez in this and all subsequent occasions to execute the provisions of the decree to the very letter!*" There exists to-day the most abundant evidence of these atrocities; not merely the official documents of the diplomatic correspondence, which in themselves are ample, and other volumes written by these authors from personal knowledge, but also a special and illustrated record, prepared by leading patriots of Mexico. It is full of pathos, written in a calm, judicial spirit, which we will now present to our readers. The volume is very large and richly illustrated, and bears the title of *El Libro Rojo*. Translated it means "The Red Book," but from the deeds recorded it might well be entitled "The Book of Blood." Its thirty-three sketches include some of the acts of the Inquisition in Mexico, and with a few exceptions relate the torture and imprisonment inflicted on the victims of Spanish and Romish cruelty as well as those inflicted by the traitors to their country on its faithful patriots. The descriptions are written by leading public men of Mexico and are signed by the authors. The pictures of the later scenes are portraits of the sufferers, and add greatly to the interest of the book, which is very costly and now difficult to obtain. It is Mexico's voice in protest against the cruelties perpetrated on martyrs of her liberties. In compiling the account of the first terrible result of "the Black Decree" of October 3, we have availed ourselves, in addition to what appears in the official correspondence and this *Libro Rojo*, of the information gathered by Colonel Evans, who accompanied Mr. Seward through Mexico two years after the death of Maximilian and the restoration of the republic. The reception of Mr. Seward by the grateful Mexican people, for the noble stand he took from the first in their behalf, was of the heartiest character. His traveling companion was desirous of writing up the actual facts of the death of Generals Arteaga and Salazar, and had, at head-quarters, so near the time, the fullest opportunity for accomplishing his purpose.

On the evening of the 21st of October, when the decision arrived from the capital, the two generals were notified that they were to die the next morning. The information was received with serenity. They occupied themselves with writing to their families and arranging their worldly affairs.

A kind-hearted priest, the curate of the place, by the name of Ortiz, who may have sympathized with their cause—as a few of his class did—came and spent the last night with them, and grateful mention is made of the consolation they derived from this good man's exhortations and prayers during its hours. He also took charge of the letters written by the prisoners to their mothers, with some little gifts, and had them safely delivered. Certainly the world is richer that these two letters were preserved, to be read and admired by those who honor true nobility and unflinching courage in the trying hour. How tender is the dying remembrance of the brave man for the young sister, who seems to have derived her sobriquet of "the little Yankee" from the way in which she stood up for the United States as her idea of a true republic!

The following is General Arteaga's letter:

URUAPAN, *Oct.* 20, 1865.

MY ADORED MOTHER: I was taken prisoner on the 13th instant by the imperial troops, and to-morrow I am to be shot. I pray you, mamma, to pardon me for all the suffering I have caused you during the time I have followed the profession of arms, against your will. Mamma, in spite of all my efforts to aid you, the only means I had I sent you in April last; but God is with you, and he will not suffer you to perish, nor my sister Trinidad, *the little Yankee.*

Mamma, I leave nothing but a spotless name, for I have never taken any thing that did not belong to me, and I trust God will pardon all my sins and take me into his glory.

I die a Christian, and bid you all adieu—you, Dolores, and all the family, as your very obedient son, JOSÉ M. ARTEAGA.

The letter of his fellow-sufferer was equally worthy:

URUAPAN, *Oct.* 20, 1865.

ADORED MOTHER: It is seven o'clock at night, and General Arteaga, Colonel Villa Gomez, with three other chiefs and myself have just been condemned. My conscience is quiet. I go down to the tomb at thirty-three years of age, without a stain on my military career or a blot on my name. Weep not, but be comforted, for the only crime your son has committed is the defense of a holy cause—the independence of his country. For this I am to be shot. I have no money, for I have saved nothing. I leave you without a fortune, but God will aid you and my children, who are proud to bear my name.

Direct my children and my brothers to the path of honor, for the scaffold cannot stain loyal names. Adieu, my dear mother. . . . My blessings for all my friends, and receive the last farewell of your obedient and faithful son, who loves you much. CARLOS SALAZAR.

Postscript.—If affairs should change hereafter—and it is possible they may—I wish my ashes to repose by the side of my children, in your town.

Things did *change* in truth. When the cause for which they died triumphed the remains of these martyrs were brought to the capital and interred near President Juarez, within the sacred precincts where Mexico honors her illustrious dead.

No relaxation of this awful decree was allowed. The assassinations went on to the very last. A well-authenticated case, within three days of Maximilian's capture at Queretaro, is given. A young gentleman of the name of Mercado, son of one of the leading families of Queretaro, was taken by the imperialist force and was executed within the twenty-four hours, as prescribed by the decree. No chance for mercy, nor for the rectification of mistakes, where only a verbal examination was allowed, and where the officer in charge was forbidden to forward any petition for pardon! What fastens the responsibility for these assassinations upon Maximilian still more definitely was his act when, seven weeks after the deaths of Arteaga and Salazar, he rewarded Mendez in the following order, which appears in the *Official Journal* of December 9, 1865: "Colonel Mendez, the captor of Arteaga, etc., has been promoted to the rank of general on account of his recent services in Michoacan." *

At this very time—November, 1865—Marshal Bazaine was humanely exchanging prisoners at Mexico city with General Riva Palacios. No wonder that he and Maximilian quarreled, and that he hated Marquez and the church party. As commander-in-chief Bazaine concedes the rights of belligerents to the forces of the republican army, and calls their leader "general," and even compliments their humanity to the French prisoners in their power. His language to the republican general is a sufficient reply to Maximilian's cruel decree. He wrote:

I am pleased at the sentiments of humanity that have animated you in this affair. . . . I will not close this letter without thanking you for your kindness and attentions toward the prisoners.

---

* *El Libro Rojo.* V. Riva Palacios y Manuel Payno. Mexico, 1870. *Diplomatic Correspondence of the United States*, 1866, p. 460, etc. *Our Sister Republic*, by Colonel Evans, p. 324. Hartford, Conn., 1870.

MONOGRAM OF MAXIMILIAN,
With Medallions of his favorite Generals.

Here we present a monogram which appeared at this time as an attempt to popularize the empire. How far Maximilian was responsible for its publication does not appear. But the bad taste expressed in it is unaccountable. The emperor and empress are seen in the central medallion, their armorial bearings are above them, and on either side are their favorite generals, Miramon, Mejia, and Marquez—men infamous for their cruelties, and who were held in abhorrence, with good reason, in tens of thousands of homes in Mexico. Two of these men shared the fate of the emperor, and the other fled his country, too guilty to be forgiven. The lower portrait is Marquez, the one on the left Miramon, and on the right Mejia. These are the generals who attempted to build up the empire by the cruelties of "the Black Decree." The last place where we should look for such faces in conjunction with Maximilian and fair Carlota would be under the motto of the empire, "Equity and Justice"—a motto which they so utterly failed to evidence in this period of their unworthy career.

The year 1866 opened in gloom for the French Intervention. Napoleon's course in regard to discontinuing the monthly grant for the support of the troops, his dissatisfaction with the progress made, joined to solicitude as to the intentions of the United States government, with their war closing, and the immense resources now free under their command, were sad facts for the young couple that occupied the imperial throne. Then, in addition, Santa Anna was prowling round, like a beast of prey, anxious to enter Mexico and start an interest of his own. For this purpose he issued a proclamation to the nation, dated "Elizabethport, N. J., June 5." He had the hypocrisy to offer his services on the 21st of May to the republican government, which were promptly declined, because, as the reply runs:

As an officer he has been disloyal to all the governments that have employed him; that as the head of the government he has been disloyal to all the parties who have aided him to power, and that as a Mexican he has been lately disloyal to the cause of his country.

He then had the audacity to address our own government on the 10th of August, asking "support" in his enterprise and promising "gratitude to our government with a liberal hand" if thus assisted! He was promptly repelled by a note from Mr. Seward. His countrymen in New York, learning of his attempts, in their organization, "The Mexican Club," at once drew up a public protest against him and his plans as "the man who was always the foe of freedom, and who, abusing all honor, begged for Mexico the shameful foreign yoke she now wears." To commemorate this man's rejection Maximilian (to whom two years before he had actually offered his services) on the 12th of July issued a decree ordering the confiscation of all Santa Anna's property in Mexico. Ordinary mortals would have been extinguished after such a tornado of repulses. But Santa Anna was not an ordinary mortal, and he was yet to make one more dash for the destruction of his country's freedom before abandoning public life forever.

How desperate the state of the empire must have become by the 1st of July may be imagined by the sudden departure of the empress for Europe in the ordinary mail steamer of that month. Her presence was very essential to her husband. Indeed, she was regarded as the prop of the whole enterprise, from her superior mental ability, for Maximilian was confessedly weak and unreliable; yet this gifted woman resolved to face alone the risks of such a journey, including the danger to her life from the yellow fever at Vera Cruz (which rages worst in July), and to leave her husband alone and exposed in her desperate effort to save their empire. What she could hope to accomplish, which could not be done by correspondence, by her personal presence in Paris and Rome, may be inferred by glancing at the leading items of the situation. Foremost of all was the expressed intention of Napoleon to withdraw his troops, in view of the pressure from the United States. Of the small force that would remain to Maximilian, the republican troops, she feared, and rightly, would soon give a good account. Worse, if possible, than the loss of the French force was the warning from Napoleon that the monthly re-mittance for expenses must soon cease, in view of his own increasing military wants and the clamor of the French parliament and press against further outlay in a hungry enterprise which swallowed up such enormous sums, and yet yielded no return in either gain or glory. The course of Bazaine, also, in refusing to recognize Maximilian as his master in his military measures—for the marshal had a contempt for the Mexican emperor's judgment, and was wont to ignore him and decide what was to be done in view of his instructions from Napoleon—was keenly felt by Maximilian, as commander-in-chief of his empire, all the more as the French were losing ground and many of the important cities had been recaptured by the republican forces. Add to this the unrelenting pressure of the church party to force Maximilian to act in the line of the papal allocution, even to the point of reimbursing the Church for her losses by republican confiscation—and this, too, at a time when he was uncertain from whence the support of his own household was to come—and we have more than enough to account for the desperation that led Carlota to cross the sea to endeavor to relieve their distressing situation. She was determined to find out if her husband was really emperor, or merely a French agent, and she flattered herself that she could sway Napoleon to her views of the case. Alas! that "imperturbable reserve" and "ambiguity" for which the "sphinx of the Tuileries" was already known proved too much even for the accomplished daughter of that Nestor of kings, Leopold. The case was even worse for her than when she left Mexico, for on her way across the ocean she may have imagined that Austria had chastised Prussian insolence and would be therefore triumphant! What a terrible revelation must the fact of the case have been when she landed and *Sadowa's* result was told to her astonished ears! Austria's power dashed to pieces, Napoleon so involved that he was preoccupied with affairs with which, in their gravity to himself, the Mexican enterprise was a mere military excursion! The attention of French statesmen

17

could not be attracted to the Mexican empire save to wish that their emperor had never originated it. The conviction was now forced upon her that help from France was out of the question, and that if their empire could not stand when the French troops were recalled and French money ceased to flow to it, then it would be hardly worth while for her to make another journey across the Atlantic! The short answers received from Napoleon could not have been a total surprise to her, nor his evident desire that she should leave Paris, while he addressed himself to the question of withdrawing from Mexican affairs with as little loss to his prestige as possible.

There was only one thing for the distressed empress to do, and that was to place herself and their cause in the hands of the pope, from whom she fully expected sympathy and such help as he could give. But here begins the dark cloud which so soon enveloped her mental powers. Maximilian's failure to carry out the stern policy of the pontiff in regard to reversing the action of the Republicans, and, worse still, in having himself, under the pressure of the nation's necessities, ordered the renewal of the sale of the church property, had enraged the curia, so that the pope at first could hardly be civil to the empress, and it is said that he condemned her husband's conduct in very strong language. The deed for which he had excommunicated Victor Emmanuel could not be overlooked in Maximilian.

Of the sad events of the days since Carlota's arrival in Europe the following letter was a melancholy report for Maximilian. It was written by his embassador at Rome on the 18th of October, 1866:

Sire: I proceed to inform your majesty of the particulars of the unfortunate and unexpected events of the last few days.

We could imagine many calamities to Mexico, but it certainly never entered our minds, when we were admiring the courage and heroic valor of her majesty the empress at leaving your majesty, enduring the dangers and fatigues of the bad roads to Vera Cruz, in the rainy season, in the midst of yellow fever, crossing the ocean and coming as a great negotiatrix to demand rights for Mexico and the execution of treaties, that she would be so ungraciously received in Paris as to affect her majesty's mind so seriously.

The effects of her reception in Paris were so strong that she had to stop in Botzen, on the way to Rome, where she imagined herself surrounded by Napoleon's spies and traitors, who had poisoned her. On the 26th her majesty rested in Rome, and the next day we called to see his holiness. This interview was solitary, as your majesty knows is the custom with sovereigns, and lasted one hour and eighteen minutes.

At eight o'clock in the morning, on the 1st inst., her majesty the empress went out, and I waited for her till three. At five and a quarter I got a note from Cardinal Antonelli, telling me to come to the Vatican immediately.

I met Cardinal Antonelli much afflicted because her majesty the empress said she would not return to the hotel until Count del Valle, her lady of the wardrobe, and Dr. Benslaveck, who, she said, had poisoned her, had left the house. She wanted to stay in the Vatican all night, for fear of the persons mentioned, but I persuaded her to return to the hotel by 7 P. M. On entering her room she perceived the keys were not in the door. In fact, the doctor had taken them away secretly, as he afterward acknowledged, to lock her majesty in her chamber, in case of a violent attack. Missing the keys, she went straight back to the Vatican, and locked herself and Madame del Barrio in the room under the pope's, where she passed the night. . . .

I have lately heard that the idea of poison originated in Paris. While visiting the Tuileries lemonade was given to her majesty, and when she got back to the Grand Hotel she said that they had poisoned her.

I am sorry to learn at this moment that her majesty the empress even suspects the Count of Flanders, and will not see him. I regret to send you such sorrowful news, but it is my determination to let your majesty know every thing, as that is true frankness and loyalty and the true way to serve you.*

It may be that the embassador makes more of the facts against Napoleon than is fair, and less against Rome. We have a letter that throws great blame on the pontiff, but it is so bitter against him that we withhold it. Two facts, however, remain for consideration. In the first place, Carlota's chief hope was with the pope. She hoped he would relax the demands made on the Emperor Maximilian, which we know he did not do, and, secondly, that after her interview with the pope her malady

* *Diplomatic Correspondence*, 1867, part iii, p. 385.

assumed a greater intensity. The poor mind completely lost its
balance. Long after her husband was dead she insisted that
he lived, was triumphant in Mexico, and would soon come for
her. She was taken to her home at Miramar, where she has
since lived in solitude and desolation.

The pending departure of the French troops would leave only
the "Foreign Legion," composed of Belgic and Austrian volunteers, with such levies as the church party might raise, and
these were utterly inadequate to meet the republican troops.
Maximilian proceeded to invite foreign volunteers, under large
bounty and extra pay, from Cuba, Austria, and Egypt. Napoleon
had initiated the effort of this latter class; a battalion of them,
four hundred and forty-seven strong, was already in Mexico.
Maximilian desired a large increase of this Egyptian force, as
they were bold and ferocious fighters. Juarez appealed to
our government to put a stop to such an outrage, and Mr.
Seward ordered our representative in Egypt " to protest against
any more Nubian Negroes being supplied for Mexico, to subvert established political institutions or disturb society on the
American continent." It was bad enough to invite Austrians
and Cuban negroes, but to have Nubians, and probably savages
from the Soudan, to murder American republicans was worthy
of the traitor to freedom who originated it and wished to carry
it on when his own soldiers were recalled. The protest of our
government terminated the effort for volunteers from any quarter, and left Maximilian to be sustained by the foreign legion
and such adherents of the clerical party as would fight for him.

On the surrender of Lee, Maximilian attempted to strengthen
his position by offering great inducements to the leaders of the
South to colonize in Mexico. Colonel M. F. Maury (formerly
of the United States navy) was appointed " Imperial Commissioner of Colonization." The idea took amazingly with some
of the Confederates. It is amusing to read now the names of
those who shook off the dust of their feet against the United
States—men like Generals Sterling Price, John O. Shelby,
and Governor Isham G. Harris, of Tennessee, Judge Perkins,

Generals Hardman and Terry, of Texas, and many others. It is entertaining to see by their letters, published in the *Diplomatic Correspondence*, what facile converts to monarchy they made, and how they laud "his majesty the emperor," a "much-admired and praised monarch," and all that sort of thing! This is mingled with denunciations of the United States, and even contrasts drawn in favor of the order prevailing in the land where their "new and delightful homes" were situated! About two hundred such men availed themselves of the magnificent offers of land in some of the choicest spots of Mexico, and might have prospered, but their rough treatment of the Indian laborers soon produced a revolt which ended in the overthrow of this scheme and the return of nearly all to the once despised territory of the United States.* By October, 1866, Maximilian became apprehensive of coming disaster. His solitary condition, combined with the failure of French aid, led him suddenly to resolve to leave the country before the French could interfere. Some of his effects were sent down to Orizava, and, probably under color of having a change of climate for a while, he soon followed. From Orizava he opened communications with the commander of the Austrian war-ship *Dandolo* at Vera Cruz, informing him that he would leave Orizava at half past twelve on the night of October 31, and warning him to have his frigate ready by five o'clock the following afternoon, at which time he would arrive and embark at once. As soon as day dawned the captain went to the house of the French commander, Peyrau, and in confidence communicated the message he had received. The Frenchman was amazed, and, suspecting something wrong, immediately telegraphed the news up country to Marshal Bazaine, who was equally surprised. Bazaine at once telegraphed his orders to Orizava and Vera Cruz that the emperor and his luggage were to be detained, and also informed Maximilian that he had discovered what he was attempting, but that unless he abdicated in due form he would not let him embark. Indeed, Napoleon, despairing of success under the cir-

* *Diplomatic Correspondence of the United States*, 1866–67, p. 202.

cumstances, had already sent General Castlenau to advise Maximilian to abdicate, which he declined to do.

For some time past the French had had their suspicions that Maximilian was intending to deceive them, and Bazaine had been instructed how to act in such a case. They would not hinder him from leaving if he chose to do so, but it must be on the condition of abdication. The position taken was, " Maximilian abdicating, French engagements are at an end; but Maximilian going off without abdicating and renouncing the throne, and declaring, as they say was his intention, all ' his griefs against the French,' which then rested in a very bad position, immense ridicule would have fallen on them from which abdication would save them." * Into what a ridiculous situation would Maximilian's quiet escape have turned the entire situation had the French and the church party waked up next morning and been informed that their " emperor " had fled and was then a couple of hundred miles off upon the broad Atlantic ! The meeting between Maximilian and Bazaine was a stormy affair and ended in open rupture. The clericals, alarmed by the prospect of the complete failure of their plans, now came forward with offers of money and men if the emperor would only renew the struggle. To his council, who had been hastily summoned to Orizava, Maximilian propounded the question whether it would not be advisable for him to *abdicate ?* This raised intense excitement among the adherents of the empire. What occurred at the council, in view of the terrible results, shall be stated by one who stood on the side of Maximilian and the Intervention, and who had no partiality for the republican cause. This was Captain Elton, of the French army. The reader will not fail to note what he says of the character of the two clerical generals, now advanced to power, and the irresponsibility with which they were clothed. He says :

The council, influenced by their own dangerous position, and backed up by the church party, who were beginning to see that unless they could

* *Diplomatic Correspondence of the United States,* 1866, p. 392. *Historia de la Intervencion,* por. E. Lefèvre, vol. ii, p. 349.

succeed in propping up the tottering foundations of the empire their rights, property, and privileges must inevitably go by the board, opened their eyes at last to the absolute necessity of immediate action. They found themselves on the point of falling from the frying-pan into the fire —from the hands of an emperor inclined to conciliate them, and who only desired to establish some sort of order and morality among their ranks, into the power of the Liberals, who decidedly would make the very fact of their having invited Maximilian into the country an excuse for ill treatment and the legal plunder of what property still remained to them. Foreseeing all this, they made the first overtures of conciliation and offers of substantial aid to the imperial government, the bishops, as a commencement and guarantee of their good faith, giving thirty millions of piasters toward the establishment of the army. They declared it necessary for the preservation of order that the present government should be sustained, offering to Maximilian the services of Miramon and Marquez, the two champions of the church party, who, good soldiers and brave men, though not overscrupulous as to the means they employed, undertook to raise troops and lead them against the enemy, provided *they were given full powers and not rendered accountable to any authority for illegal acts.*

Finally Maximilian agreed to a compromise, and matters stood thus:

The services of Marquez and Miramon were accepted, full power being delivered to them to raise troops by whatever means they chose to adopt; every assistance in the way of supplies of arms and money was to be furnished them from all available resources, and authority was given them to raise forced loans whenever and wherever they pleased, in order to defray the expenses of their armies. On their side Marquez and Miramon engaged to march at once with all the men they could collect, and in conjunction with Mejia endeavor to strike an effective blow and recapture the towns and territory lost to the empire by the French evacuation.

It was thus by a curious combination of circumstances that the emperor again found himself trusting for support to this still powerful clerical party. From this moment the aspect of matters underwent a violent change, for suddenly his army sprang into new life, money was plentiful, and the two most able generals in Mexico declared for his side.[*]

The report of this fearful and irresponsible power thus conceded to these two generals to stamp out the republicanism of Mexico, together with their well-known character as compromised traitors, and the power of the Black Decree of October 3,

---

[*] *With the French in Mexico,* by J. F. Elton, pp. 177–181. London, Chapman & Hall, 1867.

to be wielded in full at their will, soon spread over Mexico
and carried anxiety and distress in all directions. It revived,
too, the recollection of the horror caused by the assassination of
Generals Arteaga and Salazar and their associates, and of many
others since. But the combination did not work just as the
church party and their agents expected. On the contrary, a
fearful revulsion set in, and men grew desperate in their resolve
to overthrow these murderous agents of Maximilian and save
their country. The homes filled with mourning under that
black flag that floated so freely now were not commending the
imperial cause to the men and women of Mexico.

General Grant had a broad view of the events transpiring in
Mexico, and a few lines written by him will show his opinion
of the crime perpetrated by Louis Napoleon against Mexico
and the United States. He writes:

The governing people of Mexico (the Imperialists) continued to the
close of the war to throw obstacles in our way. After the surrender of
Lee, therefore, entertaining the opinion here expressed, I sent Sheridan
with a corps to the Rio Grande, to have him where he might aid Juarez,
. . . much to the consternation of the (French) troops in the quarter of
Mexico bordering upon that stream. This soon led to the request from
France that we should withdraw our troops and to negotiations for the
withdrawal of theirs. Finally Bazaine was withdrawn from Mexico by
order of the French government. From that day the empire began to totter.
Mexico was then able to maintain her independence without aid from us.
. . . To erect a monarchy upon the ruins of the Mexican republic was
the scheme of one man, an imitator without genius or merit. He had
succeeded in stealing the government of his country, and made a change in
its form against the wishes and instinct of his people. He tried to play
the part of the first Napoleon without the ability to sustain that role. He
sought by new conquests to add to his empire and his glory; but the
signal failure of his scheme of conquest was the precursor of his own overthrow. . . . The beginning of his downfall was when he landed troops
on this continent. Failing here, the prestige of his name—all the prestige he ever had—was gone. He must achieve a success or fall. He tried
to strike down his neighbor, Prussia, and fell. The third Napoleon could
have no claims to having done a good or a just act.*

* *Personal Memoirs of U. S. Grant*, vol. ii, p. 545.

CHAPTER VIII.

Mr. Seward's firm stand compelled Napoleon to name the date for the evacuation of Mexico as the 11th of March, 1867. His subsequent effort to defer this until November was met with a firm refusal. In a brief dispatch Napoleon's embassador was informed that our government would expect a satisfactory answer, pending which a "military force of observation" would "await the president's directions." This was perfectly understood at Paris. The whereabouts of Sheridan were known to Napoleon. Therefore the French army withdrew at the appointed time, the republican forces following closely and occupying the cities which they had held for the empire.

Some of our people, who were not acquainted with the cruelties now daily perpetrated in Mexico by these wretches, were inclined to regard Mr. Seward's present pungent messages as rather risky and dictatorial. But our government was fully informed by Señor Romero, and was aware that the protection of the French should be withdrawn in order, among other reasons, that these frightful assassinations might end. Even at the risk of war, the United States must at this point help Mexico. By the 1st of May only a single line remained in the power of the empire, the other parts of the country being occupied by the republican forces. The city of Mexico and Queretaro, with the towns between, were still held by the Imperialists, but the intervening towns were soon taken by the advancing Liberal army.

The capital was defended by the traitor Marquez, while Maximilian, with his foreign legion, occupied Queretaro. The last outside conflict was near Zacatecas, where Miramon was defeated by General Escobedo. Miramon returned and joined Maximilian at Queretaro. General Escobedo laid siege to that city with an army of about twenty-five thousand men, while General Porfirio Diaz surrounded the capital with a sufficient force. Escape from either city was practically impossible, and famine soon began its horrors in each place.

Amid the difficulties existing in the way of obtaining reliable information at this most important point it seems very fortunate that, in entering upon the final scenes of the Intervention, we are not left to rely upon fragmentary or unreliable statements, but that full evidence in regard to the capture, trial, and execution of Maximilian became available to us. There lie before us as we write a dozen volumes on the subject, six of which were written in the interests of Maximilian and the Intervention by competent authors who were with him and who did their best for their subject. These authors are: Dr. Basch, the emperor's physician; Alberto Hans, one of his prominent officers; Count de Kératry, his friend; the Princess Salm-Salm, wife of a member of his staff, who was devotedly attached to the interests of the empire, and the two lawyers who defended him at his trial, M. Riva Palacios and M. de la Torre. On the other side we have the republican cause defended in the volumes of E. Lefèvre, H. Frias y Soto, the report of the attorney-general and the secretary of the court-martial, by Lorenzo Elizaga, and Rafael M. de la Torre, in the *Libro Rojo*. Two of these are chiefly occupied in traversing the statements of the defenders of the empire and pointing out their inaccuracies. Additional facts have been gleaned from the works of Schroeder and Colonel Evans, from the *Diplomatic Correspondence*, and from the newspaper *La Sombra de Arteaga*, of Queretaro, which published a full account of the trial as it progressed.

We condense the information regarding the eventful night of the 14th of May. Maximilian had become convinced that further resistance was hopeless. A report received that day from his generals, Miramon, Mejia, and Castillo, on the situation had greatly excited him and led him to doubt the fidelity of these officers, and to fear that they were disposed to save themselves by abandoning him in the emergency if an opportunity occurred. He concluded he would do well to save himself, leaving them to their fate. To this end he selected Colonel Miguel López, once a republican officer, but who had during the empire been in his service in command of the regiment of the empress, and had served him faithfully. Maximilian took him into his confidence, directing him secretly to open communications with General Escobedo, the commander-in-chief of the republican army. This López did, from La Cruz, the part of the works which he defended, and was admitted to the headquarters of the republican army during that night. He delivered his message, which was that Maximilian, despairing of the situation, was ready to surrender at once if his own life was guaranteed and Escobedo would grant him leave to pass out, escorted by fifty horsemen only, to make his way to the coast, and so leave Mexico, offering the most solemn assurances never to return. General Escobedo could not accede to such a proposition. Maximilian must surrender unconditionally, leaving the government to judge of his case. His willingness to avoid further bloodshed was, however, appreciated by General Escobedo, who, having learned from the admissions of Colonel López the desperate condition of the besieged, took measures at once for a final assault upon the city in order to force surrender.

López returned to Maximilian with the news of General Escobedo's firm refusal, which greatly depressed the emperor. That he could have entertained the hope of such a concession, under such circumstances, is another evidence of his weakness of mind. But he had judgment to realize, after reflection, that he had seriously compromised his dignity and his honor by a proposition which contemplated the forsaking of those who had followed his fortunes and risked their lives in his service. It was, however, kindred in character to his attempt in the previous year to escape by the *Dandolo* from Vera Cruz, and to leave the French to face the results of his desertion of their cause.

The next morning before daylight the final assault was made, one column entering without resistance at the post held by López, who assured his command that further resistance was useless, and they therefore quietly surrendered. In the confusion Maximilian mounted a horse and tried to escape, but was surrounded and captured at the Cerro de las Campanas. General Corona soon came up and guarded Maximilian until the arrival of General Escobedo.* One account states that Maximilian drew his sword with formality and said, "I am Maximilian, Emperor of Mexico, and I surrender to you," offering the sword. On which Escobedo replied, "No, Maximilian, you are not Emperor of Mexico, and never were, nor could you be against the will of its people." He intimated to his chief of staff to receive the proffered sword, to be sent to President Juarez, and directed that Maximilian should be taken to suitable quarters and carefully guarded. The archduke (we shall henceforth call him) was apprehensive that he would be insulted, and even appealed to General Escobedo that he "should be treated with the consideration due to a prisoner of war;" to which Escobedo replied, "That you may trust to me." Later in the day Maximilian asked for a private conversation with General Escobedo, and renewed the request which Colonel López had already negotiated in vain. The short reply, "I am not permitted to concede what you request," ended the matter.

A telegram was at once sent to President Juarez, informing him of the capture of the city and that the archduke, Miramon, Mejia, with fifteen other generals and over eight thousand men, were made prisoners. Head-quarters were soon crowded by those who had been cruelly bereaved and injured by the Imperialists, who demanded the fullest penalty upon them for the crimes they had committed. General Escobedo asked for in-

---

* *Official Documents from the Private Archives of Maximilian*, by E. Lefèvre, vol. ii, p. 390. Brussels and London, 1869.

structions from the supreme government. The president had come from Chihuahua to San Luis Potosi, which was within a comparatively short distance from Queretaro and connected by telegraph. He directed that a court-martial should try the three chief offenders, that every thing should be done legally, and that full publicity should be allowed. A competent lawyer of Queretero, Señor J. M. Vasquez, was retained on behalf of Maximilian, and on the expression of his desire for additional counsel he was allowed to name three of the leading lawyers of the capital, Señores E. M. Ortega, M. Riva Palacios, and R. M. de la Torre, who were at once sent for, and in company with the Prussian embassador, Baron Magnus, and other gentlemen were permitted to pass out of the besieged capital by General Diaz, and forwarded under a safe conduct to Queretaro. Maximilian was well and ably served, and at the close expressed his gratitude for their efforts to each of those lawyers. Seven officers constituted the court-martial, the president being Colonel Platon Sanchez, with Colonel M. Aspiroz as attorney-general.

After consultation, having approved the line of defense, the lawyers agreed that two should remain to conduct the case, and the other two should go to San Luis Potosi, to be near the government to use all the means available there in the interest of the archduke. Maximilian claimed that the court-martial was incompetent to try him, and that another month of time was necessary for a full defense. He declined to appear in court, and was not compelled to do so. His generals, Miramon and Mejia, were there, but his seat between them remained vacant. Morning and evening his lawyers reported proceedings and received instructions. He addressed a long and rather rambling statement to the commanding general, in which he argued his views for a change of tribunal, the withdrawal of the present charges, and the formulation of others to be held before a "tribunal of the federation," and made use of the case of Jefferson Davis to indicate the course which should be pursued toward himself, though he was unable to find facts to institute a parallel between them. It was replied that Davis did not cross the ocean as a foreigner at the head of a large army to overthrow the government of a country and establish a monarchy on its ruins, and this without a declaration of war, and then, when fair fighting could not accomplish his purpose, raise the black flag, and, by the authority of a mere decree, send those who fell into the hands of his agents to death within twenty-four hours, without tribunal or appeal for mercy, and not even allow their names to be reported till after their execution had taken place! The parallel could not apply.

It seems that he supposed himself to be in better case than that of Jefferson Davis, as the following curious extract may show that he claims exemption from punishment on the ground " that the death penalty can be imposed upon the traitor to the country in foreign war, but it is clear that Maximilian, not being a native of Mexico, but of Austria, the charge of traitor to the country cannot be made against him ; therefore he is in the case, not as an exception, but of the general rule." He concludes his rambling statement in this curious style :

Having time for no more, I conclude by requesting, first, that you declare yourselves incompetent, and, second, that you command all proceedings being instigated against me in accordance with the law of January 25, 1862, to be withdrawn; third, that the ordinary council of war created by that law be not appointed nor installed, as I do not recognize but do deny its competence, declining now its jurisdiction under any form ; fourth, and last, that reports be made to the proper persons for ultimate effect; and, finally, I will say that, in accordance with the frankness of my character, I should not conceal from you that a copy of this letter is in the possession of the consul of Hamburg to be transmitted, when possible, to the diplomatic corps of my court. (Signed) MAXIMILIAN.*

The archduke misunderstood his surroundings. He expected rough treatment, which did not come. On the contrary, he was treated courteously and reasonably provided for as to all personal comforts. Sufficient time was allowed for preparation before the trial began ; all legal forms were duly observed as

* *Memorandum sobre el proceso Del Arquiduque Fernando Maximiliano de Austria,* by M. R. Palacios and R. M. de la Torre, part ii, p. 3. Mexico, 1867.

the procedure developed in his case; he was free from all annoyance, and was fairly and even deferentially treated. So that, with his views, he was liable to imagine that his personal safety was not much compromised. In fact, Maximilian had a contempt for what Mr. Lincoln called "the common people," and was disposed to believe occasionally that this "democracy" would not dare to lay its hand upon his life. Somewhat harsher treatment, it might be, than Jeff Davis received might be dealt in his case. He might be expelled from Mexico, but no worse was at first feared by him. His "rank" and royal blood would surely protect him. This fond notion clung to him to within forty-eight hours of his death, as we shall see, and then only the earnest assurances of the two generals who were to die with him could convince him that his life was in danger!

These are the chief counts of indictment on which he was tried:

1. The first charge against Maximilian consists in having lent himself to serve as an instrument to the intervention of the French in the political affairs of Mexico.

2. The title of emperor with which he came to support the aims of the French Intervention. The illegality of this title makes him a usurper of the rights of a sovereign people.

4. That of having disposed, with the violence of armed force, of the interests, rights, and life of the Mexicans.

5. The kind of war which he made upon the republic, together with the French; the responsibilities which he contracted on account of the excesses committed by the French army in the name of the emperor.

6. In having himself made war with foreigners, subjects of powers who were not in war with the republic.

8. The publishing of a decree on October 2, 1865, in which he falsely asserted that the republican government had abandoned the national territory, from which falsehood he deduced that the republican forces had no known flag, that they were bands of robbers, and should be treated in accord with the decree he issued on October 3.

9. In having continued the war after the French army had withdrawn from Mexico; with the aggravating circumstances of having surrounded himself with men who had made themselves famous for their crimes in the civil war of Mexico, and of having continued to employ means of violence, death, and destruction until he fell, surrendered at discretion in this town.*

The claim for a change of tribunal was not allowed. The procedure was being impartially applied to the two generals indicted with him, and could not be altered in favor of him who was the chief of the rebellion against the constitutional government of the country. The trial lasted two whole days. All that his able lawyers could do, under the circumstances, for his defense was done, but in vain. They could not lift the weight of guilt against the nation which pressed upon him. They tried mercifully to insinuate that "the Black Decree" of the 3d of October was intended merely to be used *in terrorem*, to frighten men into submission to the empire, but not to be made effective or to last too long. When the evidence of this was demanded it could not be furnished. The very contrary was proved by evidence found in the prince's archives, giving the names of leading Mexicans who had perished under his decree, even up to recent dates, as in the case of young Mercado. The decree was never suspended and never disavowed. The families of these victims were demanding stern justice on the man whose warrant sent them to swift and illegal execution, and also upon the guilty wretches who were the willing instruments of this sanguinary decree—Marquez, who at Orizava stipulated that he should be clothed with irresponsible power; Mendez, who was rewarded with higher rank after the assassination of Generals Arteaga and Salazar; and Miramon, whose cruelty was continued to the very last of his power, and many others. The nation, in sympathy with the bereaved families, maintained that these men were murderers, and demanded how

* *Causa de Fernando Maximiliano de Hapsburgo*, Attorney-General Aspiroz, p. 289. Mexico, 1868.

much better was the prince who gave them the authority and rewarded their acts.

Some facts brought out in the trial were regarded as grave crimes against the republic, as even the formulated charges. The regency was one of these. When leaving the capital to take command at Queretaro, on the 7th of March, in view of the contingencies of war and his liability to death, Maximilian drew up a decree of regency. Though the French army had withdrawn from him, though he had seen the whole republic (save two cities) rise up against him, and in spite of the fact that the legations of Spain, France, Prussia, Belgium, Italy, Austria, and England at the capital had united in an earnest protest against continuing the hopeless struggle, and against the rule of the reckless men Maximilian had put in power, he determined to arrange for a continuation of this bloodshed! He actually provided that in the event of his death a *regency* should come into power, naming as its members Señores Lares, Lacunza, and General Marquez, with two vice-regents to fill vacancies. This regency was to carry on the war and the government until a Congress was assembled. As this could not be called until the war was over he thus aimed to prolong this arbitrary power even when he was in the grave!* The horror of the nation on the discovery that he intended to continue thus the cruel struggle was greatly intensified by the fact that the universally hated traitor Marquez was to be elevated to the position of ruler over the people he had so bitterly wronged. The "Decree of Regency" was published in *La Sombra de Arteaga* at Queretaro, during the progress of the trial, and no doubt aided in his condemnation.

"The Inviolability of the Constitution of Mexico," an article accepted by the nation in February, 1857, filled a very decisive position in this trial. The language runs thus:

Article 128. This Constitution shall not lose its force and vigor even if its observance be interrupted by any rebellion. In case that, by means of

* *Documentos Oficiales*, E. Lefèvre, vol. ii, p. 446.

18

such an event, a government shall have been established contrary to the principles which it sanctions, immediately upon the people recovering their liberty its observance shall be re-established, and according to its provisions and the laws which have been framed in virtue of it they shall be judged, as well those who have figured in the government emanating from the rebellion as those who have co-operated with it.

The law of January 25, 1862, was for the defense of this article of the Constitution, and it was shown on the trial that Maximilian was entirely without excuse. He knew all this before he left his home for Mexico, President Juarez having warned him to this effect. Here is the evidence of Mr. Lerdo, secretary of state, to the two lawyers who, in an interview, hoped to break the force of the application of this heavy charge against their client:

Having so reasoned with Mr. Lerdo, he replied that the law of January 25, 1862, was a pre-existent law, and that its several dispositions must have been perfectly understood by the archduke before coming to Mexico. He also stated that an agent of the constitutional government, Señor Don J. Teran, a gentleman well known for his intelligence and integrity, went to Miramar and demonstrated to the archduke the dangers of the enterprise of founding a monarchy: that there was no basis in Mexican society upon which to set up such a project, as Mexico had become too thoroughly republican in manner; that democracy had become profoundly rooted in the New World and was thoroughly wedded to republican institutions; that those who might uphold an empire were not those who had a secure following in the country, nor could they ever command sufficient elements to make it popular; that it would lose its prestige from the fact of the necessity of an intervention (French) to uphold it, and would fall flat as soon as that support was withdrawn.*

On ascertaining that his brother was to be put upon his trial, and hoping to help the solution of the case somewhat in his favor, the Emperor of Austria communicated, through the United States government, to President Juarez that he was "ready at once to reinstate Maximilian in all his rights of succession as archduke upon his release and renouncing forever all

* *Memorandum sobre el proceso Del Archiduque*, etc., por M. R. Palacios y R. M. de la Torre, p. 29.

projects in Mexico." In addition to this, but with a more grave sense of the prince's danger, the Queen of England and the Emperor of the French appealed to the United States government "to use any legitimate good offices within its power to avert the execution of Prince Maximilian." These messages had to be very cautiously and deferentially communicated, for the government and people of Mexico were then in no mood to tolerate any thing that looked toward outside dictation in any shape or form, in the duty which the nation in that hour owed to itself and its future. Mr. Seward carefully and delicately "requested Mr. Romero, if compatible with his convictions of duty, to make these sentiments known in a private and confidential manner to the republic of Mexico."

Sixteen months previous, on learning of the execution of Generals Salazar and Arteaga, Mr. Seward had asked that the influence of the French government might be thrown against the decree of the 3d of October, and the merciless manner of its application, but the imperial minister declined to recognize any responsibility for France in the matter, saying that "Maximilian was an emperor like any other, and that France had nothing to dictate to him respecting his conduct." *

A similar answer might have been returned by Mr. Seward, but it was not so done. The offer of the restoration of Maximilian to his rights of succession did not reach President Juarez until after his death, but was of no moment in the case.

The court-martial commenced at eight o'clock on the morning of the 13th of June, and on the afternoon of the 14th the verdict of guilty was pronounced against Maximilian, Miramon, and Mejia, and they were sentenced to be shot on the morning of the 16th. Three days were added to this by President Juarez. An appeal for pardon was made by the two leading lawyers for Maximilian, but was refused in these terms :

This application for pardon, and others presented with the like object, having been examined with all the deliberation which the gravity of the

* *Documentos Oficiales recogidos en la Secretaria Privada de Maximiliano*, por E. Lefèvre, p. 402.

case requires, the president of the republic has been pleased to determine that he cannot accede to them, because the weightiest reasons of justice and the necessity of assuring the peace of the nation are opposed thereto.

There are things that a powerful and trusted president may not dare to do, and to pardon this crime against a nation's life was one of them. He and his cabinet knew better than their critics the limitations of mercy in the case. They realized the deep indignation, on account of the acts of the so-called empire, which the developments of the trial had produced in the heart of the nation, and knew the danger which a failure of justice might involve to the future of the republic. Mr. Otterburg, then our embassador to Mexico, in a dispatch informed Mr. Seward that the government was aware how the Conservative party had been talking, and "giving evidence of a determination never during the prince's life to cease from advocating his claims to the crown of Mexico and from disturbing the quiet of the country by agitating his return." *

No act of injustice was desired or contemplated on the popular side. Reduced to the last analysis, the foreign archduke had shot their generals, taken in arms against his government; had they not the right to shoot *him*, taken in arms against theirs? Their first emperor (Iturbide) had pledged his honor, when they exiled him and provided him with an ample pension, never to return from Europe or trouble them again; but, under encouragement from this same Conservative party, he had violated his word, and what assurance could they have that their second emperor would not violate his and return to plunge the nation once more into the horrors of a civil war?

After hearing the appeals made to them for pardon on behalf of the archduke it was decided that it could not be granted, and the reasons were given by the supreme government of Mexico in justification of its conclusion that the sentence against Maximilian should be carried out. Señor Lerdo, the secretary of state, in reply to the lawyers of Maximilian, when

* *Diplomatic Correspondence of the United States,* 1867, part ii, p. 434.

they came to reiterate their appeal for pardon for their client, gave this decision of the cabinet in the following language:

The pardon of Maximilian might be very detrimental to the country, because, owing to the well-known vacillating nature of his character, there could be no great probability that he would abstain from another attempt. Civil war can and should end with the reconciliation of the parties; but in order to do this it is necessary that the government remove the chief disturbing elements that might lead to a probable uprising. In this process justice fulfills one of its functions. The country would call us to an account for an indulgence that might expose it to the dangers of a renewed agitation. The government has thought, previously and at present, with the greatest caution, upon the dangers of pardon as well as upon the consequences of death; and if it denies pardon, be assured, gentlemen, that it believes it demanded by national sentiment, justice, public welfare, and the need of giving peace to a country which, without this new element of monarchy, had had sufficient disturbance for the last fifty years. Who would believe that men of revolutionary intent, to whom the progress of society, its advance, its institutions, are a sin and only serve to excite them to revolt, would settle down to quiet? Who would assure us that Maximilian would live in Miramar, or wherever Providence might take him, and not desire to return to a country by which he believes himself chosen? What guarantees could the sovereigns of Europe give that we should not have a fresh invasion to sustain the empire? Europe is not willing to see in the Mexicans men worthy to form a nation. It holds the very poorest idea of us; it thinks that republican institutions are an idle dream of the demagogues. It is not impossible that Maximilian might be induced to again attempt the founding of an empire. The fatal inspirations which animated the Intervention might be revived, and the governments of Europe, under the pretext of civilizing us (in itself a blow at true morality) would arm new legions, which, though composed of foreigners, would carry the Mexican flag in order to establish again the power of him whom they called emperor. Consequently the pardon would be a misfortune for us, and to the disdain and dissatisfaction with which such a grant would be viewed we would have to add the stirring up of hatred between the parties and the cry of treason upon all sides. One party would constantly turn its eyes toward Miramar, and a fresh violation of the principles of public justice would be imminent. Then might the independence of Mexico pass through greater dangers than those which it has recently passed through at so great a cost. The existence of Mexico as an independent nation must not be left to the will of the governments of Europe. Our reforms, our progress, our liberty must not stop at the wish of any foreign sovereign who might take a notion to father an emperor who should endeavor to regulate the amount of liberty or servitude he thought best to bestow upon us. The life of Maximilian might be the excuse for an attempt at a viceroyalty. . . . The return of Maximilian to Europe might be a weapon for the calumniators and enemies of Mexico to bring about a restoration and the overthrow of the institutions of the country. For nearly fifty years Mexico has pursued a policy of pardon and leniency, and the fruits of that policy have been anarchy among ourselves and loss of prestige abroad. Now, or never, may the republic consolidate itself.*

We now reach a point in this sad history which for Maximilian's own sake we heartily wish he had never allowed to occur. We refer to his active co-operation with some of those friends whom the government had allowed to have access to him to promote his comfort, and whom he desired to use in order that he might make his escape and avoid execution. Foremost of these was the Princess Salm-Salm, wife of Maximilian's first aid-de-camp. This prince was a German, a sort of "soldier of fortune," who had taken part in our civil war, and while in the United States had made the acquaintance of this lady, a Roman Catholic of Georgetown, D. C. Though an American, she seemed to take wonderfully to the theory of the divine right of kings and its kindred doctrines. After their marriage, at the close of our war, she accompanied her husband to Mexico, where he went to offer his services to Maximilian. On the capture of the archduke she attached herself to him to look after his wants, which was kindly permitted by the commanding general, under the express condition, however, that she was not to take advantage of her position to do any thing illegal in regard to the prisoner. But her book, soon afterward published, shows how lightly these engagements rested upon her conscience. She relates all her efforts, including the most questionable ones, where untruthfulness and deceptive measures were used by her, without a blush, and even glories in them in view of her object, which was to secure the archduke's escape by some means or other.

* *Memorandum sobre el proceso*, etc., Riva Palacios y de la Torre, p. 58.

Her first effort was with the president, going to San Luis Potosi to interview him. Here she evidently did her best. But David's desire and prayer in one of his psalms, "Let integrity and uprightness preserve me," was so thoroughly embodied in Juarez's character that she could not shake his sense of duty. She returned to Queretaro to pursue her plan for the escape. Every thing depended upon a Mexican officer, Colonel Palacios, who had charge of the prisoners. She delayed her visit at his quarters that afternoon till it became dark, and then, professing fear to go home alone, requested him to escort her, which he did. On reaching the house she asked him to enter and be seated. She adroitly gained his confidence by talking of his wife and newly born baby, and of their necessities in the future, and then came to what she wanted to propose. She first made him swear "by the life of his wife and babe" not to divulge to any one what she was about to confide to him, even if he rejected her proposition. Little suspecting the character of the affair, he gave his engagement to respect her secret. She then drew from her pocket two drafts on the imperial family in Vienna for $100,000 each, to be paid to him and the other colonel (Villanueva) on condition that the archduke should regain his liberty by their means. These drafts Maximilian had prepared and signed, and had given the princess his signet ring to be handed to Colonel Palacios, to be returned to the archduke at once by the colonel as a token that "all was right." The amazed colonel hesitated as he held the drafts in his hand. He was poor, and here was what seemed to him boundless wealth for his wife and child in all their future. But he hesitated. The princess assured him it was for his country's good to do this thing, and not stain her record with the blood of the archduke, and, besides, he "would not be asked to do any thing; he would have only to turn his back and close his eyes for ten minutes;" others, who would be ready outside, would arrange for the rest of the escape. He declared himself unable just then to accept the drafts or the ring. He would reflect upon the matter in the night and give her his decision in the morning.

She had $5,000 in gold ready for the escort, who stood ready
to move in the matter. Greatly to her disappointment, the
whole affair must be left over until the next night.

The distracted colonel went to bed, but not to sleep. At
midnight he rose, went to head-quarters, and divulged the plan
to General Escobedo. At daylight the next morning a carriage
was stationed at the door of the house where the Princess Salm-
Salm was staying. Dr. Basch and the other two foreigners in
the secret had been roused from their beds and sent off with the
assurance that if they returned sooner than five days they would
be shot. The lady was allowed to sleep until she was ready to
rise, but on coming down-stairs she was ordered to enter the
carriage to be driven to head-quarters. The account of the interview is as follows:

In polite but sarcastic tone, General Escobedo observed that the air
in Queretaro did not seem to agree with me, that it was, indeed, very
bad. I assured him that I never felt better in all my life; but he
insisted that I did not look well at all! He had a carriage ready and
an escort to take me to San Luis Potosi, where I should feel much better.
I told him I had no desire whatever to go there, but thanked him for his
kindness.

Seeing that she was not willing to accept the opportunity of
withdrawing, and unable to endure her insincerity any longer,
General Escobedo spoke out and upbraided her dishonorable
conduct and her wicked attempt to bribe his officers and bring
him into an embarrassing position. She tried to defend herself,
and insisted on remaining in Queretaro. Orders were then
given for her departure.

She was permitted to return to her lodgings and pack her
valise before leaving, and an officer in citizen's dress was detailed
to escort her to San Luis Potosi. Before leaving her lodgings
she had a scene with the captain, who was ordered to keep
her in sight until she left. In her anger she drew her re-
volver to shoot him on the spot. She might well remark after
she cooled down and reflected on her whole conduct, as she
does in closing the account:

If I consider what I attempted to do, and that I was by no means yielding, I must acknowledge that I was treated throughout with great forbearance and courtesy, not only by General Escobedo, but also by Señor Juarez and his secretary and all Mexicans with whom I came in contact.*

Flight and bribery and falsehood, all sanctioned or concurred in by himself, are very unworthy associations to have identified with Maximilian's name and last hours, especially when we recall the high standard of honor by which he wished to be known and remembered.

On her arrival in San Luis Potosi the princess resolved to make one more of her efforts to save the archduke's life. Notwithstanding the serious way in which she was compromised in the effort for Maximilian's escape, the president consented to give her the interview she sought. We will let her describe it in her own words. She writes:

The last day before the execution had come; the emperor was to be shot on the following morning. Though I had but little hope, I was resolved to make another effort and to appeal once more to the heart of that man on whose will depended the life of the emperor. It was eight o'clock in the evening when I went to see Mr. Juarez, who received me at once. He looked pale and suffering himself. With trembling lips I pleaded for the life of the emperor, or at least for delay. The president said that he could not grant it; he would not prolong his agony any longer; the emperor must die to-morrow.

When I heard these cruel words I became frantic with grief. Trembling in every limb and sobbing, I fell down on my knees and pleaded with words which came from my heart, but which I cannot remember. Mr. Juarez tried to raise me, but I held his knees convulsively and said I would not leave him before he had granted his life. I saw the president was moved; he, as well as Mr. Iglesias, had tears in their eyes, but he answered me with a low and sad voice, "I am grieved, madam, to see you thus on your knees before me; but if all the kings and queens of Europe were in your place I could not spare that life. It is not I who take it, it is the people and the law, and if I should not do its will the people would take it and mine also." (P. 223.)

Her failure led her to regard Maximilian ever after as "my august martyr."

* *Ten Years of My Life*, by the Princess Salm-Salm, pp. 211–220. New York, R. Worthington, 1877.

Even at this late hour Maximilian was still clinging to his belief that the Republicans would respect his *rank* and not dare to execute him. His companions tried to undeceive him. They were confined in rooms which were so situated that by looking diagonally across they could see each other's faces as they stood at their windows. Colonel Evans was taken to the premises by a gentleman who was present when the following took place. He writes:

When my friend entered they were conversing. Miramon called out to Maximilian :

"Emperor! I beg you to prepare for death; I tell you they will certainly shoot us!"

Maximilian replied confidently, "No; they dare not do it; they may shoot you, possibly, but Don Benito Juarez will not let me be killed. He will send me either to the United States or to Europe!"

Miramon replied, "I assure you that you are deceiving yourself; they will certainly shoot us all !" (P. 235.)

This assurance decided the matter in his mind; he accepted the inevitable, and the rest of the time was devoted mostly to the remaining duties in a spirit which exhibited the better attributes of his nature. All efforts for pardon or escape had closed, the 18th of June had come, and at seven o'clock next morning he was to die. He addressed a telegram to the president pleading for the life of Miramon and Mejia, and that "he might be the only victim." He then addressed a copy of the following note to each of the lawyers who had defended him :

MY DEAR SIR: The energetic and valiant defense which you made on my behalf demands that I assure you of my profoundest gratitude for your noble and generous service, which is deeply graven upon the heart of yours affectionately,   MAXIMILIAN.

And this letter to the president :

QUERETARO, *June* 19, 1867.

SEÑOR BENITO JUAREZ : Being at the point of death, in consequence of having wished to make the experiment whether new political institutions would put an end to the bloody civil war raging for so many years in this unhappy country, I will give up my life gladly if by its sacrifice peace and prosperity shall come to my new country. Profoundly persuaded that nothing permanent can be founded upon a soil soaked with blood and torn by violent commotions, I implore you in the most solemn manner, and with the seriousness becoming my position, that my blood be the last to be shed, and that the same perseverance (which I was glad to recognize and fully esteemed in the midst of prosperity) with which you have defended the cause that has triumphed shall consecrate that blood to the noble task of reconciliation and of founding in a permanent and stable manner peace and tranquillity for this unhappy country.*

(Signed)   MAXIMILIAN.

It will not be wondered at that some sad reflections clouded his closing hours that morning, and that he was unable to keep them to himself. Here he was left to die in a land of hostile strangers without a word of sympathy from either those to whom he stood related beyond the seas, or from those whose purposes he was brought here to work out; lured to his death by clericals whom he had tried so zealously to serve, but who, because he found it impossible to serve them in the despotic manner and extent which they required, had here left him alone and friendless to face all the consequences. Perhaps harder than all this to endure was the bitter remembrance of that imperial pair at Paris who had first fired his ambition to attempt the impossible task, and made it still more impossible by withdrawing the help on which they led him to rely; and, last but not least, to recall for the closing time on earth that supreme and "infallible" papal power whose will he was sent here to accomplish under the assurance that "the blessing and protection of Heaven" would rest upon the enterprise to which he was consecrated, and perpetuity be granted to the dynasty and empire which he came here to found!

Dr. Basch, his physician, tells us how bitterly he remembered Padre Fisher, who had done so much to induce him to change his mind and return to the capital to renew the war when he was already at Orizava on his way out of the country, and who had promised to proceed at once to Rome and complete the

* *Memorandum sobre el proceso*, etc., p. 74.

concordat which he had sketched, and whose mild requirements would, Maximilian was assured, have satisfied the nation and saved the empire; and yet, swayed by other influences, proved false and returned from Rome without it. Here are the doctor's words as to how Maximilian regarded this man in these last hours in that prison in Queretaro:

"Father Fisher, with his concordat, has lied and has deceived me." These words of the emperor are the most implicit condemnation of the conduct of the father.*

There were also some others to whom, no doubt, some of these dying thoughts were given. Frias y Soto has voiced this remembrance, and we quote him, merely adding in explanation that the closing name refers to Eugénie, the French empress, by her original title. She was understood to have promoted zealously the origin and establishment of this Catholic empire in Mexico. The author says:

In that supreme moment of the life of one sentenced to death a century is lived.

Maximilian must have thought then, with that instantaneous vision that can hardly be conceived, of the insane woman at Miramar; of Napoleon, feeling, on learning of this execution, terror touching his heart and the red wave of shame covering his face, ... and of Rome cleansing with her papal mantle the drop of blood that would spatter from the scaffold at Queretaro on the infallible tiara of the pope-king.

That look encompassed all the drama the secret thread of which began to be woven in the boudoir of "La Montijo."†

At seven o'clock on the morning of the 19th of June, 1867, the execution of Maximilian, Miramon, and Mejia took place outside the walls of the city, at a place called the Cerro de las Campanas. The archduke bore himself with dignity in the terrible ordeal. We give a picture of the spot where they suffered and the little memorial erected upon it. His body was carefully embalmed and laid away for future disposition.

* *Recuerdas de Mexico,* by S. Basch, M.D., 1870, p. 74.
† *Notes on De Kératry's Elevation and Fall of Maximilian,* by Frias y Soto, 1870, p. 370.

CERRO DE LAS CAMPANAS,
Scene of the execution of Maximilian, June 19, 1867.

It is now our duty to refer at this point to the case of a man who through all these intervening years has borne a heavy and peculiar cross for this dead prince—a man whom the world meanwhile had branded as guilty of the charge, until two years since, when the highest authority in the case has proved him innocent of the alleged wrong. The reader will remember the effort made by Maximilian to gain the sanction of the republican general for his own escape before the capture of Queretaro. That request was, of course, refused. But in brooding over the situation the archduke soon realized how unworthy was that attempt, and how fully he had compromised himself with his adherents there and with his friends in Europe should the facts become known. In order to save his own credit, he resolved upon a course that was to load down an officer in his service, for long years to come, under the terrible charge of "treason and dishonor." The world has widely heard of Colonel López "selling his imperial master and his cause to the Republicans for thirty thousand dollars," and so ending the war in Mexico. For nearly twenty-four years he bore the weight of this burden, conscious all the time that he did not deserve it, but was merely the scape-goat of Maximilian's vanity. So satisfied were even good men that he richly deserved this opprobrium that when he died a few months ago (April 26, 1891) one of the leading Christian journals of this country headed an editorial on his departure with the words, "The Mexican Judas." It now is evident that this man's mouth was closed in his own defense from a sense of honor by which the archduke had bound him to save his own credit for courage and chivalry. People simply accepted the charge without examination, and López bent down under it; and so the years went on until the burden became intolerable. That life which was to have been, by the stipulation imposed upon him, the *limit* of his silence, was most mysteriously prolonged. At last, when feeling his own end approaching, and not being willing to go into the dark grave of a traitor, he made his appeal to the one man in all this world who could clear his character by an honest statement of the facts, to do him this justice without further delay.

If those who regarded his crime with such detestation and shrunk from him had reflected, there certainly were several things that might have led them to be more cautious in their judgment, and to give him the benefit of the doubts they raised. For instance, thirty thousand dollars was a great sum of money in the year 1867 for the republican government or its army to have at its disposal for any thing but the strictest necessities, and much more to be able to spare for any such purpose as this. Even if the cash were plentiful and available for such purpose it would be hard to prove that it was really *necessary* for the object to be gained. Escobedo and his army did not *need* this help to finish their work. He had only to close his hand, and every thing and every body in Queretaro was held and could not escape. Why purchase, and at such a price, what was his when he chose to take it? Then, again, Colonel López was constantly under the eye of his countrymen during all these intervening years, and those who knew him intimately asserted that no evidence of any such wealth as this meant was ever exhibited by him or in his condition.

In the spring of 1889 López appealed to General Escobedo, the republican commander at Queretaro, with whom the interview took place before the fall of that city, to state the facts of the case. General Escobedo compiled his report in answer to the request, and placed it in the hands of President Diaz, who ordered its publication in the volume *Mexico á travez de los Siglos*, from which it was copied into one of the journals of the capital, on the 13th of July, 1889. We present the most important items of the document, so that the reader can judge. The real proposition of Maximilian we have already stated on page 223.

MR. PRESIDENT: The imperialist colonel, Miguel López, published in one of the journals of this city a letter addressed to me asking me with all sincerity to express the truth regarding those events (the supposed treason). The reactionary press of Mexico takes from the book [referring to a work of Victor Daran, lately published at Rome, reviving the scandal against López] that which shall most affect the history of our struggle against the so-called empire. They are working hard, with a vehement obstinacy, to have divulged the secret part of that affair relating to the supposed treason of López and the taking of the town of Queretaro, claiming that, owing to the direct part which this officer was to take in it by betraying his sovereign and selling the countersign for gold, the town was to fall into the power of the Mexican army. . . .

I divulge my knowledge of the affair for my own satisfaction, preferring to deposit the secret with the supreme government of the republic in order that this historical document may be preserved in the archives of the nation. . . .

The imperialist colonel, Miguel López, though unfaithful to his country, *did not betray the Archduke Maximilian of Austria, nor did he sell his office for gold.* On the 24th of May, 1867, Colonel López came to me, asking permission to speak with me in private. I agreed, and accordingly sent away my adjutants, and remained alone with him. He told me that the emperor had requested him to come to me to beg me to keep the profoundest silence regarding the conference he (López) had had with me as the emperor's agent on the evening of the 14th, because the emperor wished to save his prestige and reputation in Mexico and in Europe, which would be injured if the terms of the said conference and its results were made known. I replied to the envoy of the archduke that it would be totally indifferent to me whether or no I should keep the reserve as requested; that neither way would my own honor or that of my cause be affected; that he would certainly be directly affected by my silence, for it was already well known that he was being accused by his companions of disloyalty to the archduke, whom they said he had miserably betrayed; also, that as I was in doubt as to the legality of such a request, having no proofs to believe him, I did not wish to effect any agreement with him, deeming that improper and unsuitable for me.

López replied that he cared little for the premature judgment passed upon his conduct; that he would keep silence, because it was his duty to yield in all things to the desires of the emperor, to whom he owed very much, and to whom he could not be ungrateful. He added that he was provided with a document which cleared him of any stigma that might be cast upon him; and in order only to set at rest the doubts which I had expressed he showed me the document referred to, which consisted of a letter addressed to him by the archduke, the authenticity of which appeared to me to be beyond all doubt. I took a copy of it, and it is as follows:

"MY DEAR COLONEL LÓPEZ: We charge you to maintain the most pro-
19

found secrecy regarding the commission we gave you for General Escobedo, because if divulged our honor will be sullied.

"Yours affectionately,   MAXIMILIAN."

Then López asked me if I had any objection to keeping the secret, as it would not injure me in the least. I replied that I would reserve the right to divulge it when I might think it proper, without promising any definite time.

This was all confirmed in an interview which the general had with the archduke before his execution, when he earnestly entreated him to agree with what Colonel López desired on his behalf. We quote further from the general's narrative what Maximilian said on the subject :

He entreated that I should grant him a special favor, the obligations of which would entail no consequences upon me, but which if I would grant he would be relieved of the weight resting upon his mind, as, in spite of possessing liberal ideas, he always bowed before the respectful recollections of his illustrious ancestors. He calmly said that he would probably be sentenced to death, and that he feared the judgment of history in dealing with his brief and stormy reign. He asked me if Colonel López had spoken to me. Upon my replying in the affirmative he went on to say that he was not possessed of sufficient mental force to bear the reproaches which his companions in misfortune would heap upon him if they should know of the conference held between López and myself by his orders (in regard to the desired escape from Queretaro), and that, therefore, not appealing to aught save to his situation, he begged me to keep silence regarding said conference, which would neither be difficult nor dishonorable for me to do. I said to him that it appeared as if he was a victim to the treason of López toward his person, an infamous act already stigmatized with all the horrors of an execrable disloyalty. I said I had no object in revealing any thing of the past, but that rather than appeal to me he should do so to López, who was the one morally injured in these events.

The prince replied that López would *not* speak so long as I kept silence; that the time to which he would bind me not to reveal the results of the conference was short, being until *the Princess Carlota had ceased to live*, and her life would be extinguished when she should learn of the execution of her husband. As a final answer to the requests of the archduke I stated that it seemed to me quite impossible to keep the secret even if López should remain silent, because his defenders, his generals, the foreign ministers, or the Princess Salm-Salm, who had done every thing in their power to save him, would not fail to make use of the current versions of the treason of López and his inexplicable conduct toward himself as his chief and protector. In spite of this the archduke again insisted that I should keep the secret as requested, saying that the Princess Salm-Salm was prepared, not only to say nothing regarding that, but also to prevent the people interested in him from in any way referring to the disloyalty of López, assuring me that all those persons would strictly keep their word and not mention the colonel.

The condition in which the prince was, with his broken health, a prisoner about to be brought to trial and condemned to death, his desire to preserve, even after death, a stainless name, moved me, and, yielding to a sentiment of consideration for the unfortunate prisoner, I promised to keep his secret so long as circumstances did not oblige me to lift the veil which I have this day lifted upon the facts which precipitated the fall of Queretaro, May 15, 1867. . . . The lengthy exposition of the facts just narrated, taken from the journal of operations of the general head-quarters of the army of operations, is historic truth, and I herewith deposit it in the hands of the supreme magistrate of the nation to dispose thereof as he sees fit. (Signed) M. ESCOBEDO.

This evidence clears the character of Colonel López from the stain so long and unjustly resting upon him, under a sense of duty to a man whose vanity and pride of family could impose such a burden upon one who had served him faithfully to the last hour.

The city of Mexico was not captured till the 20th of June, after a siege of seventy days. It was cruelly prolonged by Marquez for his personal purpose. The two hundred thousand inhabitants were reduced by him to the extreme of oppression and distress. He kept up recruiting his force by all the violence of the press-gang. Forced loans (some of them for immense sums of money) were extorted. False news of imperial victories in the columns of the *Diaro Imperial* was circulated, with "the approach of the emperor's army to relieve the capital," and even fire-works and joy-bells gave forth their jubilation in honor of these monstrous lies, while for thirty-six days of the seventy Maximilian and his generals were prisoners or under trial.

General Porfirio Diaz was conducting the siege with a force

of thirty-five thousand men. He could have thus taken the city any day in June, but he humanely shrank from proceeding to the extremities of serious bombardment in which so many innocent people must suffer, expecting that a few days more of the terrible pressure would bring surrender. At length the foreign ministers and members of the city government, ignoring Marquez and his army, resolved to make an effort to open negotiations with the republican general outside. None of the ministers could do it except the American minister. Their governments had recognized Maximilian's empire; his government had never done so, and he was therefore in full relations with the republican government. The effort was made, and the entire truth of the whole situation became known, and the terms which General Diaz would offer to those willing to lay down their arms. This message was delivered to the commander of the foreign legion (chiefly Austrians), stipulating that if during the night they would cease their hostility, shut themselves up in the national palace, raise the white flag, and remain there until General Diaz should enter and receive their surrender they should all be spared and be escorted to Vera Cruz and allowed to embark without molestation. All, with one exception, gratefully accepted the generous conditions, and the next morning the white flag was seen over the "Halls of Montezuma." General Diaz, at the head of a portion of his army, rode peacefully into the city, and the war was over!

The liberal conditions were all fulfilled. The most surprising thing about the capture of the city was the non-appearance of the infamous Marquez. Every gate was guarded to secure him, but he was not found. On investigation it was learned that he had suddenly disappeared during the night, leaving his second in command, General Tabero, to bear the odium of a defense protracted beyond all reason. How he got away with his plunder has never been revealed. There are few crimes of which wicked men are guilty that were not laid to his charge by his countrymen—violence, robbery, and murder among them—and yet it was to a wretch of this infamous character that the arch-

duke extended his highest patronage and exalted him (as commander-in-chief and military member of the regency) to positions where he could most irresponsibly and powerfully exert
his baneful influence to promote the misery of his country.
That such a man could effect his escape and be living to-day
on his ill-gotten gains in the city of Havana is one of the mysteries of the Providence that governs this earth.

This man—the trusted and favorite general of the clerical
party—the republican government would certainly have executed had they caught him. But for all the rest of his countrymen who had been deluded and led astray the government
provided a merciful penalty. After nearly four months of
patient investigation of those who were compromised, on the
2d of November, 1867, the government issued its decision in
a general order by the minister of war covering every case, as
follows:

For native Mexicans who took service under the empire, either as officials or in the army, the penalty was to be:

1. To those who held the higher offices, or whose names were signed to
the decree of October 3, 1865 (the Black Decree), with regents and presi-
dents of council, the penalty was made banishment, subject to trial if
they returned to Mexico. The number under this head were about fifteen
persons.

2. Those of lesser rank in the service of the empire, under-secretaries,
etc., to the number of twenty-five, banishment until permitted to return.

3. To all below these, but above the rank and file of the service, imprisonment for from two to four years, being about two hundred in all.

4. For all the rest, in the army, civil service, etc., they were allowed to
go free and return to their homes, only being required to register their
addresses and pursue a quiet course of life in obedience to the laws of the
country.

Only two hundred and fifty persons in all were subjected to these penalties. For the foreigners, all were permitted to leave the country without further molestation.*

The bishops and compromised clergy had fled, fearing the
vengeance of the government for the prominent part they had

* Dispatch of United States Minister Plumb, *Diplomatic Correspondence*, 1867,
part ii, p. 469.

taken in the rebellion.   They were not able, however, to assume
much of the martyr aspect in their exile in view of the comparatively gentle treatment dealt out by the government to those
who had the courage to remain at home and face the results.
These churchmen, after recovering from their scare, began to
glide back again to their places.   They were not interfered
with, but it was understood by both sides that political Romanism was henceforth dead in Mexico, and that they must now
and forever keep their hands off the nation's affairs and mind
their religious work, and that alone—a hard lesson for them to
learn, but a necessary one.

The general amnesty, proclaimed in 1871, closed the last of
these retributions.   The death penalty was not imposed in any
case by the government, and thus the request of the Archduke
Maximilian was fully conceded.

It may be doubted whether, in view of all the fearful prov-
ocations to vengeance in the case, any government has ever
been more forbearing, and even lenient, in the hour of victory
than was this of Mexico in 1867.   It will stand, when fully
understood, in the future history of the world as a high honor
to the true character of constitutional republicanism.

What a contrast is suggested by the following fact!   Two
or three days after the capital was occupied by the republican
forces some of the proprietors of the mercantile houses and
other capitalists waited on the United States minister, and proposed that in view of the necessities for money which must
exist to meet the immediate wants of the army, until the
revenue from the custom-houses began to come in, they would
be willing to furnish a voluntary loan of $200,000, without
interest, payable at the convenience of the government.   General Diaz was surprised at such a proposition, especially from
people who had been so recently and repeatedly fleeced by the
traitor Marquez.   He gratefully accepted the generous offer,
making only one stipulation, that no part of this loan was to
be accepted from any person compromised by connection with
the imperial party.   This was guaranteed, the money was forth-

with paid, and in due time it was gratefully returned by the government.*

One would naturally expect that in this hour of triumphant peace and rest no disturbing element could possibly arise to put such conditions in jeopardy or attempt to fling the nation back into the fearful chaos from which it had just emerged ; but there was one man who would fain attempt even this diabolical work. The surrender of Vera Cruz to the republican army under General Benavides had already been arranged for, and in a few days more the Mexican flag would have floated unchallenged from the Gulf to California.

War-ships of England, France, Austria, and the United States were at anchor in the harbor, waiting to witness the close of the requisite negotiations, when, unexpectedly, on the 3d of June, the mail steamer *Virginia* hove in sight, having on board General Santa Anna, with a staff of five officers and a supply of munitions of war and a stock of proclamations for his purpose. General consternation was the result. Knowing the man, they could anticipate nothing from his advent at such an hour but confusion and destruction. The imperialist General Gomez was in command of the Castle of San Juan de Uloa, which dominates the city and harbor. He had formerly been a friend and adherent of Santa Anna, and promptly invited him to land and remain there till arrangements could be made for a grand reception in the city. Within an hour after the band in the fort was playing marches of welcome and the garrison shouting, " Viva el General Santa Ana ! " The foreign soldiers on the shore responded, and all saw that he had but to land, and a hostile force, which he so well knew how to attract and increase, would be around him, and all other authority at an end. Fortunately, before he landed he invited a conference of officials on board the *Virginia,* and there announced his purpose " to set up a republic in place of the tottering empire, and with the assurance that *he came under American protection*," " after interviews with President Johnson and Mr.

* *Diplomatic Correspondence,* 1867, p. 431.

Seward, and at their solicitation, Maximilian having offered to
deliver up the government of the country to him." These
outrageous falsehoods opened the eyes of all present. He had
overreached himself in asserting that the American government sustained him. A council of war was called that night at
the city hall by the naval and military officers, with the consuls
stationed at Vera Cruz. The conclusion was practically unanimous that Santa Anna should *not* be allowed to land and attempt to spoil all that had been accomplished. Captain Roe, of
the United States war steamer *Tacony*, was requested by the
entire company to take charge of the matter and see Santa
Anna sent off again in the ship that brought him. This he did
in thorough style next morning, to Santa Anna's amazement
and indignation. He escorted the *Virginia* for the first twenty
miles, and parted from her with injunctions to her captain not
to land the old general anywhere in Mexico. At Sisal Santa
Anna sent a letter, inclosing one of his proclamations, to the
Governor of Yucatan, with the request to give it publicity.
The governor was aroused to the danger involved, and as soon
as Santa Anna landed he arrested him, sending him off, for
greater security, to the State of Campeche, to await the action
of President Juarez. Our own government, under the circumstances, approved the action of Captain Roe.*

Afterward Santa Anna was tried (for the fourth time) for
treason and sentenced to death. This was commuted by
President Juarez to banishment for eight years, but under
the general amnesty of 1871 he was permitted to return, and
passed the remaining five years of his life in obscurity in
the city of Mexico.

On the evening of the 14th of July, as darkness settled down
on the city of Vera Cruz, rockets were seen in the offing. A
pilot was sent out, and when the vessel reached the harbor it
was ascertained that it was the United States revenue cutter
Wilderness, having on board the wife and family of President
Juarez, after their long exile in the United States. Our gov-

* *The Fall of Maximilian's Empire*, by Lieutenant Schroeder, p. 66, etc.

ernment had offered the vessel, through Señor Romero, to this
devoted woman, to take her back to her country. They landed
on the morning of the 15th, the very day when the honored
president arrived at the city of Mexico from the North. The
Vera Cruzanos made a joyful demonstration at the landing of
Mrs. Juarez and her children. Every boat was in requisition as
an escort fleet, while the ringing of bells, the booming of cannon, and the display of flags testified to the general rejoicing.
This last act of courtesy from Mr. Seward touched many Mexican hearts.

Beyond description were the rejoicings at the capital when
the president and the people who had so fully trusted him met
to celebrate the victory of constitutional republicanism. The
future safety of their political system was guaranteed from interference of outside foes, the power of political Romanism
was broken, while civil and religious freedom were won for all
the future. The worthy instrument of all this mighty victory
for freedom was here again, preserved through all the toil and
danger and sufferings of those five dreadful years, to rejoice
with his people, whom he had served so well and so faithfully.
He was made, by the supporting mercy of God, equal to the
height of his great mission, and in its closing triumphs showing
himself to be equally generous and humane. To him truly,
without qualification, might be ascribed the brilliant words
which Victor Hugo addressed to him on the 20th of June,
1867:

America has two heroes, Lincoln and thee—Lincoln, by whom slavery
has died, and thee, by whom liberty has lived. Mexico has been saved by
a principle, by a man. THOU ART THAT MAN !

We would not be doing justice to the subject should we fail
to recognize the religious character of Benito Juarez. No
detailed statement exists of his belief, but his devout faith is
constantly shown in the reverential manner in which he proclaims his victories or recommends his people to seek the help
of God in their emergencies. An irreligious man, as his cleri-

cal enemies have called Juarez, would not have used such expressions as the following in his proclamations to the nation:
"Providence concedes me the satisfaction of announcing a victory over the enemy." "Let us give thanks to Providence for
having aided the Mexican people to reconquer their liberties."
On account of his demand for the benefit of the State of some
of the vast wealth held by the Church of Rome in Mexico,
he was denounced as an enemy of true religion by the
papal faction. Far from this, Juarez believed that in free-
ing the Church from the political strife that had absorbed
its energies to the detriment of its spiritual work he was
aiding the Church to regain its lost mission to the souls
of its people. To this belief all unprejudiced Mexicans
hold firmly, and claim that Juarez's name shall be honored
not only as a great leader, but as a devout worshiper of
Jehovah.

He believed himself an instrument in the hand of God to
work out the liberty of his country. The simplicity of his life
and actions was the result of this conception of his mission.
Is there aught in the writings of any leader more admirable
for his reverential tone and all absence of self-seeking than Juarez's words to the nation at the close of the dreadful struggle
of the Intervention? "Let the Mexican people fall on their
knees before God, who has deigned to crown our arms with
victory. He hath smitten the foreigner who oppressed us
sorely. He hath established this his people in their rightful
place. For he who hath this habitation in the heavens is the
visitor and protector of our country, who strikes down those
who came with intent to do us ill. The excellent, the only
just, almighty, and eternal One is he who hath dispersed the
nations who like vultures had fallen on Mexico."

This far-seeing patriot did not live to see the grand success
of evangelical missions in the land, yet he realized the benefit
which a purer faith would be to his people. Shortly before
his death he said to an intimate friend, now a government
official, from whose lips we have heard it, that "*upon the de-*

velopment of Protestantism largely depends the future happiness of our country."

Juarez was greatly influenced by a sincere priest, Father Palacios, who, unable to accept the errors of the Roman Church, had come out from it with a little band of followers, and had established a service where the Bible was read. Thus a simple evangelical Church arose, which later joined our mission, and Brother Palacios labored faithfully as pastor of one of our churches until his death, in 1890.

After the death of Maximilian effort was made by several parties to get possession of his body in order to convey it to Vienna. His physician, Dr. Basch, the Princess Salm-Salm, Captain Groller, of the Austrian corvette *Elizabeth,* then at Vera Cruz, and some others, made application for it to the Mexican government. All were refused. The body, carefully embalmed, was still lying in the church at Queretaro. The reason why this refusal was returned was, first, that these parties were not authorized by the Austrian government to make such a demand, and, secondly, that the Mexican government could not, consistently with its own dignity, thus privately dispose of the mortal remains of the archduke. "An official act of the Austrian government or a petition from the family" was the proper procedure, and would be at once responded to. Of course, this was not pleasant to these parties, whose kinsmen, following Louis Napoleon's lead, had even denied the existence of a national government in Mexico or treated its claims with contempt. Now they had to face the consequences of their own injustice by " recognizing " that government and asking from it respectfully the favor desired.

Finding that the only way to succeed was the just and honest one above intimated, the Austrian court laid aside its pride and the false purpose by which it was misled, and, in a candid and worthy manner, made its appeal by the chancellor of the Austrian empire, Baron von Beust, to the government of Mexico through its secretary of state, Señor Lerdo, for the body of the prince. It was promptly conceded by the Mexican government. The following is the reply of the Mexican secretary of state :

DEPARTMENT OF FOREIGN RELATIONS, }
MEXICO, Nov. 4, 1867. }

MR. MINISTER: Vice-Admiral Tegethoff has delivered me your note. In it you say that his majesty, the Emperor of Austria, feels the very natural desire that the mortal remains of his brother, the Archduke Ferdinand Maximilian, should find a last resting-place in the vault that holds the ashes of the princes of the house of Austria; that the father, mother, and brothers of the deceased archduke, as well as other members of the imperial family, participate in the desire; that his majesty, the emperor, hopes the government of Mexico, from a feeling of humanity, will assist in realizing this desire, to effect which Vice-Admiral Tegethoff has been sent to Mexico to request the president to permit the remains of the archduke to be taken to Europe.

Conscious of the just sentiments expressed in your excellency's note, the president of the republic does not hesitate to gratify this natural desire of his majesty, the Emperor of Austria, and the imperial family.

Instructed by the president, I have informed Vice-Admiral Tegethoff that the mortal remains of the Archduke Ferdinand Maximilian will be delivered to him immediately to be carried to Europe, in compliance with the object of his mission.

I have the honor to offer your excellency the assurances of my distinguished consideration. S. LERDO DE TEJADA.*

The remains were transported from Queretaro to Vera Cruz at the expense of the Mexican government, and were attended by an escort of one hundred dragoons, with a number of officers. They reached Vera Cruz on the 25th of November, the body was identified on the 26th and delivered to Admiral Tegethoff on board the frigate *Novara*, the same vessel that three years and a half before had brought Maximilian and Carlota across the ocean to that very port. Now it takes back to Miramar the lifeless form of him who came with such high hopes, while the poor demented wife will not comprehend what they are doing as they lay him in the tomb of his ancestors!

It is but fair to add here the testimony borne by the two

* *Diplomatic Correspondence of the United States*, 1867, part ii, p. 478.

leading lawyers, Señores Palacios and De la Torre, who defended Maximilian, as to the course pursued by the Mexican government through the trial, and the spirit of fairness shown by the president and secretary of state in all the interviews which they sought with them from first to last. Their own report of the trial, printed as a volume, was published at the expense of the government and every facility given them. They say:

So numerous were the inaccuracies of the European press in referring to the tragic death of the archduke, so much that was offensive to our country was published, that we could not, in conscience, leave the history of the trial of our defendant buried in his tomb. All Mexico saw the consideration granted to the chiefs, officers, and soldiers of the Austrian army who surrendered at discretion to the general-in-chief. The representatives of France, England, Spain, Austria, Italy, Belgium, and the United States were witnesses of that consideration, and also saw that all the foreigners enjoyed full liberty and all sorts of guarantees. Yet, in spite of this public action of the authorities of our country, Mexico has been calumniated and held up to the world as unworthy of being a nation.

It was the death of Maximilian that raised this cry, and we who were his defenders feel called upon to present the history of that painful event such as it is. The responsibility and the comments can then be placed upon their true ground. . . .

As faithful narrators of this sad history we must acknowledge that the president, Juarez as well as his ministers, always granted us all the time we desired for many and lengthy interviews, and that to all our reasonings they replied with other arguments which betrayed a profound and patient study of all the elements which contributed to the tragic end of the empire. The same tranquil reasoning that Mr. Lerdo had shown, though expressed in different words, we found in the president. He let fall not a single word of enmity or vengeance, but there was underneath his replies an inflexible resolution which augmented our fears. He generally closed by saying that all that we had set forth would be weighed in the cabinet so that a just conclusion might be reached.*

* *Memorandum sobre el proceso,* p. 4.

CHAPTER IX.

"Vengeance is mine, I will repay, saith the Lord "—" So that men shall say,
Verily there is a God that judgeth in the earth "—The conspirators against
freedom—Could only be reached by the retributions of Almighty God—The
pontiff—Temporal power for one thousand years—Decree of infallibility—
Declaration of war—Downfall of Napoleon—The pope's temporal power extinguished—Italy unified—Papal coin—Scene in San Angelo—Emperor William denies the pope's claim—Napoleon rushes to ruin at Sedan—End of his
glory—Death of the Prince Imperial—Eugénie in exile—France republican—
Religious liberty—Expulsion of the Jesuits.

Had the guilty parties which had so desperately attempted to
crush constitutional freedom in Mexico retired from their effort
after the death of Maximilian, there was not a power in Europe
which would have called them to account or inflicted any
penalty upon them. And yet every one of those parties was
held to a *terrible responsibility*, while a chastisement was inflicted upon each of them that was an amazement to Europe and
will never be forgotten. But *who* was it that thus took cog-
nizance of their crimes against freedom and visited them with
such condign vengeance? Not the aggrieved and injured
party, for Mexico could not follow them across the sea. God
Almighty himself espoused her cause and answered for her in
his own way and time. Let us look at the facts of this wonderful retribution and see the evidence of the divine hand that
punished them.

There were six leading and responsible parties to this conspiracy against Mexican freedom and against the right and
duty of the United States to evangelize her neighbors. The
Most High, as we judge by the providential results, allowed not
one of them to escape the penalty due. These parties were, the
pope—in whose interest the whole enterprise was undertaken;
Louis Napoleon, the pontiff's willing instrument; Eugénie, that
"power behind the throne," who had more to do with this most

unwomanly work than yet appears; Maximilian and Carlota, heart and soul devoted to the object to be accomplished; and the Jesuits, those wily schemers, who had developed the enterprise and were to utilize its consummation, when the sword had fully opened their way and done its work upon prostrate Mexico and a bleeding and divided United States.

With reverent heart we bow before the divine Majesty and his work of vindication and vengeance. First, as to the pontiff. It was hardly necessary that Prince Bismarck should give the world his assurance that "the papacy has been *a political power* which, with the greatest audacity and with the most momentous consequences, has interfered with the affairs of this world," though his doing so carried corroboration of the fact where it might not otherwise have reached. The claim of temporal sovereignty has been to the pope as precious as the apple of his eye. He had held it for a thousand years as an essential element of his power, knowing well that a large portion of his peculiar immunities were held to him by this secular bond. To strike him *here* first of all, and so let loose the "rights" which he had gathered up and bound under this broad girdle, from the people he had so long misruled, was an act within the divine power alone. Let us mark the steps by which this was brought about. The convention of September, 1864, was a treaty between Louis Napoleon and Victor Emmanuel, secretly consummated, which bound Napoleon to withdraw his troops from Rome in two years from that date. The secret was carefully kept for six months, and when announced it fell like a bombshell upon the Vatican. The anger of the papal party was unbounded at what they designated as the "desertion of the pope by the emperor." Every one else was delighted, and the exultation of the people broke out on all sides. It was seen that it was the beginning of the collapse of the temporal power. It was stipulated also in the convention that the capital of Italy was at once to be removed from Turin to Florence, a more central position, and nearer to Rome. Napoleon hoped that the pope might thus "be led to reconcile himself to accom-

plished facts and bow with some grace to manifest destiny."
Vain hope! The pontiff, instead of taking counsel of expedi-
ency or being guided by the light of the nineteenth century,
took his stand in the eleventh by the side of Hildebrand,
and developed his now famous "*encyclical.*" Napoleon, it
will be remembered, answered this by appointing Jerome
Bonaparte to the regency as well as to the presidency of the
Corps Legislatif.

The indignation of the pope at Napoleon's action was unbounded. But he held his displeasure in restraint, knowing
that the emperor would bear little abuse from him. He could
anathematize Victor Emmanuel to his heart's content, and did,
for the king could do no more harm to the temporal power
than he had done in this convention. It was different with
Napoleon. If provoked he could order the immediate evacuation of Rome by the twenty thousand troops which held it for
the pope-king and leave him to the tender mercies of his own
people, which was what Pius IX. feared above all else. In the
volume of his published speeches the pope had characterized
them as "communists" and "demons let loose from hell!"
The people of whom he thus so violently spoke were the liberty-loving statesmen of Italy, who were wisely leading their
countrymen on to constitutional liberty and peace, and who had
addressed to him the vigorous document found on page 111. It
was truly said at that time, "Had it not been for these and
their constitutional government the red republicans and Roman
communists would have made short work of the papacy, and
neither the pope nor Antonelli nor one of the Roman curia
had dared to breathe Italian air. To-day his Vatican had been
ashes, and instead of the mock imprisonment which he parades
he would have gone to prison or to death." * It is wonderful
what power for good these patriots whom he had thus maligned
had over the masses, to keep them from excess and violence.
The people only wanted the Church to attend to her proper
work in the spiritual realm and leave secular affairs to them;

* *The Modern Jove,* by William Arthur, p. 48.

but when the head of the clergy insisted on being the temporal ruler as well there was "confusion and every evil work," under which what was good withered and what was evil flourished.

The pope alone could not see the danger arising from these facts, and supposed nothing more was necessary for peace and order except military power enough to hold in subjection to his will the three and a half millions of people within the Roman State, and as his own people refused to accept military service under him foreign mercenaries were necessary. All Italy had gladly accepted a constitutional sovereign, and the Church State was almost a unit in the same desire, as the vote taken shortly after this proved.

Failing to bring the nations of Christendom to his will by the thunders of the "encyclical," Pius IX. issued a call for an ecumenical council to pass the decree of his infallibility as an end of controversy, and as an authoritative voice that would subdue all dissent in the religious world as well as save his temporal power at home. Eight hundred bishops came together, and after deliberating six months the vote was ascertained on the 13th of July, 1870. It was during the eighty-fifth secret session of the council, 601 members being present. The vote was:

Placet (Yes)...	451
Placet juxta modum (with modification)..................	62
Non-placet (No)...	88
	601 *

On July 18, when the vote on the final adoption was taken, the disaffected and absentees reduced this number to 533, by whom, many of them under heavy pressure, the doctrine was accepted and the dogma proclaimed that afternoon. This in a Church which, according to the *Annuario Pontifico* of Rome, has 1,400 bishops and archbishops. Eight hundred and sixty-two took no part, or refused to vote "yes," so that the minority

* *Rome and the Newest Fashions in Religion*, by Hon. W. E. Gladstone, p. 74.

20

of 533 ingrafted this dogma of papal infallibility upon their
creed. Yet this is called the act of an ecumenical or universal
council!

This was the hour chosen by the Almighty to pour confusion
on this blasphemous decree, in its attempt to subordinate the
government of the world, in his name, in all things human and
divine, to an individual will! "And, behold, the day after the
proclamation of the dogma, Napoleon III., the political ally
and supporter of Pius IX., unchained the furies of war, which
in a few weeks swept away the empire of France and with it
the temporal power of the infallible pope." * The 533 prelates
departed hastily from Rome, as it was rumored that Napoleon
needed the twenty thousand men that garrisoned that city and
that they would be left unprotected! What a sarcasm to call
such a system a *Roman* Catholic Church, when in this emergency these prelates knew that they could not find fifty *Romans*
in the whole city willing to fight for their protection or that
of their infallible head!

Many supplications were offered before many altars to God,
the Virgin Mary, and the saints, to crown the "eldest son of
the Church" with victory and enable him soon to lower the
prestige of that Protestant king. It was not long—from
the 15th of July to the 1st of September, forty-seven days
only—until two of the greatest armies that Europe ever saw in
conflict met and made their appeal to the Lord of hosts to
judge between them and grant victory to the side which he
espoused. At least the Prussians made this appeal, and with
great earnestness. How the French acted is not stated, but we
know what great confidence they had in their equipment and
their leading. Truly has inspiration said, "Some trust in
chariots, and some in horses," but in war there is something
more to trust in. The right, and Him who defends it, is more
than all besides, as was here shown when a German empire
arose from the victorious battle-field and Protestantism sprang
to the political and military leadership of Europe.

* *Rome and the Newest Fashions in Religion*, by Hon. W. E. Gladstone, p. 79.

The complete overthrow of Napoleon at Sedan opened the way for the Liberals of Italy to enter Rome. All Italy saw that the hour had come for her to claim her capital for her constitutional government, and entreated their king to occupy it. Victor Emmanuel was cautious, and before yielding to the voice of the people tried once more to conciliate the pontiff. Count Pondodi di San Martino was selected to offer the pope, in exchange for the temporal sovereignty,

Leonine Rome as a residence, including St. Peter's, the Vatican, with all its treasures, the Church of Santa Maria Maggiore, Castle Gandolfo, and their dependencies; and these were all to be exempted from taxes and common law jurisdiction. This immunity was to be extended to any temporary presidency of the pope, conclave, or council. He was to have his own post-office and telegraph, choosing his own officials, to prefer benefices without royal permission, his seminaries were to be free from Italian scholastic authorities. Besides these he was to be freed from the entire papal debt, which the nation would assume, and he was to be provided with an income of 3,255,000 lire per annum and guaranteed the right of diplomatic representation, free ecclesiastical jurisdiction, and immunity of cardinals and embassadors.*

This liberal offer was contemptuously rejected.

Seeing that Pius IX. was unwilling to concede any thing, the people of Italy laid siege to Rome and captured it. Victor Emmanuel entered it on the 31st of September, 1870. His reception was enthusiastic, accompanied by every manifestation of joy that a glad people could show to their deliverer and constitutional king. In order that no doubt should remain as to the fact that he was the accepted ruler of the Roman people Victor Emmanuel left the city until a vote could be taken. In due course the *plebiscite* was proclaimed that surprised the world. Forty-nine votes only were cast for the retention of the papal government, and fifty thousand against it, in favor of the king.†

If ever a question was settled by the people it was in this case. No political madness could be greater than the attempt

* McClintock & Strong's *Cyclopædia*, vol. iv, p. 708. *Christian World*, vol. xxiv, p. 52.

† *Christian World*, vol. xxi, p. 355.

of the pope and the Curia Romana to override its decision. Yet this was done and is being done. At once a most inflammatory appeal was issued by the pontiff to every European government to unite to place him again on his throne! Antonelli followed his master's appeal with another of the same class. Thus the demand was made, not only to crush the Romans, no matter what suffering and bloodshed might be necessary, but also to provide a standing force to permanently sustain the papal throne!

Men paused and waited in surprise to see what response would be made to these furious demands of the papacy, but their hearts were relieved as hour after hour went past and no response came out of that ominous silence of the nations. No, not a protest was uttered, and *not one hand was raised to help him* in his dire emergency. All Europe concurred in what Roman freedom had done, in closing forever this hybrid government, and leaving Victor Emmanuel free to enter and reign over a "willing people," who had so cordially accepted and chosen him as their sovereign. Amid the glad rejoicings of his people, a few days after he entered the city of Rome and papal misgovernment dropped into the dust.

The institutions of united Italy were transferred from Florence to the capital. Lovers of freedom from many lands sent their congratulations to the rejoicing sons of Italy. All were happy save the pope, and he was overflowing with rage. The language in which he condemned the whole affair was simply awful. As to "the people," now enfranchised and free, he acted as if *they* were nothing in the case, and had no rights that he was bound to respect. The leading men of Italy felt themselves forced to give up all attempts at conciliation and to advance in the way they deemed best for the welfare of their country. Any plotting in the interests of his former power was sure to bring out the firmness of the government and of public opinion. Shortly after the establishment of the constitutional *régime*, a banquet was given in Rome, attended by members of both houses of parliament, the foreign embassadors, and prominent men. The speech of the evening was delivered by the mayor, Count Bianciani, whose closing words ought to have ended all uncertainty when he declared that "the people of Rome would rather see their city perish in ashes than again be subjected to papal domination!" This declaration was heartily applauded. The sentiments of the Romans have not changed, as a recent speech by ex-Prime Minister Crispi shows:

He declared that it was necessary to combat all persons, high or low, who were seeking to undermine the political edifice of Italy. The temporal power of the pope, although it had existed for centuries, had been only a transition period. Rome existed before it, and would continue to exist without it. Complaints or threats either from home or abroad would have no effect. He declared unassailable the utterance of King Humbert, that Rome forms an integral part of Italy, just as law forms a part of the modern world.

He asserted that the pope possessed perfect religious liberty, and was only restricted—and less harshly than in other Catholic States—from encroaching upon the sphere of national right.

The hand of God is especially seen in the events which transpired at this period. The rapidity of the movements, the relation which they lent each to the other, and their accumulated power for the purpose, all argue to an observing world that there was something more than *human* force behind the chain of events which so soon completely answered the preposterous claim advanced, in the name of God, on the 14th of July. Consider it, and say if Europe ever before saw any such chronology as this:

1870, July 14. Infallibility proclaimed by the pope and his council.
 " July 15. War proclaimed against the only leading Protestant power on the continent by Napoleon III., "the Eldest Son of the Church."
 " Sept. 1. This eldest son captured by this Protestant king.
 " Sept. 20. The pope and his capital captured by a king whom he had excommunicated.
 " Oct. 2. The appreciation by the Roman people of the pope's paternal rule expressed by their almost unanimous decision against it!

Divine Providence permitted this consummation of pontifical and imperial folly to proclaim itself in its pride and vainglory during those fifteen days of July, and then showed the world his overwhelming confusion of their claims in September. Well might devout men exclaim, as they did, "This is the LORD's doing, and it is marvelous in our eyes."

The work to be done in Italy was identical with that Mexico was engaged upon—the abolishing of the censorship and the Inquisition, the proclamation of freedom of the press and of worship, the provision for education and the public debt, the sale of monastic properties, sending the swarms of indolent monks to earn their own living. The beneficent effects of these changes were soon manifest. Some incidents in the author's experience may show the changes as well as any thing else. On our return from mission work in India, Rome was still famous for her intolerance, only holding her people down by the presence of foreign troops. Fourteen years later, on our second return from the mission field, we resolved to pass a few weeks in Rome, and see the effects of the happy changes that had occurred, and which our experience in Mexico had prepared us more fully to appreciate.

The first indication of the changed state of public opinion was given as we drove up to St. Peter's, and in paying the coachman I handed him, among others, a soldi bearing the inscription of the papal government. To my surprise the man objected to take that copper. When I said that it was one of the holy father's own coins he shrugged his shoulders as he repeated contemptuously, "Holy father! Please change it, sir." He preferred one bearing the image and superscription of his king, Victor Emmanuel. We were within sight of the windows of the Vatican, and yet this cabman ventured to show his animosity toward the government of the pope in a way that might have sent him to the Inquisition had he uttered it a few years previously.

On entering the Castle of San Angelo we shuddered at the thought of the cruelties perpetrated within its walls for hundreds of years past. Our attention was called to the soldiers on guard; they were bright, intelligent-looking men, and—wonder of wonders!—away on the far side of the room we noted many of them grouped near a large case of books, which proved to be a depository of the British and Foreign Bible Society, and the Holy Scriptures in Italian, French, and other languages, on sale for all who wished to buy, right here in the former prison of the Inquisition. Shades of Alva and Torquemada! Was this real, or only a dream? It was indeed wrought out by more than human power, by the "mighty working of Him who is able to subdue all things unto himself." In the cells of this castle our brethren had suffered, not for wrong-doing, but for their evangelical sentiments such as we cherish. What an answer to the martyr's cry, " How long, O Lord, how long?" was the entrance of Victor Emmanuel, bringing religious liberty to "them that were bound," and letting "the oppressed go free!"

It was delightful to see the Protestant churches already erected (our own in Piazza Poli) where so recently none were allowed, nor were evangelical services permitted to be held in a private house.

We found nine Protestant churches. Since then this number has been increased, and at present there are few towns of importance in Italy where a congregation of converted Italians cannot be found. Rev. William Arthur, of London, was then in Rome. Few foreigners have done more to help Italian freedom than has this distinguished man. It was a great privilege to meet him and have his assistance to realize the wondrous changes that have transpired since the fall of the pope from his temporal power. One of the most remarkable of these was to occur in the Wesleyan Methodist church on the following day under his own presidency. When we were parting he said to us, "Would you not like to be present at our soldiers' sacramental service in our church to-morrow?" It was in connection with the removal of this brigade from Rome to another city. We well knew that the Wesleyan Mission had been devoting much attention to the Italian military and sustains a regular chaplain for them. Hundreds of these men have been converted under this ministry, and in their changes to new stations take their notes of removal and report themselves for pastoral care where they go, the incoming men doing the same, and thus sustaining the services held for their benefit. It was the expressed and positive resolve of Victor Emmanuel that his soldiers should have the fullest religious freedom. The officers sympathize with their sovereign's wishes, and so the men enjoy their privileges.

We had no correct idea how far this had been successful with them, though we had evidently touched this matter at San Angelo. We were therefore rejoiced to have a nearer view. Had we found even a dozen or a score of such men it would have been a joy and delight. Our surprise may therefore be imagined when on entering we found the center of the little church filled with happy-looking men wearing the uniform of Victor Emmanuel, William Arthur presiding over the beautiful service and using Italy's own sweet language in doing so. One of the soldiers read the yearly report of the progress of the work among them. I counted the exact number present, and found there were one hundred and thirty-two; and the report accounted for the difference between that number and one hundred and fifty, for those who were unable to attend that day by duties from which they could not be excused, and other causes. The service closed by the gift from Mr. Arthur to each of a new pocket Bible, for all of these soldiers had been taught to read as well as having been led to Christ. This was the most thrilling and significant sight on which we had gazed during our visit to the old city. Think of it! Here we were among one hundred and thirty-two of Victor Emmanuel's soldiers—the men who take care of the pope, that nothing may harm him, and who garrison Rome, "sitting together in heavenly places" in a Methodist church, with open doors, speaking their experience in love-feast fashion, within rifle-shot of the Vatican! We concluded that "the right side of the world was coming up."

If any fact is needed to render all this still more emphatic as a suitable consummation of the penalty of Providence in the abolition of his temporal power it may be found in the correspondence which so soon after took place between the pope and the venerable Emperor William of Germany. To understand the deep significance of the claim insinuated so adroitly by the pope—that baptism, any baptism, Protestant as well as Romanist—gave him claims and control over *all* who had received the rite, to compel conformity to the rest of Rome's requirements, we must remember that such *is* the doctrine of Romanism, and one of their justifications for the persecution of Protestants. Secretary Thompson's valuable work presents the claims, and gives the authorities relied upon, from the Council of Trent down.* To have that claim conceded in any way, even by silence on the part of Emperor William, would have been counted as a great gain by the pope, but the emperor was too vigilant to be thus entrapped, and meets the claim, as we shall see, very effectively. Lord John Russell, then British premier, was equally ready to repudiate the audacious claim of "lordship over all baptized persons," when he said in Parliament, "Rome, no longer satisfied with equality, claims ascendency. This would include the queen and the Parliament. *I decline it!*"

The unhesitating reply of the emperor is refreshing—and in such a quiet, friendly way, too—when he plainly tells this "infallible" old pope that he is mistaken and has fallen into some errors on the subject mentioned in his letter, and that the trouble is from his own clergy "assisting the enemies of all law." He closes with the assurance that his own difference of opinion with any of his neighbors did not hinder him from "living in peace with them." A very broad hint to his venerable correspondent, while his repudiation of papal headship in Christianity in favor of that of the divine Saviour is grand and most appropriate!

The letters were regarded of so much importance that as soon as they appeared in Berlin they were telegraphed to the

* *The Papacy and the Civil Power*, p. 613. New York, Harper & Brothers.

New York Times.   The date of the pope's letter is the 7th of August, 1873, and is as follows:

YOUR MAJESTY: The measures which have been adopted by your majesty's government for some time past all aim more and more at the destruction of Catholicism.   When I seriously ponder over the causes which must have led to these very hard measures, I confess that I am unable to discover any reasons for such a course.   On the other hand, I am informed that your majesty does not countenance the proceedings of your government, and does not approve the harshness of the measures adopted against the Catholic religion.   If, then, it be true that your majesty does not approve thereof—and the letters which your august majesty has addressed to me formerly sufficiently demonstrate that you cannot approve that which is now occurring—if, I say, your majesty does not approve of your government continuing in the path it has chosen, of further extending its rigorous measures against the religion of Jesus Christ, whereby the latter is most injuriously affected—will your majesty, then, not become convinced that these very measures have no other effect than that of undermining your majesty's own throne?   I speak with frankness, for my banner is truth; I speak in order to fulfill one of my duties, which consists in telling the truth to all, even to those who are not Catholics; for every one who has been baptized belongs in some way or other, which to define more precisely would be here out of place—belongs, I say to the pope.   I cherish the conviction that your majesty will receive my observations with your usual goodness, and will adopt the measures necessary in the present case.   While offering to your most gracious majesty the expression of my devotion and esteem I pray to God that he may enfold your majesty and myself in one and the same bond of mercy.

(Signed)   PIO.

The emperor wrote in reply from Berlin on the 3d of September:

I am glad that your holiness has, as in former times, done me the honor to write to me.   I rejoice the more at this since an opportunity is thereby afforded me of correcting errors which, as appears from the contents of the letter of your holiness of the 7th of August, must have occurred in the communications you have received relative to German affairs.   If the reports which are made to your holiness respecting the German questions only stated the truth, it would not be possible for your holiness to entertain the supposition that my government enters upon a path which I do not approve.   According to the constitution of my States, such a case could not happen, since the laws and government measures in Prussia require

my consent as sovereign. To my deep sorrow a portion of my Catholic subjects have organized for the past two years a political party, which endeavors to disturb by intrigues hostile to the State the religious peace which has existed in Prussia for centuries. Leading Catholic priests have unfortunately not only approved this movement, but joined in it to the extent of open revolt against existing laws. It will not have escaped the observation of your holiness that similar indications manifest themselves at the present time in several European and some transatlantic States. It is not my mission to investigate the causes by which the clergy and the faithful of one of the Christian denominations can be induced to actively assist the enemies of all law, but it certainly is my mission to protect internal peace and preserve the authority of the laws in the State whose government has been intrusted to me by God. I am conscious that I owe hereafter an account of the accomplishment of this my kingly duty. I shall maintain order and law in my states against all attacks, as long as God gives me the power. I am in duty bound to it as a Christian monarch, even when to my sorrow I have to fulfill this royal duty against servants of a Church which, I suppose, acknowledges no less than the evangelical Church that the commandment of obedience to secular authority is an emanation of the revealed will of God. Many of the priests in Prussia subject to your holiness disown, to my regret, the Christian doctrine in this respect, and place my government under the necessity, supported by the great majority of my loyal Catholic and evangelical subjects, of extorting obedience to the law by worldly means. I willingly entertain the hope that your holiness, upon being informed of the true position of affairs, will use your authority to put an end to the agitation, carried on amid deplorable distortion of the truth and abuse of priestly authority. The religion of Jesus Christ has, as I attest to your holiness before God, nothing to do with these intrigues, any more than has truth, to whose banner, invoked by your holiness, I unreservedly subscribe. There is one more expression in the letter of your holiness which I cannot pass over without contradiction, although it is not based upon the previous information of your holiness, namely, the expression that every one that has received baptism belongs to the pope. The evangelical creed, which, as must be known to your holiness, I, like my ancestors, and the majority of my subjects, profess, does not permit us to accept in our relations to God any other medium than our Lord Jesus Christ. The difference of belief does not prevent me living in peace with those who do not share mine, and, offering your holiness the expression of my personal devotion and esteem, I, etc.
(Signed)   WILLIAM.*

* *Christian World*, 1873, vol. xxiv, p. 363.

This manly Protestant letter totally ignores and brushes aside all claims of "temporal power" and personal "infallibility," and must have opened the eyes even of the pope himself for the moment to the amazing changes that had transpired in his condition!

Let us now look at the retribution upon *Napoleon*. His course showed that his ambition was to be the dictator of Europe, as his uncle had been. He was not trusted by France, and six attempts were made to assassinate him. His patronage of the papacy, his intervention in Mexico, his desire to help the Confederacy, and his interference with Italian affairs all were for his personal aggrandizement, yet not one of them redounded to his credit or increased his popularity. His greatest ambition was to loosen the bonds of German unity and arrest her aspiration to be the leading power in Europe.

Napoleon did not dream of the results when he invited this quarrel with the liberty-loving Germans. He had prepared for it for years, and the miserable pretext of the "Spanish marriages" furnished the occasion. A fancied insult to his embassador was sufficient for him to rush into war, but unexpectedly to him the Germans were well prepared to meet him, not at Berlin, as he supposed, but on French ground, for they had crossed the Rhine before he could reach it. The battle between these two great hosts was soon begun. Three days it raged, till the French were driven back on Sedan, and their magnificent cavalry—the steel-clad cuirassiers—held in reserve as Napoleon's last hope, had been overwhelmed, and lay a shattered wreck in the open space between. This was the supreme moment of Prussian valor. Forbes, the famous war correspondent of the London *Daily News*, was present and thus describes it. With the Prussian sovereign were Von Moltke, Bismarck, and the royal staff and some privileged persons. "King William had risen to his feet and was intently watching the issue. The strained silence was curiously broken by the snap of a closing binocular, followed by the decisive words, 'It is all over with the French now!' Every eye turned on the speaker, a resolute man in blue undress uniform that was not German. He was none other than General Phil Sheridan, representative of the United States army attached to the royal head-quarters. At the word the German chiefs ran to shake the foreign soldier by the hand, for they knew the comment came from the past-master in the art of war."

The sad contrast of the two monarchs as they met next morning is marked by Forbes: "The German tall, upright, square-shouldered, with flush of health on his cheek and flash of victory from the keen grey eye under his helmet, . . . the Frenchman, bent, with leaden face, eye drooping and lip quivering, ailing in body and ill at ease in mind."

The language of Napoleon's surrender is pitiful indeed. He said, "Unable to die at the head of my army, I tender to your majesty my sword." The interview was brief. Twenty minutes sufficed, as Bismarck and Von Moltke had the documents ready for signature. Early the next morning Napoleon entered the waiting carriage, and with an escort of sixty German dragoons took his departure as a life-prisoner for Wilhelmshoe, a German fortress near Cassel, never to wear a crown again!

Appropriately does the author of the article in the *Libro Rojo* of Mexico comment upon this utter downfall of this enemy of his country's freedom, when he writes:

Napoleon III. must have comprehended, as he surrendered at Sedan, the great exaltation of victory, the great agony of defeat; all the inexplicable bitterness of a capitulation, and the futility of conflicts between nations who shed their blood, spend their treasure, and shatter the elements of life in the struggles which excite their evil passions, in the unbridling of which all is lost, in spite of the will of the masses. (P. 146.)

How bitter must have been his reflections as he afterward learned of the capture of Paris, the cession of Alsace and Lorraine, the victorious king crowned in Versailles emperor of united Germany, and the Rhine made the permanent boundary between the two countries! What makes all this more significant is the fact that it was the Teuton triumphing over the man

who, eight years before, announced, with such a flourish of trum-
pets, his intention to open out a career for the Latin race and
all that it implied on the soil of the New World, which was
to be "one of the most glorious enterprises of the nineteenth
century" and "the most brilliant event" of his career! Poor
man! What a "bubble" reputation was his! It began in the
fortress of Ham and now closes in the fortress of Wilhelmshoe,
while France resuscitates the republican government which he
had so foully dissolved! Well might Mr. Gladstone remark, as
he did at the time, "History records no more striking example
of swift retribution of chimerical ambition."

Usually it is not considered appropriate to subject a lady to
hostile criticism, unless she willfully steps beyond the bounds
which propriety prescribes for her action and subjects others
to injury. Unfortunately for the Empress Eugénie, she early
began to assume the role of a partisan of the papacy and to
throw all her influence against religious freedom. It was not
French Protestants alone who had reason to complain that her
beautiful hand was heavy against their rights, and that Napoleon had placed "a frivolous Spanish bigot at the head of
the French court."

Shortly after the *coup d'état* she was married to the emperor (30th of January, 1853) in the Cathedral of Notre Dame,
in royal magnificence. If fidelity to the pope could have
secured providential care and blessings, then she should have
greatly enjoyed her lot in life instead of sinking to be the unhappy creature which she soon became and is to-day. Madame
Carette, her lady of honor, in her volume entitled *Recollections
of the Court of the Tuileries*, which is understood to have
been issued under the permission of the ex-empress, tells us of
her great devotion to her religion—how, for instance, "every
year on Palm Sunday the empress received from the holy father
at Rome a palm branch, blessed by him, which was hung at the
head of her bed as a protection from evil during the year;"
also of her many prayers and religious observances. But
she was to learn erelong what mere "fables" these things

amounted to in the storm of realities to which her surroundings and her course of life was leading her. While people were
admiring her beauty, who could imagine that the "canker and
the grief" had already laid hold on her, or that the following
sentence would ever publicly describe her condition? Madame
Carette writes:

A Spanish tradition has it that the pearls with which brides adorn themselves on their wedding-day become the symbol of the tears which they
must shed during their married life. The empress, scorning the superstition, wore on that day a superb collar of incomparably beautiful pearls
which almost covered the satin corsage. Alas! the tradition was but too
completely fulfilled! This collar was sold among her other jewels by her
majesty after the war.

What was the cause of this terrible realization? The authoress
continues and makes the best representation she can of the emperor, as loving Eugénie after a sort, but frankly admits the
true reason that had blighted her existence. She says:

Nevertheless, after eight years of married life, the empress had already
experienced more than one conjugal affront. The emperor, yielding to his
former easy indulgence in unworthy pleasures, and influenced by the lax-
ity of morals in those by whom he was surrounded, did not always sufficiently consider her sensitiveness as queen and woman. In the very height
of her youth and beauty she was made to taste the subtile poison of infi-
delity, which corrupts the most delicate and secret sensibilities of a woman's heart. After abandoning himself to these temporary distractions,
one of which gained such unhappy notoriety, the emperor, who, like most
men, attached no importance to these passing caprices, always seemed
surprised that they had troubled his wife, since she alone occupied a really
important and honored place in his life. She became irremediably as-
sailed by melancholy. Dating from that time a marked change took place
in her majesty's tastes and habits. It seemed that her youth had quite
vanished, while the consciousness of her rank, hitherto scarcely discern-
ible, was now plainly visible on the ever-charming features of the grief-
matured woman. (P. 61.)

This man was viler than the world imagined when he could
thus injure this beautiful woman and consign her to premature
old age, and then defend himself by the fact of his prefer-

ence of her and the position to which he had raised her as sufficient to condone his conduct!

Notwithstanding, she was the "power behind the throne," after events proving that she was the great upholder of the Jesuits. She influenced Napoleon in his inimical position toward Italy and Mexico, sustained the pope to the last degree, and fomented the animosity with which the growing strength of Prussia was regarded. She cherished intense confidence that this Protestant power was to be broken, and that her husband was the instrument to accomplish this great work for the papacy. She identified herself thoroughly with the effort, and much is contained in the words attributed to her when the campaign against Prussia opened, and she raised her hand with the significant words, "This is my war!" Then began the prolonged prayers at the shrine of "Our Lady of Victory," which she so zealously kept up during the entire period of the conflict, accompanied with offerings of great value. A large number of ladies assisted her in these intercessions, and they confidently expected the most decisive victories! Before this time, when she and her husband were at the height of power and influence, Horace Greeley had visited Paris and studied the situation, especially in the part taken by the empress, and on his return, while delivering a lecture on France in the Westminster Church in Brooklyn, he was quite carried away by the convictions which crowded upon him. We quote from the report his remarkable utterance:

Near the end of his discourse Horace Greeley seemed to become elevated almost like a seer, and his words appeared like prophesies as he spoke of a day coming when, "as sure as there is a God in heaven, Napoleon III. will pay the penalty for having outraged moral and civil law. And thou, Eugénie, beautiful queen of power and of fashion, when that day does arrive, thou wilt have thy share in the penalty!"

When the blow came that so overwhelmingly shattered the power of the empire she escaped from Paris by the kind help of an American, Dr. Evans, a dentist in Paris, and made her home in England, to which Napoleon soon came, it being understood that his escape from the fortress at Wilhelmshohe was not unwelcome to the German government.

Meanwhile Italy had reached her capital and consolidated her power. Mackenzie tells us that Eugénie was so enraged at this fact that she exclaimed, "Rather the Prussians in Paris than the Italians in Rome!" (P. 67.) But the world was then no longer ruled by her preferences. Madame Carette's book shows the estimate in which Mexico's public men were held at France while she was at the head of its gossip. Benito Juarez was "that ambitious barbarian whom the arrival of Maximilian in Mexico had temporarily reduced to powerlessness;" the republican forces were "savages" and "bands of ferocious adventurers, who exercised neither justice nor mercy." (P. 260.)

Perhaps in her bigotry Eugénie most of all regretted that France should re-establish the republic and maintain true religious liberty. The fall of her power was good news for evangelical Christians. That grand Scotchman, Mr. McAll, was soon in Paris beginning the work that has had such a development, reporting now forty-four halls in Paris and eighty-six in the surrounding towns, with two hundred and fifty-nine helpers, while about two hundred and fifty thousand people regularly hear the Gospel preached on week-days and the Sabbath in those places. The writer had an opportunity of seeing some of these audiences in 1879, and can testify that not merely the "wearers of the blouse," but all sorts of people, avail themselves of the privilege. On reaching such a place one evening I found the hall well filled, and the audience singing with great satisfaction French adaptations of *Gospel Hymns*. There was a delay in the service, as the preacher had not arrived, so they still sang on. The gentleman in charge was watching the door for the expected help, and finally he left the desk and came to inquire if I was a minister. He requested me to preach, which I was willing to do, but could not in French, so he asked if some one in the audience who spoke English would interpret for me. A gentleman came forward and stood by my side in the pulpit. Meanwhile I had determined to take a theme of an

21

experimental character—the witness of the Holy Spirit to the sonship of Christian believers.   While I tried to present it in as simple a manner as possible, yet I felt the subject might be "strong meat" for people who might have come to this service without some good measure of religious feeling and intelligence; but, to my delight, I found I had the most earnest attention of the audience, and that my translator never seemed at a loss for a word, that the theme was evidently not new to him or them.   At the close I was told he was a banker of the city.   This in Paris!   It was gloriously free and has continued so, while Eugénie sits deprived of all power to dictate in the sacred rights of any human being there or elsewhere.

After Napoleon's death, in 1873, Eugénie's hopes were bound up in the life of her son, "the Prince Imperial," who might, she hoped, some day restore the fallen empire.   As his education was about completed, in 1879, the Zulu war broke out.   His father, years before, in a dispatch had lauded the military spirit of the lad, and had spoken enthusiastically of him as having passed unflinchingly through his "baptism of fire" on the field, and the youth was ambitious to win military fame.   His mother encouraged his desire, and application was made to the Duke of Cambridge for a position on the staff of Lord Raglan, the general commanding, which was at once refused as dangerous.   The prince insisted upon going, even as a volunteer, and finally was permitted.   Shortly after his arrival in Africa he and a little party of scouts were surprised by the Zulus, and the prince lost his life.   This was the culmination of the misery of this unhappy woman.   There was nothing left her but to go and seek the body of her son and bring it home to be buried beside Napoleon III.   There they will remain, doubtless, as France is not likely to desire to restore their dust to her own soil, as she did in the case of the great Napoleon, to lay his body under the dome of the "Invalides" in Paris.

Eugénie, alone in a foreign land with her dead, discrowned, widowed, and childless, is a sad but striking memorial of the penalty dealt out to the oppressors of Mexico, and may well rank with the retribution imposed upon the pontiff. These penalties were not inflicted by human hands. They are the judgments of God, and are a wonderful evidence of the truth of his own words, "Vengeance is mine; I will repay, saith the Lord."

Poor Maximilian and Carlota! The events that deprived the one of life and the other of reason oppress us in the contemplation of their calamitous magnitude, and all the more when we reflect that they sacrificed the substance for the shadow. Had they declined to do this wrong to Mexico and patiently waited, crown and throne and empire would all have been theirs if they had lived. Meanwhile they might have continued to enjoy what Madame Carette so justly describes as "the tranquil shades of that charming retreat on the borders of the Adriatic, where, at the foot of the Tyrolese mountains, they had delighted in constructing a fairy palace to shelter their happy and harmonious union." (P. 252.) The suicide of Rudolph, the only son of Francis Joseph, two years ago, would have left Maximilian and Carlota heirs to all the honors of the Austrian empire. But this too was sacrificed, as well as life and reason, by the course that was urged upon them so determinately by the pontiff and Louis Napoleon for their own purposes. No wonder the divine judgment fell so heavily, as we have seen, upon those who thus misled this young couple to their complete undoing, and that all alike shared in the terrible catastrophe which so completely overthrew papal despotism and saved constitutional freedom in the New World!

Our view of these providential retributions will close with a few words in regard to the Jesuits. This hateful society, whose machinations give the religious world no rest, prepared the plan which God reversed in Mexico. Standing back in the shadow, they work unseen day and night for their purposes. By the use of the confessional they can lay their hands on every secret of social and personal life in every family where they have a representative of their religion. And as to politics and public men, no power in this world is so debasing as that

of Jesuitism.   The attention of thoughtful men was intensely
drawn to this prompt and overwhelming series of calamities
which overthrew these parties.   Seldom has the world witnessed
a more manifest fulfillment of the utterance of inspiration,
that "When thy judgments are abroad in the earth the inhabitants of the world learn righteousness," and that "There is a
God that judgeth in the earth."

In evidence of their frequent rejection of the order of Jesuits by all the states of Christendom (and by heathen nations as
well), which found their presence intolerable to their peace and
order, let the following list bear witness.

This society, founded by Ignatius Loyola, August 15, 1534,
conditionally sanctioned by the bull of Pope Paul III., September 25, 1540, unconditionally approved by him in 1543, has
had a most troubled existence, and has in some way succeeded
in winning a vast amount of ill-will of both rulers and people.

For their crimes, intrigues, and conspiracies the Jesuits have been banished from various countries again and again, as will be seen by the following table, compiled from *A Short Sketch of the Jesuits*, also from the
Encyclopædia of Chronology, by B. B. Woodward and William L. R.
Cates, and from other trustworthy authorities.

JESUITS EXPELLED FROM

Saragossa.............. 1555	Russia.................. 1723	From entering Saxony.. 1831
La Palinterre.......... 1558	Savoy.................. 1724	Portugal............... 1834
Vienna................. 1566	Paraguay.............. 1733	Spain again............ 1835
Avignon............... 1570	Portugal.......Sept. 3, 1759	Rheims (by the people). 1838
Antwerp, Portugal, etc. 1578	Prohibited in France.... 1762	From entering Lucerne. 1842
England............... 1579	France again 1764	Lucerne again.......... 1845
England again......... 1581	Spain, colonies and Sici-	France again........... 1845
England again......... 1584	lies, and Naples....... 1767	Switzerland............ 1847
England again......... 1586	Parma and Malta....... 1768	Bavaria and Genoa..... 1848
Japan................. 1587	All Christendom, by bull	Papal States, by Pius IX.,
Hungary and Transylva-	of Clement XIV., July 21, 1773	Sardinia, Vienna, Aus-
nia.................. 1588	Russia................. 1776	tria.................. 1848
Bordeaux.............. 1589	France again 1804	Several Italian states.. 1859
The whole of France.... 1594	Canton Grisons 1804	Sicily again........... 1860
Holland............... 1596	Naples again........... 1810	Spain again............ 1868
Touron and Berne...... 1597	France again 1816	Guatemala............. 1871
England again......... 1602	Moscow, St. Petersburg,	Switzerland............ 1871
England again......... 1604	and Canton Soleure... 1816	German empire 1872
Denmark, Venice, etc.. 1606	Belgium................ 1818	Mexico (by the viceroy). 1853
Venice again.......... 1612	Brest (by the people) ... 1819	Mexico (by Comonfort):. 1856
Amura, Japan 1613	Russia again........... 1820	Mexico (by Congress) ... 1873
Bohemia.............. 1618	Spain again 1820	New Granada......since 1879
Moravia 1619	Rouen Cathedral (by the	Venezuela 1879
Naples and Netherlands. 1622	people) 1825	Argentine Republic..... 1879
China and India....... 1623	Belgium schools 1826	Hungary.. 1879
Turkey 1628	France, 8 colleges closed. 1828	Brazil................. 1879
Abyssinia............. 1632	G't Britain and Ireland. 1829	France again. 1880
Malta................. 1634	France again........... 1831	

The last report shows that there are 2,377 members of this order, 1,130 of them being in the United States, and a large portion of the remainder in England.

These are the gentlemen, polite, plausible, and trained, the spies, the vassals, the sworn minions of a foreign despot, who, having been expelled from all Catholic countries again and again by popes, princes, and kings, both Catholic and Protestant, now swarm into England and America, and, under the protection which the influence of an open Bible gives to honest men, are proceeding to destroy the public schools, debauch the government, and work the mischief which has ever been their legitimate business.

The clearance which Mexico made of all monastic orders was so complete that I once asked a Mexican gentleman if it was really necessary to be thus thorough and expel even the "Sisters of Charity." He promptly replied that the nation so regarded it, adding:

Do not mistake us. We are not opposed to religion, as such; far from it. But we have learned by bitter experience that the ultimate object of these confraternities and sisterhoods is not religion. Religion is only a means for reaching the ends which they aim at. Their object in being here is to work for the subjugation of our people to a foreign despotism that has its seat at Rome. We have suffered so much from this source that we want no more of them.

Being in Mexico at the time of the final expulsion of the Jesuits (August, 1873), I naturally desired to witness the enforced departure of the last band, and so went to the railroad station to see them off. No demonstration was made save by a few of their devotees, who went on their knees occasionally to receive their parting benediction. It looked rather theatrical and tiresome. On the morning after their departure there came out in the columns of *El Monitor Republicano,* one of the leading dailies of the city of Mexico, an article bearing the title " Adios Jesuitas ! "—" Jesuits, farewell ! " It contained a fearful arraignment of the miseries which this order of foreigners had inflicted upon Mexico during the years when their baneful influence was intruded into her social and public life ; how they had identified themselves remorselessly with the enemies of her freedom, and aided in sending some of her noblest and best to premature graves.

The gist of the article, and of others which were published at the same time, may be thus expressed : "Jesuits, farewell! In this hour of your departure we have sympathy and compassion, but that sympathy and compassion are not for you. We reserve both for the people among whom you will now fix your homes, and with whose religious, social, and civil life you will endeavor to tamper, as you have tampered with ours, with similar results of misery and distress. Jesuits, farewell!" Thus Mexico, instead of being—as she was twenty-five years ago—the most priest-ridden country on earth, has worked her way up, by the help of God and the valor of her sons, to the position of the most free of all Roman Catholic lands, while her existing laws now sanction no monastery or nunnery, sisters of charity or Jesuits, within her bounds.

In connection with the expulsion of the Jesuits a law was enacted by Congress to facilitate prompt action in any case of return. It was entitled "The Pernicious Foreigner's Act," and certainly was sufficiently offensive as a title. It was designed to save time, so that, without waiting for processes of law, the person could be met and promptly told to leave. Not only so, but all foreigners coming to reside in the country were required to appear before a magistrate and be duly registered, with name and abiding-place, so as to leave no loop-hole for undesirable (or "pernicious") people to remain. It became my duty as superintendent, as our missionaries arrived, to see this regulation complied with. Invariably the smile would pass round when we appeared, and the magistrate would courteously ask us to excuse the trouble which the act gave us, observing, "Of course, señor, the law is not meant for you missionaries. We have no anxiety about *your* coming in. But we have to act in a way that is impartial. Please excuse the trouble of this attendance here." They knew we did not, as law-abiding people, regard it as any hardship, and we were respected accordingly.

CHAPTER X.

The star on Orizava—Summary of what Mexico has gained—Her resources—Improved financial condition—Porfirio Diaz—Evangelical missions—Miss Rankin—Circus of Chiarini—Providential help—Purchase of Inquisition—Popular vengeance—Buried martyrs—General Assembly—Statistics of Protestantism—Persecution—Interview with President Diaz—Santa Anna—Epitaph—Tomb of Juarez—Memorial services of the Emperor William—Madame Calderon's prophecy.

On the 19th of February, 1873, an hour before daybreak, we stood on the deck of the steamer approaching Vera Cruz. The object of our gaze was the peak of Orizava, towering up in majesty three miles and a half in height above sea-level (17,879 feet). The cone, covered with its perpetual snow, shone in the azure vault of heaven, above all obscurity of mists or vapors, recalling the glowing lines:

> " As some tall cliff erects its awful form,
> Springs from the vale and midway meets the storm,
> Though round its base the rolling clouds are spread,
> Eternal sunshine settles on its head."

At that time Orizava's majesty was farther glorified by the brilliant morning star resting on its brow, radiant light enthroned on spotless purity! We gazed in rapt attention until the star

> "Melted away into the light of heaven"

and the early rays of the sun gilded the mountain's summit. Never can that vision be forgotten. Often have we dwelt upon it, accepting it as an omen for good of that coming hour when the smile of Him who is " the bright and morning star " shall rest on the heart of redeemed Mexico.

We stand at last amid the GRAND RESULTS for which Mexico has so long struggled and suffered. Let us look at some of the

evidences of her wonderful progress since 1857. The fruits of
her victories over civil and religious despotism have been thus
summarized by outsiders, who rejoice with her in the victories
which she has won:

1. They have firmly established a free Constitution, embodying those
essential guarantees of liberty which we Anglo-Saxons regard as funda-
mental, including an entire divorce of Church and State.

2. They have secularized the vast and ill-gotten estates of the Church,
from the revenues of which it was always able to pay a mercenary soldiery
in the interest of despotism, and by which it virtually controlled the
country and kept it deluged in blood.

3. They have placed on an enduring basis the rights of free speech, a
free press, speedy public trials, and, above all, liberty of conscience in religious worship, and are establishing universal suffrage and trial by jury.

4. They have in operation, and are steadily extending, a system of
primary schools, which could never have been done while the priestly
tyranny continued.

5. Already the fruits of these beneficent victories are visible in the press
of the country, and are expanding literature in the growth of education
among the youth. In another and grander aspect the change is so remarkable that a volume might well be devoted to its discussion. This is the
great religious awakening, standing perhaps without a parallel in this
century. From small beginnings, in 1846–47, the sacred Scriptures have
been finding their way to Mexican homes, till their circulation has become
openly and remarkably rapid. Already thousands of her people have
wholly abandoned the old religion in which they were born and organized themselves into evangelical Churches, in harmony with the leading
Churches of the United States, and taking the Bible only as their rule of
faith. They have spiritual leaders of their own race and language. Their
influence is rapidly extending by means of the pulpit, religious societies,
and the press.*

In the presence of such results, wrought out by the endurance
and heroism of such a people, how just and appropriate is the
conclusion of Dr. Ellinwood at the close of his address before
the General Assembly! He says:

I have marked the struggle of the Mexican people for their independence
in order to meet the flippant talk which we sometimes hear about annex-
ing their country to the United States. I have wished to show that men

* *Putnam's Magazine*, July, 1870.

whom the armies of Europe could not compel to accept even the most amiable of rulers, men who could carry the life and soul of their republic with them, though driven all over their domain, are not of a class to be handed over easily to a neighboring power, exchanging their independence for a few railroad lines and a little commerce.

We would not attempt to annex Mexico, but would rather take a generous pride in her independence, while by every means we extend our aid in securing for her all the blessings of Christian enlightenment which we enjoy. But chiefly it is my desire to emphasize those wonderful providences which have wrought out her religious liberty.

Those who have examined her unique and magnificent *resources* are well aware that Mexico is worthy of the progress at which she aims. Baron Humboldt's testimony, after his full and scientific inspection, has been justified by all subsequent discoveries and experience. He wrote: "This vast empire, under careful cultivation, would alone produce all that commerce collects together from the rest of the globe." Her scientists to-day assert "that there is not a mineral known except *cryolite* that is not found in Mexico." Her very formation wonderfully favors her wealth, the railways on both sides concentrate the productions from the tropics with those of the temperate belt, and bring them to the mart of the capital.

Here is a partial list of her products which she exports: Cereals and fruits, sugar, rice, cotton, tobacco, dyewoods, coffee, indigo, cocoa, cocoanuts, India rubber, vanilla, chili, cochineal, mahogany, rosewood, ebony, lemons, limes, pine-apples, jalap, salts, vegetable waxes, medicinal gums, cinchona bark, anise-seed, Sisal hemp, madder, ramil, hennequin, dyes, nuts, oils of commerce and for the table, and, in fine, every variety of produce known in the temperate and torrid zones. Her wheat is regarded as almost the finest in the world, next to that of Egypt; Indian corn, maize, and barley are of excellent quality, and one of her specialties is the bean, of all kinds and colors, from black to white. The beautiful marble or onyx from Puebla is coming into great use for clocks and different ornaments.

In return she wants our petroleum, clocks, and watches, quicksilver, lamps, and gas-fixtures, silks, woolen goods, hardware, printing-presses and type, books, paper, rails, locomotives, tools, machinery of all kinds, well-boring apparatus and pumps, canned meats and preserves, scientific instruments, pianos and organs, educational appliances, plated-ware and cutlery, telegraph wire, agricultural machinery of all sorts, railroad carriages for passengers and freight, maps, globes, and charts, mining fuses, seeds and plants, slates, lithograph-stones, and a hundred other articles which she does not produce but constantly requires, and for which she is now paying the highest prices, in addition to the cost of four thousand miles of freight charges, to English and German importers.

At the close of Maximilian's empire Mexico had but one railroad, with 260 miles of track.   To-day she has them running in all directions (see the map), with an average of 10,025 kilometers (about 6,300 miles), and is building more.   Of telegraph lines in 1867 she had but a few short connections, under 3,000 kilometers; now she has telephone and telegraph lines which aggregate between 60,000 and 70,000 kilometers.   So satisfied was General Grant, after thorough examination, of Mexico's coming prosperity that he stated to her government that subsidies for the building of her railroads might soon cease entirely, and the lines be built relying on the trade they would develop for their support.   That hour has now come, and his confidence in the prosperity of Mexico is fully justified.

In his last message to Congress (1891) President Diaz said:

It is gratifying to me to be able to inform Congress that the financial situation of the republic continues to improve.   The receipts of the treasury during the past fiscal year exceeded $36,000,000, the receipts from the frontier and maritime custom-houses reaching $24,000,000.   This shows the magnificent impulse that mercantile traffic has received, since, without increasing the tariff, the custom-houses now collect $9,000,000 more than they did four years ago.

Of the nation's credit, once so low, he said:

The loan of £6,000,000 sterling was issued September 9 in Europe, and taken many times over.   The banks having the subscriptions in charge had to close their registers almost immediately without giving the general public a chance to subscribe.

The revenues of the republic have more than doubled in the past twenty years. In 1870 they were $16,000,000; they are estimated now at over $36,000,000. Reviewing Adolfo Salina's valuable work, *Mexico and her Riches*, the reviewer says:

The figures should prove of great interest not only to those who are actively engaged in Mexican trade, but also to all who wish well to Mexico. They are conclusive on two points, namely: (1) The volume of Mexican exports since 1872 has largely increased year by year, being twice as much in the fiscal year 1889–90 as in 1879–80. (2) The major part, over two thirds, in fact, of the exports go to the United States. The last-named country received during the fiscal year 1889–90 three times the quantity of exports from Mexico that it did in the year 1879–80. These facts show that Mexican trade with the United States increases more rapidly than it does with any other country. This is not to be wondered at, seeing that Mexico and the United States adjoin, and that each country has products which the other requires and does not produce. Each country is, in fact, the complement of the other, and both together produce all known products.

The spread of education, the extension of the railway system, the increase of industries under the protection of an enlightened government, with the increasing consciousness of the rights and duties of civil and religious freedom, are fast bringing the country to the orderly and peaceful development of her great resources.

From a table showing the exports from Mexico to the United States and the total exports to all countries, we select the exhibit of every fifth year since she entered upon the control of her own circumstances, and have this grand result:

YEARS.	Exports to the United States.	Total Mexican Exports.
1872–73	$11,367,859	$31,594,000
1877–78	12,340,689	29,285,000
1882–83	16,739,097	41,807,000
1887–88	31,059,626	48,885,000
1889–90	43,022,440	63,276,395

MEXICAN IMPORTS, 1888–89.

From the United States		$22,669,420 71
" England	$6,337,980 30	
" France	4,956,568 41	
" Germany	2,842,932 35	
" other countries	3,217,992 55—	17,355,473 61
		$40,024,894 32
Of the above, free-list imports during 1888–89 amounted in value to....................................		$13,506,230 23
Giving as dutiable imports during 1888–89, in value ...		26,518,664 09
		$40,024,894 32

MEXICAN DEBT, JUNE 30, 1890.

Mexican foreign debt................................	$52,500,000 00
" domestic debt, consolidated under laws of 1883 and 1885..................................	23,052,550 00
" indebtedness represented by certificates........	2,906,076 32
	$78,458,626 32

The remarkable man now honored by his fellow-citizens by a third presidential term demands our attention at this point. Porfirio Diaz (see portrait opposite) was born in the State of Oaxaca, in 1830. His intercourse with Juarez in his early manhood inspired him with the ardent patriotism of that great reformer, and he began his efforts for the freedom of the country by resisting Santa Anna's despotic measures in 1854. During the succeeding years of conflict his valor won his advance to the highest position in the army, and at the overthrow of Lerdo, in 1876, he was elected to the presidency. In 1880 he relinquished the office to General Gonzales, and for a short time served as minister of public works, carrying out many excellent reforms. Resigning his position in 1883, he made an extended tour through the United States, where he was received with great cordiality. In 1884 he was again elected president, and in 1888, so rapid had been the advancement of the country under his rule, the amendment to the Constitution, advanced by Diaz himself in 1878, against re-election

GENERAL PORFIRIO DIAZ,
Mexico's brave soldier and honored president.

was changed, in order to keep this exceptional statesman at the head of the nation. The term now drawing to a close has been one of great prosperity. The commerce of the country is rapidly extending; the credit of the nation has risen until now they can borrow money in any market; the public debt has been reduced, railways have been built, and all classes are enjoying the benefits of justice and peace.

As we write popular demonstrations are being made in favor of another term. Certainly no other man in Mexico shows such ability as General Diaz, and the universal respect paid him by foreign residents, as well as by Mexicans, testifies to his impartial and just dealings. During his administration all forms of worship have been protected. While carrying out the laws for freedom of opinion he has been justly severe with those who interfered with the rights of others, and this may have caused some opposition to him among fanatical people. Mrs. Diaz is a daughter of Manuel Romero Rubio, a prominent lawyer of the capital, and is very active in charitable work and much esteemed.

The present prosperity of Mexico is very largely due to the efforts and incorruptible character of her noble president, Porfirio Diaz. A recent biography written by Hubert Howe Bancroft, gives an excellent view of the life of General Diaz and of his association with Benito Juarez. To this we refer our readers who wish to know more of the subject.

The incoming and results of evangelical missions in Mexico, consequent upon the establishment of religious freedom, will now, in closing this record, claim our attention, as the highest aspect of that happy transition which has crowned all the efforts and sufferings of the past forty years.

That devout Christian woman, Miss Melinda Rankin, who shortly after 1850 established herself in Brownsville, Texas, and employed colporteurs to sell and distribute copies of the Scriptures in the Spanish, was the providential agent to open the way for the Bible into northern Mexico. For twenty years she prayed and toiled and suffered. The bigoted priests tried to meet her work at every point, while again and again the sad story of the destruction of the sacred volumes was borne back to her by the faithful agents who often risked their lives in their work. Little congregations grew out of this Bible work, and her helpers were enabled to go farther into Mexico; the work in the city of Zacatecas being started by these, and at Cos also, where they were aided by a Christian physician from the United States located there. The long strain of this service began to tell on Miss Rankin's strength, and after her sister's death and her own severe attack of yellow fever she realized the need of stronger hands to lift the burden, which by its very success had grown so heavy. It needed also regularly ordained workers to organize the churches and administer the sacraments, in order that an evangelical form of worship might extend through the country. Therefore, after due deliberation she made over the results of her labors to the American Board of Commissioners for Foreign Missions. She published a book giving some of her experiences, entitled *Twenty Years Among the Mexicans*, and from her home in Bloomington, Ill., she went, as much as her strength would permit, to visit the churches, interesting the people in the cause of the Gospel in Mexico. On the 7th of December, 1888, she passed to her reward, leaving a name that will always be associated with the earliest efforts for the redemption of Mexico.

Toward the close of Miss Rankin's service the American and Foreign Christian Union was led to institute a union movement in Mexico city, but after a trial of this method the work was found to be more in the line of promoting the services of one denomination than the contributors desired, and also bore a somewhat exclusive aspect. Therefore, at the close of 1872, a conclusion was reached to discontinue this union effort and allow each Church to go in and do what it could in the use of its own forms to enlarge the work. Success has amply justified the change, and, as we shall see in our closing pages, far more has been accomplished in behalf of Mexico than by the methods of any professedly undenominational plan.

The writer was appointed by Bishop Simpson in November, 1872, to proceed to Mexico and establish a mission there for our denomination. We reached the city of Mexico on the 23d of February, 1873, and for three weeks had the help of Bishop Haven's presence and advice in acquiring property at the capital and at Puebla. A reference or two at this point will illustrate the amazing changes that had occurred, and in what an extraordinary manner divine Providence was leading the liberty party in Mexico to open the way for Christian missions. The first necessity of the hour was to find suitable places, in the right locality, for the work to be done and to secure them, escaping all the risks of false titles, extravagant prices, and the wicked interferences of Jesuitical enemies, who toiled day and night to get between us and the available property and thus defeat our purpose.

Secularized church property, particularly the convents, were in demand in suitable localities. Two of these which fell to our share may be referred to briefly as being in themselves most uncommon purchases for Protestant missions. These immense establishments were generally structures of the most enduring character, adapted for a scenic worship, but usually gloomy, with windows fifteen or more feet from the ground, beneath which hung great pictures. The light and airy appearance of Protestant places of worship was absent, and great expense was necessary to adapt them to our purposes, especially where the walls were so thick and solid.

One of these properties which we secured was part of the monastery of San Francisco, as we described elsewhere. It had been sold to a theater company, which had failed, because the ladies expected to attend, much as they liked the performances, regarded it as somewhat sacrilegious to have them in a building once consecrated to religious uses. The Chiarini Circus company shared the same fate for the same reasons. So closely were the missionaries watched to prevent them from acquiring property that, when any one of us was seen looking at a desirable place, before it could be decided upon it was

22

"out of the market." Hearing that the Chiarini Circus was for sale, I was eager to see if it could be adapted for our use. Not daring to go near it in the day-time, for fear of being seen and losing the chance, I waited until ten o'clock at night, then went and knocked at the great door. The sleepy janitor opened the portal a little way only, and was reluctant to admit any one at such an hour. However, a silver dollar proved quite persuasive to compensate him for his interrupted sleep, and upon my saying that I only wanted to see what the circus of Chiarini was like the drowsy creature woke up to considerable willingness and by the light of his lantern showed me the premises.

To my great satisfaction I found the property just what we required, and at once made earnest efforts to secure it. But I learned that one of the parties whose signature was necessary was a fanatical old lady who would rather see the building go up in smoke than sold to Protestants. What to do I could not imagine. We needed the place so much, the location was admirable, central yet quiet, and our work, already begun, was suffering for lack of a proper center of operations. But here was delay and uncertainty. We could only seek divine help and wait. Three weeks later I was standing at a street corner, conversing with a friend, when a gentleman passed on the other side of the street. My friend signaled, the stranger crossed over, and we were introduced. During the conversation India was mentioned. "What!" said I, "have you been in India?" "Yes; I fought under Havelock, and was one of the volunteer cavalry that rode with him into Lucknow." Instantly it flashed across my mind that here was help at last if I could win him! "Well," I replied, "I have done my best to immortalize you and your gallant comrades." "What do you mean?" said he. Asking him to remain where we were for a few minutes, I hurried to the hotel and took a copy of *The Land of the Veda*, which I carried back and showed to him, opened at the portrait of General Havelock. He looked at it astonished, and said, "That is indeed our illustrious commander," and commenced at once to read the pages that refer to the bravery

HEAD-QUARTERS OF THE MISSION OF THE METHODIST EPISCOPAL CHURCH,
Calle de Gante, City of Mexico.

of the heroes, led by their devout general. I stood prayerfully and anxiously waiting. Finally, turning to me he said, "How much I would like to possess this book!" "Please, sir, then, accept it as a gift from the author." Thanking me with genuine heartiness he exclaimed, "Is there not something I could do for you to show my gratitude?" I had learned that he was an Irishman and a Catholic, but Providence led me to feel that he could and would help me, so I replied, "You are probably the only man in this city who can do something very necessary for me." "What is it?" I explained the circumstances, how we were anxious to secure a suitable property for our work, but that the bigoted old lady would not be willing to sell it to us, and I feared to trust any broker in the city lest they should be induced to fail us. He asked, "Would you trust *me?*" I felt free to say I would. "Have you the money?" Yes; the money was ready in the bank. "Well, say nothing until I come to you to-morrow morning, and I will arrange it all for you." I reminded him that I was a Protestant missionary and that he was a Catholic, but he said, "What of that? Have five hundred dollars ready for me to-morrow." He came the next day, took the money, paid the installment, and obtained his receipt. The property was his and all secure. As soon as the papers in the case were ready he took me to the government office and made out a deed to me as agent of the missionary society of our Church, and the circus of Chiarini was ours! He had meanwhile, when his purpose leaked out, an enticing offer to be unfaithful to us, but he spurned the temptation and in due time and form made it over to us.

Surely "the hearts of all men are in the hands of God," and he has his own way of answering the prayers of those who seek his aid. Here, when I needed it so much, after all my anxiety, was this warm-hearted Irishman brought in good time twelve thousand miles across the world, attracted to me by a common interest which that "Land of the Veda" represented to us both, ready to do a service that I could not safely ask any lawyer or broker or other Romanist to do in the city of Mexico!

One of the clerical papers came out a few days after with the following note, under the title, "Each Time Worse:"

It is said that the Protestants have purchased the Chiarini Circus. As is known, this place is formed out of a *patio* of the monastery of San Francisco. O, venerated shades of Belaunzarán and Pinzon! You will wander lamenting around that place which was sanctified by the presence of the sons of San Francisco, and which is profanated in a descending scale, by rope-dancing, immoral shows, licentious balls, and the ceremonies of a dissenting sect which is the enemy of the Church. It is a real profanation, but it cannot be remedied, for power protects the profanators.

Preceding page 291 is a view of the newly erected façade of this church. The beautiful interior will be shown farther on. It increased our interest to discover, as we did, from the pages of the Jesuit historian Clavijero, that these premises were part of the very site of the famous palace of Montezuma.* Afterward in relaying the floor we found confirmation of this fact near the front door by discovering one of the fish fountains which Clavijero describes. Could Montezuma and his historian rise from the dead how amazed would they be to witness the transformation that has taken place! Here, in place of the pagan palace and the Romish convent, there stands to-day the beautiful evangelical church, complete in all its appointments, with chapel, vestries, printing-office, schools, besides two comfortable parsonages and other accommodations for this work. Mexico has had many "transitions" during the past twenty-five years, but none more wonderful than that which we witness here.

Equally remarkable was our purchase of the property secured for our work in the city of Puebla. While Mexico city is the political capital, Puebla may be considered as the ecclesiastical capital of the country. A branch of the Inquisition of Rome had been established in each city with equal powers. No Protestantism existed then in either city or in either

---

* *Ancient History of Mexico,* by Abbé D. F. S. Clavijero, book v, p. 213. London, 1810.

THE INQUISITION, CITY OF PUEBLA,
Purchased by the Methodist Episcopal Church in 1873.

COVERED WAY OF THE INQUISITION,
Connecting with the Examining Chapel.

section of the country for this diabolical institution to expend its energy upon, during the first three hundred years of its existence. Its watch-care then was directed toward its own people, and evidently extended to more than questions of religious opinion, thus enabling the priesthood to lay a heavy hand upon those who dared to make themselves prominent in the advocacy of civil and religious freedom. But these inquisitors had such ability to cover their tracks that the whole truth can never be known until the books are opened in the judgment-day! We are about to uncover dark transactions which "that day" will fully reveal, when the sightless eyeballs and the dumb lips on which we have gazed with horror shall open, and the truth of their tortures shall be brought before those who thus inflicted them!

We present two views of the Inquisition building in Puebla. The photograph was taken from the roof of one of the corridors. On the left hand appears the dome of the Examining Chapel, where the victims were tried, and beneath, on the ground floor, were the cells, which we must soon mention. The second picture shows the covered way leading to the Inquisition over the tops of the houses. The face of it remains open as it was left when the government cut a street through the premises. Certainly those who erected these buildings, with walls of masonry some of them over six feet thick, and arches and trimmings of cut stone, expected that they would endure for all time. In some of the changes necessary to adapt them to our use crowbar and pickax seemed weak tools to make any impression upon their hardness. These immense premises of the Dominican monks (the Inquisitorial order) fell at last into the hands of the republican forces, and the people, especially those from whose homes father, brothers, or sons had disappeared, and of whose fate something might be learned within those walls, demanded permission to search, as did the Parisians at the Bastile. The request was granted and the excited searchers went through the whole establishment from the ground to the roofs; a few survivors were found, but the majority of seekers were disappointed. Baffled and enraged, they were about to leave when some one remarked on the amazing thickness of the walls. A new train of thought was started. The walls were struck and at places seemed to sound hollow to the blow. Tools were procured, openings made, and within narrow cells were found those whom they sought, manacled and ghastly, not arrayed in grave vestments, but in their daily clothing, as when last seen. Twelve such cells were found and opened, each with its occupant. Truly this was "bringing to light the hidden things of darkness." These victims of Rome's cruelties, buried alive for freedom, or for Christ, or both, it may be, were tenderly lifted out into the open *patio* and a photographer called. A flower-stand was near, and four of the martyrs who were recent enough to be handled without breaking up, though not recognizable, were placed against it, and the sun has painted for us the faithful and enduring proof which the Liberals of Mexico can hand down in evidence to future generations of what the Church of Rome did with their fellow-countrymen. From one of these photographs in our possession the picture opposite was copied.

The cells were four feet six inches on the square, and seven feet high. The need for the thick walls was thus explained. These spaces were left open when building until the victim was condemned and bound in the Examining Chapel above, and brought down to the corridor where the cells were located. He or she (for women were among the number) was placed in the cell, a "brother" of the order who was handy with the trowel was ready to build up the entrance before their face and leave them to a horrible death, while a coat of plaster and whitewash made all invisible, and these fiends in human form may have supposed that they had sealed up their crime forever and buried their secret beyond discovery. Two bodies of such sufferers may still be seen in a glass case in the National Museum in Mexico city.

One cell, making the thirteenth, was overlooked and not opened until we came into the possession of the premises. We found it occupied and had the body removed and buried. Like

MARTYRS OF THE INQUISITION,
Taken out of the cells in the walls, where they were buried alive.

the other large ecclesiastical properties, this had been divided
into lots for sale, and a street cut through the premises. A German Jew, living in Puebla, bought this portion of the Inquisition. When we came to Puebla to look for property, such even
then was the clerical influence that people were timid about
renting or selling to us. With the Jew it was different. He
cared nothing about their fulminations, and was eager to make
a trade with us. Both in India and in Mexico I have made all
sorts of purchases for our society, but when we stood beside
this man on the dais of the Examining Chapel in Puebla, and
realized that a Jew was actually offering the Inquisition for
sale to a Methodist preacher, this seemed about the most extraordinary transaction in real estate which we had ever known!
To have purchased the great cathedral itself would not have
been more amazing. Around us were the evidences of the
popular vengeance that had been wreaked upon the accursed
building; the doors, windows, and floors had been torn up and
smashed to pieces, and the plaster defaced. But all this could
soon be repaired. On the upper floor to the right was a suite
of rooms which would make a comfortable parsonage, and on
the left the Examining Chapel could be made into the first
Methodist Episcopal Church in Puebla. It was capable of holding about one hundred and fifty people. On the floor below a
room as large as the chapel would give us a good school-room, and
the apartments and corridors to the right would afford accommo-
dation for the boys' orphanage and a theological seminary. We
were thus—at least for the time being—amply provided for in
the work which our Church was to undertake in Puebla.

It was while engaged, a few months later, in laying out the
rooms on the ground floor for a theological seminary that we
made that additional discovery of those dead secrets which
have ever since been such a perplexing remembrance to us.
The leading impression produced has been that they represent
"deeds of darkness" that certainly double the guilt and cruelty
which we already know to be justly chargeable to the account
of this horrible institution. In front of the rooms where the

cells were there runs a covered corridor with outside pillars, about twelve feet wide. Our purpose then was to divide this space by a wall into two rooms. Having indicated where the foundation was to be laid, we left the spot, but were soon after met with the startling announcement that the workmen in digging had come upon a number of human skeletons packed together in rows. They were about two and a half feet below the surface, covered with earth, and over this a layer of mortar in which large floor-bricks were firmly laid. They were packed close together and occupied about two feet in depth, the trench running the entire length of the corridor. They were lifted out into the *patio*, and the mayor of the city notified to send the municipal carts and grant them proper burial.

People were annoyed that Protestant strangers should make such a dreadful discovery. They thought that they knew all the horrors of that establishment and had removed them. We discussed the situation, but could find no innocent cause for their being there and in such condition. They were not more than twelve feet in front of the martyrs' cells, all under cover of the roof, with less than thirty inches of earth over them, and the mortar and floor-brick resting on this shallow protection, the whole bearing the aspect of utter secrecy. As a probable explanation it was suggested that at certain intervals, when the cells were full, the floor would be opened and the contents of the cells emptied into the space made, and then closed up like the rest, leaving the cells ready for new occupants. The one fact seems to bear a relation to the other in guilt and secrecy, but of the character of the manacled martyrs of the cells there is no doubt whatever.

It is with much concern that we are contemplating parting with this locality; but, notwithstanding all its interest, the place has become too small for our growing work in Puebla. We have secured a large lot in the best part of the city and are erecting a church adequate for our congregation. These incidents will suffice until we come to the close to speak of the work done by all the missions operating in the land.

PERSONNEL OF THE ANNUAL CONFERENCE IN MEXICO IN JANUARY, 1888,
Seventeen of the number being natives of the country.

What an utter failure those Dominican and Franciscan monks were! After their three hundred years of power the conquered race expels them from New Spain, and some of their palatial abodes, wrested from the hands of pagan royalty for their endowment, pass into the hands of heretics, who there proclaim the word of life under the ample protection of Mexican law. Had they done their work as God willed it to be done their time would have endured forever, and our services would not have been required. They failed to elevate Mexico, but made her a land of ignorance, unrest, and misery, from the galling yoke of which she could only shake herself free by one of the most extraordinary revolutions known to history, carried through by the very people they had trained in their faith and usages.

The advance which our own Mission has made under the divine blessing is indicated in the picture opposite of our Annual Conference of 1888. Eighteen of the ministers therein are native Mexicans, most of them raised up and trained under our own labors during the preceding fifteen years.

The entrance of Protestant missions into Mexico and their progress since the close of the French Intervention has claimed the attention not only of the public journals but also of the government, and is frequently referred to with approbation. There lies before us as we write the *Official Report of the Progress of Protestant Missions in Mexico,* by the government secretary of finance, dated January, 1879, in which the facts are given with entire fairness. This public and kindly notice of the Protestant propaganda in their country is given not because of any personal interest in our views, but because the facts furnish the most satisfactory evidence of the full religious freedom and progress which their country is now enjoying side by side with the United States. Any violation of these rights is denounced in the most prompt and decided manner by all save the fanatical faction who are under the inspiration of the Romish clergy, and all wrongs under it are quickly redressed on appeal for the protection of the rights of ourselves and our people.

23

As these missions stand for the highest progress which Mexico can ever know, the desire for the meeting of a General Assembly of Evangelical Missions began to take form about 1886. The purpose was

To review the results of the past fifteen years and to consult with each other in regard to the future of their common work. A committee, with power, was agreed upon to call this assembly from all parts of the land, and to take such measures as, in their judgment, would best accomplish the purposes of such a gathering. A suitable circular was prepared and sent to every missionary in the country to be filled up with replies to the questions which would bring together the information desired to be laid before the assembly.

After nine years of absence from the termination of my own work in Mexico (in 1879) I naturally desired to be present on this occasion, as well as to have the opportunity of collecting the information which was needed for writing this work. Five months of delightful privilege was thus improved, especially in witnessing the advance made by the country during the period from 1879 to 1888. From all quarters of Mexico these servants of God, American and Mexican, came to represent the work in which they were engaged for their common Lord and Master.

On the morning of January 31, 1888, this remarkable body of Christian men and women assembled in Trinity Methodist Episcopal Church in the city of Mexico, the largest Protestant church in the city. It was found that there were eleven evangelical denominations represented, as follows: The Baptists, North and South; the Friends; the Presbyterians, North and South; the Methodist Episcopal Church, South; the Episcopalians; the Associate Reformed Presbyterians; the Congregationalists; the Cumberland Presbyterians, and the Methodist Episcopal Church. The representation was from one to nine, according to the size of the missions operating in Mexico. Including two for the Bible Society, the total representation consisted of about seventy-five persons. These, with other missionaries and native ministers, who came as visitors, swelled the number attending to about one hundred and twenty-five. Deeply interested audiences, from three hundred to four hundred in number, were present at the sessions, mornings, afternoons, and evenings. It was the first occasion on which these evangelical workers had ever come together. Few of them had before met one another, and yet the meetings, lasting more than three days, were undisturbed in their delightful harmony.

It may not be too much to say that in view of the past history of this land, the interests involved, and the future which was intimated, this General Assembly was the most important event that has occurred here since the Laws of Reform were passed by the new-born nation. It presented before the people of this country and before the Church of Rome the blessed evidence of the union, affection, and the strength of evangelical Christianity in a way that must have astonished them. Certainly, if there really was (as was supposed by many) any treasonable purpose of the Reactionary party to employ the opportunity of December 12, 1887, in connection with the crowning of the Virgin of Guadalupe, to overthrow the civil and religious liberties of this nation, that party found a surprise of which they never dreamed, and one which they cannot soon forget. How like it seems to a direct answer of the Almighty to the enemies of his cause—giving them to understand that he has taken Mexico out of their hands and is to accomplish her redemption after her long night of sorrow!

The programme was carried out almost to the letter, and a wonderful unanimity realized in the conclusions reached upon each item by the Assembly. These "watchmen saw eye to eye."

We have not space for an outline of the deliberations or of the work accomplished except under one head, that of the statistics. Many Romanists came in to see the Assembly, and it was evident that they were surprised at the order and thoroughness of the deliberations and the size and attention of the audiences. They must have realized that their methods of contempt and persecution could not frighten these people from their convictions, and that the intelligent and sincere aspect of their countrymen who had become preachers and members of these Protestant Churches had some claim upon their respect.

Great interest was excited by the reading of the report of "The Statistics of Protestantism in Mexico." The utmost care had been taken to have the exhibit as accurate as possible. The forms which were supplied were of the fullest and most exact character. Each mission filled out its own forms, and then the whole was carefully tabulated, so that every item of every

mission in Mexico was fully presented from its own records. I
have resubmitted these statistical tables again to each of the
missions represented, requesting them to correct and add to
their figures the growth of the past four years, so as to present the numerical standing of Protestantism in Mexico at the
close of 1891. The tables are too voluminous to be given in
full for each mission. It may be enough to present the results
in two columns, the first showing the grand total of the eleven
Protestant missions in Mexico, and the second the statistics of the missions of the Methodist Episcopal Church by
themselves ˙alone. No one who has prayed and contributed
for the spread of the Gospel in this land but must rejoice over
"what God has wrought" during the past twenty years in
Mexico. If such a glorious result has been reached in twenty
years, in the face of vigorous opposition and fanaticism, what
may we not expect in the future as a result of the work now
so well established under the ample protection of the law of
the land?

ABSTRACT FROM THE REPORT OF THE STATISTICS OF PROTESTANT MIS-
SIONS IN MEXICO, 1888 (REVISED TO 1892).

I. *The Field.*	Total of Protestant Missions.	Methodist Episcopal Missions.
Number of centers of operation	87	30
Number of congregations	469	125

II. *The Workers.*

Number of ordained foreign missionaries	59	9
Number of assistant foreign missionaries (that is, unordained men, and wives of ordained and assistant missionaries)	51	9
Number of foreign lady teachers	67	9
Whole number of foreign workers	177	27
Number of native preachers, ordained	111	13
Number of native preachers, unordained	161	38
Number of native teachers	177	47
Number of other native helpers	63	45
Total number of native workers	512	143
Grand total of foreign and native workers	689	170

III. *The Churches.*

Number of churches organized	385	100
Number of communicants	16,250	2,665
Number of probable adherents	49,512	6,735

IV. *The Schools.*	Total of Protestant Missions.	Methodist Episcopal Missions.
Number of training and theological schools............	7	1
Number of students in same........................	88	5
Number of boarding-schools and orphanages..........	23	4
Number of pupils in same...........................	715	125
Number of common schools.........................	164	49
Number of pupils in same...........................	6,533	2,703
Total number under instruction.....................	7,336	2,833
Number of Sunday-schools..........................	347	45
Number of Sunday-school teachers and officers........	694	90
Number of Sunday-school scholars	9,814	1,797
Total membership of Sunday-schools................	10,508	1,887

V. *Publishing Interests.*

Number of publishing-houses.......................	5	1
Number of papers issued............................	11	3
Pages of all kinds of religious literature issued since the establishment of your press.........	75,197,885	35,197,885

VI. *Properties.*

Number of church buildings........................	118	23
Approximate value of same (including furniture)	$391,675	$84,575
Number of parsonages..............................	45	19
Approximate value of same (including society furniture)	$158,835	$110,925
Number of educational buildings....................	31	8
Approximate value of same (including furniture and utensils)...	$256,940	$93,490
Value of publishing outfit..........................	$36,850	$18,000
Total value of all missionary property...............	$844,300	$306,990

VII. *Historic and Personal.*

How many martyrs, if any, has your mission had?.....	58	1
Place and date of such martyrdom?............................*		......†

The last item but one, that of the martyrdom of our preachers and people, developed the deepest feeling in our Assembly. The time and place where these cruel deeds were done is stated in the foot-note of the table, and makes the dreadful showing that an average of one murder every three months had been inflicted upon our Protestant missions from 1873 up to the period of holding that General Assembly. One of these was an American

---

* One foreigner and 57 Mexicans: Martyrs—4 at Capalhuac in Holy Week, 1873; 2 at Ahualulco, March, 1874; 15 at Acapulco, 1874; 2 at Tlalquiltenango, 1876; 1 at Guadalajara, 1876; 25 at Atzala, 1878; 1 at San José, 1879; 1 at Salatitlan, 1880; 1 at Apizaco, 1881; 1 at Progresso, 1881; 2 at Almoloya, 1884; 2 at Ahuacatitlan, 1887, and 1 at Comalcalco, 1887.   † Brother Monroy at Apizaco.

missionary; the rest, fifty-seven in number, were Mexicans, either preachers or members. One word of condemnation or reproof from Archbishop Labastida would have prevented these unprovoked atrocities, but that word was never spoken to his dying hour last year, and the cruel fanatics presumed that his silence meant consent for their deeds. Most of the cases were atrocious to the last degree. The Rev. John L. Stephens (whose picture is here given) was sent out by the American Board in October, 1872, to Guadalajara. He was a man of noble character and devoted to his work. On Sunday night, March 2, 1874, after preaching at Ahualulco, he was attacked by a party of fanatics, who broke into the place and assassinated him and one of his native preachers.

Another case we speak of from personal knowledge. He was one of our native ministers, the Rev. Epigmenio Monroy, stationed at Apizaco. This man was characterized as being of an unusually sweet spirit, avoiding controversy as far as possible, and loving to preach the Gospel in its experimental blessedness. He had opened a station at Santa Ana, about three miles from Apizaco, and one night (April 8, 1881) on returning late after holding the service, he was followed and left for dead on the side of the road, terribly mangled. Some time after his groans attracted the attention of some travelers, who found him lying in his blood in the darkness. They revived him till he could tell them where he lived, when they kindly bore him into Apizaco. Medical help was called, but it was too late, his life was fast ebbing away; he had only time and strength to bless his family and bid them farewell. The Christ-like spirit of the man was still in full possession of him. He requested his family not to prosecute his murderers in case they should be discovered, he had forgiven them, and, feebly lifting his hands and looking up to heaven, he threw the last energies of his life into the prayer, "Father, forgive them, they know not what they do!" His head rested down on his bosom, and he was gone! Surely it may be asked, What more has the Christian religion done for men anywhere in making them Christ-like

REV. J. L. STEPHENS, CONGREGATIONAL MISSIONARY,
Martyred at Ahualulco, March, 1874.

REV. EPIGMENIO MONROY, NATIVE METHODIST MINISTER,
Martyred near Apizaco, April 8, 1881.

than it did for this humble minister, whose mangled remains we laid to rest in the sure and certain hope of a glorious resurrection? At the Annual Conference his brethren, by whom he was greatly beloved, out of their scant allowances united to place a little monument over the grave of this proto-martyr of the Methodist Church in Mexico. We present a picture here of this good and devoted native Methodist preacher.

We Americans have been also the objects of this maliciousness, but the fanatics are more afraid to strike us in view of the closer guardianship which the government is able to extend to us, and of the fact that we occupy centers where the police care is more effective. For the first year or two we were exposed to their hostility, and some of them imagined that if we were only struck down the cause would die. But the government knew our danger better than we did, and was constantly on the lookout for our safety, giving us useful cautions from time to time. From the press and the pulpit, and in episcopal edicts put up on church doors, we and our work were held up to public hatred. Some of our churches have been desecrated and burned. Threats of all kinds have been hurled at us and our doom said to be decided upon. On the 9th of December, 1873, the oldest of our native helpers informed me that he had reason to believe (I understood from government intimation) that a body of these fanatics had been banded together to accomplish the assassination of all the Protestant ministers, American and native, in the city of Mexico—a "Saint Bartholomew's Day" on their own account. But the government was quietly vigilant, and had intimated to some of the leaders that they were aware of their purpose, and threatened punishment if we were injured. Thus we were left unharmed.

The tactics pursued by the enemies of evangelical faith in Mexico are identical with those followed by Romanists elsewhere. They try first to terrorize, then to deny our religious belief, then they malign our morality; and when they have thus depreciated us, and inoculated their ignorant dupes with this virus of malice and hatred, the step is a short one for these to think that to kill would be doing God service. Even if the blow is not struck their course answers its first purpose, to keep the people away from Gospel instructions and from the reading of the Holy Scriptures. From this source come the cruel names which they bestow upon us. We are not only "heretics," but "children of Satan," and are assured by the pope (in his encyclical of November 9, 1846) that "It is certain that every one who does not preserve the Roman faith entire will be utterly and eternally lost," and that bishops must inculcate unity with the Catholic Church, "out of which there is no salvation, and obedience toward the chair of St. Peter, on which the whole structure of our most holy religion reposes." No wonder they fear the reading of the Bible, where not one word can be found to sustain this assumption. They even dare to justify their cruelties toward evangelical Christians in the following language :

The Church or Christian princes are not blamed for putting heretics to death. *The blood of heretics is not the blood of saints*, no more than the blood of thieves, man-killers, and other malefactors—for the shedding of which blood by the order of justice no commonwealth shall answer.*

Let it be observed that this murderous language is not the utterance of some obscure writer, but is the rule laid down by a leading theologian of their Church, and copied into the standard work of Peter Dens, that manual of divinity in which vile and intolerant system the majority of her priests are trained.

The deeds of cruelty done in Mexico have not helped them. The thoughtful people of the land condemn the idea that, to gratify clerical malice, Protestants are to be "counted as sheep for the slaughter," and are determined that this shame must terminate. We will ever remember the interview with President Diaz on the occasion of the assassination of some of our native brethren at Atzala. After expressing his deep sorrow at the atrocities and assuring us that religious freedom would be vindicated, that the government was ready at any hour to de-

* Rhenish Test., annot. upon Rev. xvii, 6.

fend our people in the rights guaranteed by the Constitution, President Diaz assured us that not only the government but also the Congress and people generally all over the land were as indignant as we were over these instances of Romish intolerance; and he earnestly deprecated the idea that people outside should judge their nation by these instances of the rage and cruelty of their Church and its fanatical agents.

The president then made a remark that at first surprised us all. It was to this effect:

You are greatly depressed and discouraged over what has now occurred, and I do not wonder; but if you knew this country as I know it you would feel differently.

He saw our surprise and then proceeded to explain:

I have seen this land as none of you ever saw it, in degradation, with every thing in the line of toleration and freedom to learn. I have watched its rise and progress to a better condition. We are not yet all we ought to be and hope to be; but we are not what we once were. We have risen as a people, and are rising now faster than ever. My advice is, do not be discouraged. Keep on with your work, avoiding topics of irritation and preaching your Gospel in its own spirit, and believe me that twenty years hence religious murders will have ceased in Mexico and our people will be rejoicing in the peace and toleration which our Constitution guarantees to all without distinction.

The words of the worthy president have already become true. Long within the twenty years anticipated these murders have ceased and people are willing, beyond all former experience, to hear us for our cause. Blood-stains—even though only "the blood of heretics"—are no longer considered excusable or endurable on the clerical escutcheon. Popular condemnation (and, let us hope, the priestly conscience as well) has become opposed to it. The warning of our Quaker poet, uttered in 1871, when the pope issued a second call to Romish nations to come to his aid and crush and drive out Italians and King Victor from their capital, has sunk deep into the souls of men: "Woe be to the Church which mingles human blood with her wine of sacrament and breaks the peace of God among men!" It is again true that "the more they oppressed them the more they multiplied and grew." Some time since I was delighted to hear from the secretary of the American Board that the very man who held the torch to enable the murderers of Brother Stephens to do their work has been converted and is now devoted to the cause which he once destroyed.

The table of statistics on page 300 shows that, in spite of this great fight of afflictions, our work has wonderfully prospered and that we are doubling our numbers, on the average, about every *eight years*. In twenty years there have been raised up 111 native ordained ministers, 161 unordained, and a total of 512 native workers, with 16,250 communicants and 49,512 adherents in 469 congregations. Who, after this, need doubt whether Roman Catholics *can be converted* to evangelical Christianity? Thank God for the faithfulness of our Mexican converts!

During this recent visit to Mexico we went again to see the cemeteries of Guadalupe and of San Fernando, symbolizing as they do the past and the future of Mexico and the great change she has experienced. What a rush of memories came over us as we stood by the monument that covers the grave of Santa Anna, just inside the gate of the Guadalupe cemetery! Of all his desperate movements, the last—at Vera Cruz, in 1867—seems to have been the most pregnant with evil for his country. What a chapter of political ruin and ecclesiastical domination he might have added to the history of Mexico if the commander of the *Tacony* had not interposed! About two years after his return from exile, under the general amnesty granted by Juarez, we saw him in Mexico city. Ex-Governor Brown, of Georgia, and some of his friends were visiting in Mexico. They expressed a desire to have an interview with the old dictator. The visit was arranged, and we accompanied these friends. Santa Anna had not yet had his property restored, and was living in an obscure street, neglected and forgotten by all parties. He seemed gratified that Americans should desire to see him. On entering the apartment we found the old man sitting on a sofa, behind which hung the life-size picture of his wife, "her serene highness, Dolores Tosta de Santa Anna," arrayed as a vice-queen. The magnificence of the painting contrasted sadly with the poverty-stricken aspect of the room and furniture. To him, however, this could make but little difference, as we soon saw that he was totally blind as well as feeble and broken in spirit, with a tendency to mental weakness. He did nearly all the talking, and frequently referred to his interview with General Jackson, and of his being sent home on a United States war vessel, which he took care to emphasize as a mark of high respect to himself. He was still the vain and self-seeking Santa Anna!

We sat before him in a semicircle and surveyed a man who had probably more history in him at eighty years of age than any other person on this continent; one who had been the ready instrument of clerical despotism, firmly resolved to keep the Bible and religious freedom out of his native land, but who had *failed* in every point. God had overthrown him and his purposes, and here were missionaries sitting before him entirely unconcerned whether he was vexed or not that the Bible and evangelical Christianity were where he had intended that they should never come. He had every opportunity to make himself the Washington or Cromwell of his country, but proved that he was incapable of being a true reformer. Instead of this the amazing record that he built up seems matchless in modern history. It was recalled the more vividly by the picture behind him. Curtis has well epitomized the facts which in this presence were made all the more expressive:

It created a sensation in Mexico when the pretty peon girl Dolores Tosta was suddenly raised from abject poverty to affluence. Santa Anna was President of Mexico three years before she was born; she was married to him when she was only thirteen. He was then a military dictator, sleeping on his sword, beset with constant perils. In six months he had lost his leg and got into a Texas prison. For twenty years her life was spent in a camp, surrounded by the whirl of warfare. Her husband was five times President of Mexico and four times military dictator in absolute power, and in his reckless career had upset some fifteen governments of his country. He was banished, recalled, and again banished. She has seen much "glory" and received unlimited adulation, but she hardly ever enjoyed one thoroughly peaceful month in all her life.

So far Curtis is correct, but he errs in supposing that their career ended in exile. Here they were, having been permitted, on their petition, by the republican government, to return and die in their native land. That government, consolidated and strong, had nothing more to fear from this traitor or his allies, and the public had left them to sink into the neglect and obscurity in which we found them.

A short time after Santa Anna died, at the age of eighty-four. The account of the funeral is dreary enough, "only a few prominent individuals following the funeral cortege" to the cemetery of "the most Holy Virgin of Guadalupe." True to his habit, he made a modification of his title to be cut on the white marble monument (to which her name and title were added ten years after). We thought it interesting enough to be copied exactly as it appears:

Excelentísimo
Sr Grāl Antonio Lopez de Santa Ana.
Junio 21 de 1876.

Serenísima Sora
Dolores Tosta de Santa Ana.
Agósto 11 de 1886.

R. I. P.

The translation is:

Most Excellent
General Antonio Lopez de Santa Anna.

Most Serene Madame
Dolores Tosta de Santa Anna.

Truly it might be said that this man was as whimsical in death as in life and character, in view of certain solemn obsequies that transpired in another locality and of another monument that was erected years before. It might be said that he was buried in sections, while, unfortunately for his fame, the pomp and ceremonial came at the wrong end of his career. A public funeral was decreed for his "Christian leg," while the rest of him was interred almost in privacy and without ceremonial.

If the Virgin of Guadalupe is all that his clerical guides taught Santa Anna to believe, then even he may have a chance, for he served her well in his way and placed himself under her protection at the last. But if *not*—if this "holy image of the mother of God" is but a myth and will not be beside that judgment throne to own and shelter her devotees—what an awaking must be that of the man who lies here, in view of the miseries inflicted upon Mexico during the forty years of his more active life!

It was pleasant to turn from this pathetic example of Mexico's degraded past to the Panteon de San Fernando, the resting-place of many of her illustrious dead. Most prominent and rising above them all stands the worthy monument of "the Washington of Mexico," Benito Juarez. He died on the 19th of July, 1872, aged sixty-six years, and his ever-grateful country erected this rich tribute above his grave.

It is a tomb the most exacting soul might envy. As a work of art it is fine indeed, but as the tribute of an Indian sculptor to the great Indian statesman it is magnificently impressive. Out beyond the Alameda in the Panteon of San Fernando is the resting-place of many of Mexico's illustrious dead, and the eternal fitness of things in God's acre is kept when the richest tribute that sculpture could bring rises above the grave of Juarez. This monument is the work of Manuel Islas, who has succeeded in the most difficult of all fields. The unvarying testimony of those who visit the cemetery might be quoted in proof of this claim, and certainly no monumental effort in the United States tells such a story of heroic grief or so immortalizes the dignified emotion of a nation. A small but well-proportioned Grecian temple, surrounded by rows of columns, contains the commemorative group of spotless marble, the dead president lying at full length with his head supported on the knee of a female figure representing Mexico. It is the most simple and natural thing in the world, after it is done; and yet the United States has scarcely a memorial of dead greatness that does not seem conventional and strained beside it, scarcely one in any degree so good in its technical qualities, or so satisfying as a work of art.

Summer and winter this magnificent tomb is fragrant with the floral offerings laid upon it by his grateful countrymen. Around him, in this Westminster Abbey of Mexico, lie— sharing his honor and the glory of his success—such heroes as Generals Arteaga and Salazar, and many others, who struggled and died to secure to Mexico the glorious future on the threshold of which she stands to-day.

Under the gentle influence of that "timely silence" which falls on all who approach this tomb of Mexico's greatest statesman-patriot and the resting-places of many others of her noble heroes, one feels instinctively that there may not be on earth a spot where the adaptation of those wonderful words of our own martyr-president might be more justly admitted:

The brave men, living and dead, who struggled here have consecrated it far above our power to add or detract. The world will little note, nor long remember, what we say here; but it can never forget what they did here. It is for us, the living, rather to be dedicated here to the unfinished work which they who fought here have thus far so nobly advanced. It is rather for us to be here dedicated to the great task remaining before us, that from these honored dead we take increased devotion to that cause for which they gave the last full measure of devotion; that we here highly resolve that these dead shall not have died in vain; that this nation, under God, shall have a new birth of freedom, and that the government of the people, by the people, and for the people shall not perish from the earth.

Before we left Mexico there occurred a significant event which presented a providential response to the vaporing of Louis Napoleon when he tried to interfere with American affairs under the pretense of securing on this continent "a career for the Latin race and its civilization," which he alleged was "to be the glory of his reign" and "the most beneficent event of the nineteenth century." I refer to the memorial services of the Emperor William of Germany. Next to those in Berlin it may be safe to say that those so grandly solemnized in the city of Mexico were among the most significant. The lesson was so marked that we need not wonder that the papal party in Mexico resented the honor being conferred upon the memory of the man who with such Teutonic and Protestant candor and courage could so ably brush aside the hollow pretenses and antiquated claims of Pius IX. when he ventured so adroitly to impose them upon the emperor's acceptance. Nor is it strange that in the capital of Mexico memorial services should be held for the grand man who laid low the "eldest son of the Church" and all his projects, thus avenging the wrongs which Louis Napoleon inflicted on Mexico! It was gall and wormwood to the clerical party that the memory of the great Protestant sovereign of the land of Luther and of the glorious Reformation should be thus honored in the city of Mexico and in the presence of its government. In this respect it was also the grandest hour for the evangelical faith that Mexico up to that date had witnessed. From an account which we prepared at the time we present the facts of this extraordinary event.

On Friday morning, March 9, 1888, when the telegram arrived announcing the death of the Emperor of Germany, the Rev. J. W. Butler, in charge of our mission in Mexico city, went at once to wait upon the German embassador and the consul to express our sympathy and offer the use of our church for any memorial services which they might desire to hold. The Germans have no church of their own in Mexico, and on several occasions have gratefully accepted the use of our edifice. Both minister and consul expressed themselves as most thankful for the kind spirit shown by our American mission in this offer to place our church at their disposal. They arranged at once to call together the heads of the German colony (residents in Mexico city) for consultation, and to communicate with the pastor without delay. Within a few hours the colony had been consulted and their measures taken, and the committee appointed came to express their gratitude and arrange a programme. Monday evening at five o'clock was their preference. By early afternoon on Saturday their invitations, printed on heavily bordered

24

mourning-paper, in Spanish, were ready. They bore the coat of arms of the German empire, and read as follows: "The German minister, in his name, and in that of the German colony, has the honor to invite you to the religious ceremony which, occasioned by the death of his majesty the Emperor of Germany, will take place Monday, March 12, at five o'clock in the afternoon, in the temple on Gante Street." The word temple is used for all places of worship in Mexico.

This invitation was sent to General Diaz, the president of the republic, to the members of his cabinet, to the foreign embassadors and consuls and the members of their respective staffs, and also to the governor of the federal district and the various officials, civil and military, in the capital, as well as the gentlemen and ladies of the German, English, and American colonies, and others. The editors of the leading papers were also invited.

Meanwhile the leading decorator of the city had been called and instruction given him by the Germans to decorate our church suitably, regardless of expense, for the high and solemn occasion. With a little army of assistants he commenced his labors at daylight on Saturday and worked till midnight, resuming again early Monday morning, and had all ready one hour before the time for commencement of the services on Monday afternoon. The handsome audience-room was a suitable background for the rich adorning with which they draped its pillars, cornices, arches, and balconies. This is truly the land of flowers, and the fullest use was made of their magnificence to add to every other charm of the place. The gorgeous tropical plants were intertwined with the floral decorations, making a sight in themselves alone worth a journey to see and enjoy. Then the festoons of flowers were carried around, above, upon the arches and cornices, and the wreaths were hung under the center of the arches and upon each pillar. The flowers used were those which were appropriate, white roses and violets preponderating largely.

The flags and shields with the German arms were then placed

in position, and the long bannerets, with spheres of silver crystal, were suspended from the roof above. Black crape was gracefully draped every-where, and all the ornamentation was appropriate to the occasion. Black cloth hung from the balconies all around the church. But it was upon the pulpit and communion rails that their chief skill was employed. Upon the pulpit platform near the wall rose a white pedestal draped, on the top of which rested a bust (life-size) of the dead emperor, supported by a cushion of flowers. Behind the pedestal and bust hung down, some eight feet in length, a rich drapery of black velvet, studded with silver stars. The pulpit was draped with black velvet and silver trimmings, as were the communion rails, and illuminated by small chandeliers, bearing wax tapers. The kneeling-step was overlaid with the leaves of the rubber-tree, their shining green contrasting beautifully with the black and silver above them. On the communion table a superb imperial crown of roses rested on a rich cushion of white rose-buds. In front of the rails hung a large wreath formed of blue corn-flower (the emperor's favorite flower), with his monogram "W" filling the center. This was a gift of affection sent by a Swiss lady and gentleman, and was regarded as the gem of all the floral decorations. The perfume of the lovely flowers rose on the air of the church as nature's own incense, making the atmosphere redolent with their fragrance.*

Anxious to illuminate the church to the highest degree possible, the committee had some electric lights put up on Monday, to be additional to the illumination given by our own reflector, and when all was laid on the flood of splendor which filled the sacred edifice was beyond any light that ever shone there since it was erected. The rich stone carvings and harmony of the several parts, added to the effect of the decorations,

* To enable the reader more fully to realize the beauty of this scene we introduce here a photographic view of the interior of our church. The decorations shown have nothing to do with our present description. They are the usual embellishments put in by our people to celebrate the birthday of their great president, whose portrait hangs behind the pulpit.

were brought out so distinctly by the brilliancy as to attract the general admiration of the audience. It was, altogether, a sight never to be forgotten by those who gazed upon it.

No superstitious symbols were introduced to mar the simple and natural beauty of the scene; nothing out of harmony with the sincerity and reverence which was intended to be expressed. Seats in front near the pulpit were reserved for the government officials and the diplomatic corps and their ladies. The ladies of the German colony, in full mourning costume, were seated on the right hand of the pulpit and down that side of the house, while the Mexican orchestra of forty-five pieces, and the Orpheon, or German Choral Society, occupied the other side of the pulpit on a platform provided for them. The general audience filled the center behind the legations, and overflowed back into the chapel, the windows of which were lowered so as to make one audience of the whole assembly. The *Partido Liberal*, in its report, estimates the number present at over one thousand persons. Many senators and deputies of the Congress, heads of departments, and members of various societies and clubs and business organizations were in the audience.

At ten minutes past five o'clock nearly all had arrived. The reserved seats in front were occupied by the embassadors of England, France, the United States, Spain, Belgium, Italy, and other countries, with their secretaries and consuls, most of them in splendid uniforms, while a few of the leading diplomates wore on their breasts the orders of merit or honor which had been conferred upon them. A few chairs in the front row still awaited their occupants. Soon a slight buzz was heard, and Baron Von Wacker Gotter, the German minister, appeared at the entrance, escorting his excellency the President of Mexico, who was accompanied by the members of his cabinet, with several generals of division in full uniform. The entire audience rose to receive them with due honor.

As soon as these were seated the services commenced by the orchestra rendering the solemn strains of Chopin's "Funeral March." After this came the Kreutzer andante, "La Chapelle," sung with deep feeling and expression by the German Orpheon. The Rev. John W. Butler, pastor of the church, then rose and read the Scripture lesson, from the fifteenth chapter of First Corinthians. And well, and with proper emphasis, did he render St. Paul's glorious doctrine of the resurrection of the dead. The seraphic faces, sculptured in the stone over each of the twelve pillars above, seemed as though looking down upon the reader and the audience as his voice resounded among these old monastic arches, which suggested the dissimilar scenes which they had echoed in the days of yore, till the center of that assembly seemed to be that magnificent open Bible, now and henceforth unbound and free in Mexico. I wonder not that the reporter of *El Nacional*, a clerical journal, in his account of the service, innocently remarks, referring to that sacred volume, " which we suppose was the Bible of Luther."

As I sat there and looked out upon the wonderful and brilliant scene I seemed lost in astonishment at the *contrast* which it presented to the time, fifteen years before, when I first entered this building. It had been purchased from the government some time previously and fitted up as a theater. The company had failed, and we bought it from them in 1873. Its condition then was simply indescribable—dark, dirty, and reeking with the fumes of tobacco. This added to the darkness, for the daylight was purposely excluded so as to depend entirely on the gas-lights for their effects.

Such, too, was the bigotry of that time that I had difficulty to find men who were then willing to work for Protestants; so I stood amid that gloom and defilement wondering how I could evolve light and cleanliness and beauty out of such a state of things. But I knew the beauty was there, though hidden, and that it could be brought out.

Now, here I was, fifteen years after, looking, as the redeemed often do, at " the hole of the pit whence they have been digged," conscious that but few eyes besides my own in all that bright assembly before me had looked upon the disorder, ruin, and chaos out of which this present vision of light and loveliness had risen.

I also remembered how few and timid were those who at first ventured, when I did develop a place of Christian worship out of the circus, to join with us in evangelical services under this roof; and now here we were with the grandest assembly this land can produce, with its honored president and his ministers in this magnificent memorial service!

Just here my son finished his reading and turned and looked at me, intimating that the time had come to take my part. "What hath God wrought!" was on my lips as I came to the front, and, lifting up my hands in prayer, the entire audience rose to join me in the act. God helped me as I pleaded for the stricken nation with whom we sympathized in the death of its venerable monarch, and for the bereaved family and the aged widow, and especially for that suffering crown-prince on whom the imperial burden must now fall so heavily. I implored God to bless Germany, and to impart to the powers of Europe at this critical time that grace and sagacity which would lead them to indorse heartily the dying word of the grand old emperor as he pleaded for "peace"—the peace of God among the nations. I closed by invoking the benediction of the Almighty upon the land whose hospitality we were enjoying, and its honored president, so that beneath its flag of freedom, civil and religious liberty, with peace and order, should be maintained as long as the sun and moon endured. I had a consciousness that my prayer was heard and that the hearts of the great assembly were with me in the petitions presented. Some of them, especially the Germans, were in tears, and thanked me heartily at the termination of the service.

Another funeral dirge and another hymn, and then my son again took the pulpit and used the closing portion of the burial service of our ritual, in the Spanish, ending with the Lord's Prayer. A short pause, and then the whole audience rose to receive the benediction, which he gave in the German language. This ended the beautiful service. The audience remained standing while the president and his cabinet and the foreign ministers and other officials passed slowly out.

As I saw them reverently retiring I could realize the quiet and yet great advance that our cause had gained in this city during the past few years. Eleven years ago hardly one of these upper-class Mexican people had the courage to enter this or any Protestant church, so decided were their prejudice and timidity. In 1877 I conducted in this same church the funeral service of Herr Benecke, the Consul-general of Germany; but on that occasion we could not induce the limited number of these people who attended to go forward and take the front seats. They lingered round the entrance, and were timid about making any farther advance into the room. On this occasion there was no hesitation. The whole front was occupied and the church crowded. Slowly but surely the Lord's work is advancing in this land, and we can look for more candor and less prejudice as the light spreads and they come to understand us and our object in being here among them.

The General Assembly of all the Protestant missions previously held in this church no doubt did much to impress them favorably; and now came this grand service, at which the highest people of the land were not afraid or ashamed to be present. All this is a decided advance for the evangelical cause.

In the minds of many of these people on this occasion there was a fact that greatly interested them, which would not at all have been regarded as remarkable by any Protestant audience. That fact was that the two ministers who conducted the service and were together in that pulpit stood in the relation of father and son to each other. Such a fact was never seen in Roman Catholicism. No priest or bishop of that Church ever had his son to minister by his side. Here, too, is something to lead them to reflection as to one of the reasons why the clergy of their Church are what they are, denied as they are by mere human authority those relations of holy matrimony which the Founder of Christianity has expressly declared to be the right and privilege of his ministers.

The archbishop had threatened that attendance at this service would be followed by the usual penalties; but his effort to prevent people from going was a failure. He would have had a large business on hand had he attempted to carry out his threat. These were people, beginning with the president, not to be trifled with, and he knew it, and concluded that discretion was the better part of valor. Among the many evidences which we found in the reports in the papers next morning of the excellent impressions made by the service, nothing was more unique or paid a higher homage to the holy word of God than the innocent declaration of the editor of one of the leading periodicals, who evidently was a stranger to the language of Holy Scripture, and supposed, as he listened with such profound attention to my son's reading, that he was uttering something which he had himself composed for the occasion. He therefore reported upon it that "such an eloquent and pious address we have never before heard." No doubt of it, for the minister was reading St. Paul's inspired description of the resurrection of the last day in 1 Corinthians, chapter xv!

As we close, our thoughts revert to a remarkable utterance of Madame Calderon's, and nothing much more appropriate could end this book. Here was a gifted lady, sincere in her Romanism, sadly contemplating a condition of things that was a reproach to her Church. She who for nearly three years stood in that wealthy but dark past which we have portrayed, when there was no ray of light and no prospect of betterment apparent, felt, with increasing conviction, that some change was inevitable, from the necessity of the case, or her Church in Mexico must remain a standing reproach throughout the civilized world. She could discover no source from whence hope of change could arise save one, and that not from the quarter she as a Romanist would have preferred; yet, if it must be so, she bows to the inevitable and predicts its approach. Here is "the prophecy of Madame Calderon:"

The cross was planted here in a congenial soil, and as in the pagan East the statues of the divinities frequently did no more than change their names from those of heathen gods to those of Christian saints, and image-worship apparently continued, though the mind of the Christian was directed from the being represented to the true and only God who inhabits eternity ; so here the poor Indian bows before visible representations of saints and virgins, as he did in former days before the monstrous shapes representing the unseen powers of the air, the earth, and the water ; but he, it is to be feared, lifted his thoughts no higher than the rude image which a human hand has carved. . . . He kneels before the bleeding image of the Saviour who died for him, before the gracious form of the Virgin who intercedes for him; but he believes there are many virgins of various gifts, and possessing various degrees of miraculous power and different degrees of wealth, according to the quality and number of the diamonds and pearls with which they are endowed—one even who is the rival of the other—one who will bring rain when there is drought, and one to whom it is well to pray in seasons of inundation. . . .

If any one wishes to try the effect of strong contrast let him come directly from the United States to this country; but it is in the villages especially that the contrast is most striking. Traveling in New England, for example, we arrive at a small and flourishing village. We see four new churches, proclaiming four different sects; religion suited to all customers. These wooden churches or meeting-houses are all new, all painted white, or perhaps a bright red. Hard by is a tavern with a green paling, as clean and new as the churches, and there are also various smart stores and neat dwelling-houses; all new, all wooden, all clean, and all ornamented with slight Grecian pillars. The whole has a cheerful, trim, and flourishing aspect. Houses, churches, stores, taverns, all are of a piece. . . . Every thing proclaims prosperity, equality, consistency; the past forgotten, the present all in all, and the future taking care of itself. No delicate attentions to posterity who can never pay its debts. No beggars. If a man has even a hole in his coat he must be lately from the Emerald Isle.

Transport yourself in imagination from this New England village to that of ——, it matters not which—not far from Mexico city. "Look on this picture and on that!" The Indian huts, with their half-naked inmates and little gardens filled with flowers; the huts either built of clay or the half-ruined *beaux restes* of some stone building. At a little distance a hacienda, like a deserted palace, built of solid masonry. There, rising in the midst of old faithful-looking trees, the church, gray and ancient, but strong as if designed for eternity, with its saints and virgins, and martyrs and relics, its gold and silver and precious stones, whose value would buy up all the spare lots in the New England village; the *lépero*, with scarce a rag to cover him, kneeling on the marble pavement. Leaving the inclosure of the church, observe the stone wall that bounds the road for more than a mile, the fruit-trees overtopping it, high though it be, with their loaded branches.   This is the convent orchard.   And that great Gothic pile that stands in hoary majesty—what could so noble a building be but the monastery, perhaps of the Carmelites, because of its exceedingly rich garden and well-chosen site ?   For they, of all monks, are richest in this world's goods.   Also we may see the reverend old prior riding slowly from under the arched gate up the village lanes, the Indians coming from their huts to do him lowly reverence as he passes.   Here, every thing reminds us of the past, of the conquering Spaniards who seemed to build for eternity, of the triumphs of Catholicism, and of the Indians when Cortéz first startled them from their repose and stood before them like the fulfillment of half-forgotten prophecy.   It is the present that seems like a dream, a pale reflection of the past.   All is decaying and growing fainter, and men seem trusting to some unknown future that they may never see.   One government has been abandoned, and there is none in its place.   One revolution follows another, yet the remedy is not found. Let them beware lest half a century later they be awakened from their delusion, and find the cathedral turned into a meeting-house, and all painted white, the railing melted down, the Virgin's jewels sold to the highest bidder, the floor washed (which would do it no harm), and around the whole a nice new wooden paling, freshly done in green— and all this performed by some of the artists from the wide-awake republic farther north.*

"The artists" are already there and hard at work, but not in any line of interference with the political institutions.   Madame Calderon would be amazed could she return and see how literally her anticipations have been realized, and the peace, order, and prosperity that are firmly established throughout the land.   More than all would she be surprised to behold, not merely foreign artists at work, but a noble band of native Mexican ministers and teachers engaged in spreading evangelical Christianity, and with grand results.

Mexico is destined to a high mission on this continent.   Her evangelization will aid gloriously in the redemption of Central and South America.   Erelong the States beyond, who imitate her example, will receive her missionaries, who, using the same melodious language, will speak to those millions and thus consummate the evangelization of Spanish America.

* *Life in Mexico*, p. 289.

O, Church of the living God! here is the "open door," "great and effectual," which the divine Master has set before thee! It is thine to enter. God expects it as the work which "thy hand findeth to do." He sends thee to open their eyes, to turn them from darkness to light, and from the power of Satan unto God, that they may receive "remission of their sins, and an inheritance among them that are sanctified by faith in Jesus Christ." Living or dying, I appeal to thee for them. Give them, O, give them quickly, thine evangelical faith and thy saving Gospel. Give in adequate measure for the consummation of the blessed change for these millions of dying men, that Mexico may become that "delightsome land" which the Lord of Hosts has promised, where her "sun shall no more go down, neither shall her moon withdraw itself, for the Lord shall be her everlasting light, and the days of her mourning shall be ended."

Then will redeemed Mexico, her sorrows closed, rise to the greatness of her position on this continent, and, turning to the Redeemer who has saved her, and to him alone, will claim her right to crown him with the diadem of Mexico's adoring love, as "Lord of all, to the glory of God the Father." Henceforth it will be her joy to adopt as her own the rapturous strain of Cowper:

> "Come then, and added to Thy many crowns
> Receive yet one, the crown of all the earth,
> Thou who alone art worthy! It was thine
> By sacred covenant, ere nature's birth;
> And thou hast made it thine by purchase since,
> And overpaid its value with thy blood."

INDEX.

THE END.